BETWEEN BAUDELAIRE AND MALLARMÉ

Between Baudelaire and Mallarmé
Voice, Conversation and Music

HELEN ABBOTT
Bangor University, UK

ASHGATE

Published by
Ashgate Publishing Limited
Wey Court East
Union Road
Farnham
Surrey, GU9 7PT
England

Ashgate Publishing Company
Suite 420
101 Cherry Street
Burlington
VT 05401-4405
USA

www.ashgate.com

British Library Cataloguing in Publication Data
Abbott, Helen
    Between Baudelaire and Mallarmé: voice, conversation and music.
    1. Baudelaire, Charles, 1821–1867 – Criticism and interpretation. 2. Mallarmé, Stéphane, 1842–1898 – Criticism and interpretation. 3. French poetry – 19th century – History and criticism. 4. Oral interpretation of poetry. 5. Music – France – 19th century – Philosophy and aesthetics. 6. Music and literature – France – History – 19th century.
    I. Title
    841.8'09–dc22

Library of Congress Cataloging-in-Publication Data
Abbott, Helen.
    Between Baudelaire and Mallarmé: voice, conversation and music / Helen Abbott.
        p. cm.
    Includes bibliographical references.
    ISBN 978-0-7546-6745-2 (alk. paper) – ISBN 978-0-7546-9573-8 (ebook)
    1. Baudelaire, Charles, 1821–1867 – Criticism and interpretation. 2. Mallarmé, Stéphane, 1842–1898 – Criticism and interpretation. 3. French poetry – 19th century – History and criticism. I. Title.
    PQ2191.Z5A526 2009
    841'.8–dc22

                                                                                    2009007672

ISBN 9780754667452 (hbk)
ISBN 9780754695738 (ebk)

Mixed Sources
Product group from well-managed
forests and other controlled sources
www.fsc.org Cert no. SA-COC-1565
© 1996 Forest Stewardship Council
FSC

Printed and bound in Great Britain by
MPG Books Group, UK

Contents

List of Tables and Music Example

Tables

Music Example

Abbreviations

The editions of Baudelaire's and Mallarmé's work referred to throughout are the Pléiade editions (see bibliography for full details), and will be signalled by the following abbreviations:

B.*OC*   Baudelaire, *Œuvres complètes*
B.*Corr*   Baudelaire, *Correspondance*
M.*OC*   Mallarmé, *Œuvres complètes*

Certain publishers have also been abbreviated as follows:

CUP   Cambridge University Press
OUP   Oxford University Press
PUF   Presses Universitaires de France

Note on the text

Every effort has been made to trace or contact all copyright holders. The author would be pleased to rectify any omissions brought to her notice at the earliest opportunity.

Acknowledgements

With thanks to Anne Green and Craig Moyes at King's College London, and to those who humoured me with challenging conversations, book loans and advice, especially David Evans, Patrick Ffrench, Roger Pearson and Dee Reynolds, and finally to those who provided invaluable support, proofing and technical assistance, especially Anne Abbott, Steve Abbott, Veronica Holland, Felix McGonigal, Matthew O'Sullivan, Katie Playfair and Carol Tully. I am grateful to the AHRC for funding this research.

Prologue

The opening of a one-act play by Jean Cocteau, which was premièred at the Comédie-Française in 1930 and set to music as an opera for solo soprano by Francis Poulenc in the late 1950s, satirises the notoriously unreliable Parisian telephone exchange of the day. The audience hears only one side of a telephone conversation between a female protagonist and her lover. Amongst the passionately fierce outbursts directed at her lover – for she knows that her lover is to marry another woman the following day – the woman finds herself also having to fend off other parties who have been connected erroneously by the operator into her own telephone conversation:

Allô, allô, allô........ Mais non, Madame, nous sommes plusieurs sur la ligne, raccrochez........ Vous êtes avec une abonnée........ Mais, Madame, raccrochez vous-même........ Allô, Mademoiselle, allô........ Laissez-nous........ Mais non, ce n'est pas le docteur Schmidt........ Zéro huit, pas zéro sept........ allô! c'est ridicule........ On me demande; je ne sais pas. *(Elle raccroche, la main sur le récepteur. On sonne.)*........ Allô!........ Mais, Madame, que voulez-vous que j'y fasse? .... Vous êtes très désagréable........ Comment, ma faute?........ pas du tout........ pas du tout........ Allô!........ allô, Mademoiselle........ On me sonne et je ne peux pas parler. Il y a du monde sur la ligne. Dites à cette dame de se retirer. *(Elle raccroche. On sonne).* Allô, c'est toi?........ c'est toi?........ Oui........ J'entends très mal........ tu es très loin, très loin........ Allô........ c'est affreux........ il y a plusieurs personnes sur la ligne........ Redemande. Allô! *Re-de-mande*........ Je dis redemande-moi........ Mais Madame, retirez-vous. Je vous répète que je ne suis pas le docteur Schmidt........ Allô!........ *(Elle raccroche. On sonne.)* Ah! enfin........ c'est toi........ oui........ très bien...[1]

[Hello, hello, hello........ But no, Madame, there are several of us on the line, hang up........ You're talking to a lady already connected........ But, Madame, you hang up yourself........ Hello, Mademoiselle, hello........ Leave us........ But no, this is not Doctor Schmidt........ Zero eight, not zero seven........ hello! it's ridiculous........ Someone is asking for me; I don't know. *(She hangs up, her hand on the receiver. It rings.)*........ Hello!........ But, Madame, what do you want me to do?........ You are most impolite........ How is it my fault?........ not at

---

[1]   Jean Cocteau, *La Voix humaine* (Paris: Librairie Stock, Delamain & Boutelleau, 1930), pp.25–27. All translations throughout are my own. I have favoured a literal translation over more poetic renditions in order to assist the reader less familiar with the French language.

all........ not at all........ Hello!........ hello, Mademoiselle........ Someone is calling me and I cannot speak. There is someone else on the line. Tell this lady to get off. *(She hangs up. It rings.)* Hello, is that you?........ is that you?........ Yes........ It's very hard to hear........ you're very far away, very far away........ Hello........ it's dreadful........ there are several people on the line........ Redial. Hello! *Re-di-al*........ I said redial asking for me........ But Madame, get off the line. I repeat that I am not Doctor Schmidt........ Hello!........ *(She hangs up. It rings.)* Ah! finally........ it's you........ yes........ very well...]

The crossed wires involved in this conversation, and the one-sided textual and dramatic representation of it, offer an angle from which to approach the kind of problems that arise when conversing with others.

When using our voices to converse with others, we might find ourselves being misunderstood, interrupted, overheard or cut off in mid-flow.[2] These potentially negative features of a conversation are, however, such an inherent feature of the way in which we use our voices with regard to others that we are often hardly aware of the problems that they might cause. Even in the face of these risks, we still converse with others, and in fact our awareness of these negative aspects is what feeds our ability to be able to communicate, and they contribute to our naturally sophisticated system of conversational exchange.

My initial encounter with the Cocteau text in the form of a concert performance of Poulenc's operatic setting served as the impetus behind the current study, prompting me to explore questions of conversation, communication and exchange in relation to the human and textual voices used in poetry. For the poet who 'converses' with his reader, the problems he encounters are the same as those encountered by the female protagonist of *La Voix humaine*: he constantly runs the risk of being misunderstood, interrupted, overheard or cut off in mid-flow. Yet this does not put him off writing poetry. The 'conversation' that constitutes poetry is a sophisticated means of communication. Poetry embraces these risks in order to move beyond any superficial form of communication which fails to take into account the complexities of the way in which the human voice is able to interact with others.

---

[2]   Derrida comments on a particular telephone conversation in James Joyce's *Ulysses*, suggesting that the telephone conversation is an interior conversation which both constitutes and ruptures any conversation: 'Intériorité téléphonique, donc: car avant tout dispositif portant ce nom dans la modernité, la *tekhnè* téléphonique est à l'œuvre au-dedans de la voix, multipliant l'écriture des voix sans instruments, dirait Mallarmé, téléphonie mentale qui, inscrivant le lointain, la distance, la différance et l'espacement dans la *phonè*, *à la fois* institue, interdit *et* brouille le soi-disant monologue' ['Telephonic interiority, then: because before any device carrying this name in modern times, the telephonic *tekhnè* is at work within the voice, multiplying the writing of voices without instruments, as Mallarmé would say, mental telephony which, inscribing the distant, the distance, the deferral and the spacing in the *phonè*, *at the same time* institutes, forbids *and* blurs the so-called monologue']. Jacques Derrida, *Ulysse gramophone* (Paris: Galilée, 1987), p.82.

Introduction

'Voice' is a notoriously slippery concept. The trajectory that can be followed from Charles Baudelaire (1821–1867) to Stéphane Mallarmé (1842–1898) in their use of poetic language and forms has been well-documented, marking a shift from seemingly straightforward representational language, to more elusive, indirect, suggestive language. However, little emphasis has thus far been placed on how this affects reading practices, and how each poet employs and exploits both his own voice and the voices of others in order to establish a particular aesthetic response. The stark differences in the way poems by Baudelaire and Mallarmé sound to the ear or feel on the lips are an indication not simply of each poet's own distinctive 'voice', but also of how the developing aesthetic of each poet reflects a particular attentiveness to the effects created by the voice of the text itself. In this study, I shall suggest that the second half of the nineteenth century in France saw a renewed focus on the notion of 'voice' as an important aesthetic principle for poetry, and that this is especially evident in the works of Baudelaire and Mallarmé. My analysis acknowledges that the notion of 'voice' undergoes certain re-evaluations during the course of the nineteenth century, and that, as recent critical analysis has established, 'voice' remains an elusive term because it seeks to incorporate a complex range of physical, textual and symbolic ideas.[1] It is not simply a case of 'voice' defining the selfhood or identity of each poet,

---

[1]   Michel Chion, for example, criticises French theoretical writing on voice for failing to explore 'voice' in a systematic way, and opens his study *La Voix au cinéma* (Paris: Éditions de l'Étoile, 1982) by describing the voice as 'elusive'. Dominique Ducard, meanwhile, highlights that 'voice' is, by its very nature, a complex theoretical problematic: 'Le statut ontologique de la voix, à la croisée du corps et de la pensée, du sens intime qu'elle révèle et de la signification conventionelle qu'elle délivre dans la parole, du subjectif et de l'interpersonnel, en fait un objet théorique dont la problématique est nécessairement complexe' ['The ontological status of the voice, at the crossroads between body and thought, of the sense of intimacy that it reveals and of the conventional signification that it provides in the spoken word, of the subjective and of the interpersonal, makes it an object of theoretical study whose problematic is necessarily complex']. Dominique Ducard, *La Voix et le miroir: Une étude sémiologique de l'imaginaire et de la formation de la parole* (Paris: L'Harmattan, 2002), p.10. Danielle Cohen-Levinas talks of voice as a paradox, outlining how 'la voix résiste aux méthodologies musicales, à l'objectivation des codes et à la réduction sémiotique. Nous savons qu'il s'agit d'un matériau complexe, fascinant, fondamentalement ambivalent' ['the voice is resistant to musical methodologies, to the objectification of codes and to semiotic reduction. We know that we are dealing with a material which is complex, fascinating, and profoundly ambivalent']. Danielle Cohen-Levinas, *La Voix au-delà du chant: une fenêtre aux ombres* (Paris: Vrin, 2006), p.19.

rather it is the effects of using 'voice' in poetry – and the way that this can spark interactions, resonances and exchanges – that will be foregrounded in this study.

The initial underlying question behind this research is: what is the difference, if any, between reading poetry out loud and reading it internally? Since this is a very broad question which relates, essentially, to the 'performance practice' of poetry (to borrow a term from musicology), my field of analysis will be narrowed to four main areas of focus – Rhetoric, Body, Exchange and Music – in order to:

1. evaluate the importance of prescriptive rules or principles – most notably rhetoric, prosody and music – in the context of poetic production during the nineteenth century in France, and the extent to which these principles contribute to a definition of 'voice' as something which is both active and memorable;

2. consider the role of the human body or physical attributes of voice in the context of textual poetic practices; an analysis of the relationship between physical and textual manifestations of voice and the extent to which this is a dynamic process which privileges an ideal of resonance will further refine initial definitions of 'voice' as active and memorable in the context of Baudelaire and Mallarmé in particular;

3. explore the extent to which 'voice' must be considered as a process, and more specifically as a process of exchange, and to suggest that Baudelaire's and Mallarmé's models of conversational exchange begin to favour increasingly strange, foreign and abstract voices even in the face of potential risks and threats, such as infiltration by other, more seemingly powerful, voices;

4. assess whether trying to define voice as an active, memorable, dynamic, resonant, abstract process of exchange in the context of Baudelaire and Mallarmé is ultimately underpinned by a desire to create music rather than poetry, and to suggest that the forms and strategies of the song setting represent at once the ideal and yet the most problematic scenario for using 'voice' effectively.

Through detailed analyses of both the poetic and critical writings by Baudelaire and Mallarmé, I seek to add to existing critical work on the notion of 'voice' by addressing what 'voice' can mean in relation to reading and writing practices in poetry. The overriding concern, then, is the ways in which 'voice' in poetry is defined and influenced by aesthetic concerns. This study does not follow a strictly chronological path starting with Baudelaire and moving on to Mallarmé (although my opening chapter sets the scene in relation to earlier poetic and theoretical practices, and most notably the overriding spectre of Hugo); instead I have chosen to read both Baudelaire and Mallarmé closely together, looking at what happens in the 'between' spaces of their work. That Verlaine, a poet who also demonstrates a particular preoccupation with the nature and status of 'voice' in his poetic writings, has not been included as a key figure in this study is due the fact that this research relies on exploring the relationship between poetic and critical writings.

Verlaine's lack of critical writings in comparison to the wealth of texts composed by Baudelaire and Mallarmé situates him in a different mould, although his poetic influence cannot be ignored.

Rhetoric

The rhetorical aspect of this study will explore the governing principles which underlie poetic production during the nineteenth century in France, and in particular those principles which addressed how a poem was to be read. I draw from a number of key rhetorical and prosodic theories and principles which specifically preoccupied poets of the era, including Hugo, Gautier, Banville, and Baudelaire and Mallarmé in particular. I shall refer to a range of classical, nineteenth-century and contemporary theoretical concepts and treatises on poetry in order to establish the status of rhetoric, prosody and music during this period. This leads me to address a number of questions including: should strict rhetorical or metrical rules be adhered to in order to assist the reader who will 'voice' a poem upon reading? Are any diversions from poetic rules a direct result of a particular emphasis on the role of the human voice in poetic language? Should poetic composition be governed solely by the extent to which it sounds pleasing to the ear? I explore to what extent 'voice' in the context of traditional rhetorical practice is an action, insofar as it might prompt effects within a particular temporal framework that will be lasting, repeatable and, ultimately, memorable (in rhetorical terms, as I shall elaborate, this is the relationship between 'actio' and 'memoria'). The purpose of this opening section on rhetorical practices is to establish both the framework within which the poets were working, and a theoretical framework for exploring the aesthetic outcomes of the concept of 'voice' within the context of a fresh approach to Baudelaire and Mallarmé which considers their work in dialogue.

Body

If I take as my framework the notion that 'voice' is both active and memorable, how then does this affect how poets compose and readers read? I seek to answer this question in Chapter 2 by considering three core elements:

a. what performance scenarios or vocal enactments are at the disposal of the poet and his reader?
b. what do we know about the ways in which Baudelaire or Mallarmé read their own poetry?
c. what are the implications of the differing dynamic properties of the human voice in the context of verse and prose poetry?

By exploring the ways in which each poet exploits both quieter whispering voices (which are supposedly close to the internal silence of thought) and louder shouting or crying voices (which are supposedly too loud to be considered as part of internal thought) in their written texts, I seek to understand how the dynamic range of voices portrayed therein leads the reader to react physically to these voices, even when the reader does not read out loud.

Alongside my analysis of Baudelaire's and Mallarmé's own writings, I also take into consideration more recent work in a domain outside of literary studies – the field of neuroscience – which seeks to explain why the distinction between reading or speaking out loud and reading or speaking internally is so difficult to pin down. I propose that this difficulty is not only a necessary feature of the human voice, but one that begins to explain the aesthetic agenda which underlies the work of Baudelaire and Mallarmé. The human voice is bestowed with particular dynamic properties that link the physical elements of voice with more abstract connotations which derive from the poetic text itself. I shall argue, then, that 'voice' is to be understood not simply as a purely corporeal feature, nor as a purely textual or abstract notion, but as a concept that encapsulates a dynamic interaction between both corporeal and abstract properties. If we understand 'voice' as something dynamic, which has as its purpose an aesthetic outcome, then we can better contend with the manifold attributes of voice that arise within the works of both poets under consideration here.

One of the most prominent aesthetic outcomes of poetic language for Baudelaire and Mallarmé is its potentially resonant effects. I turn, in Chapter 3, to study the implications of creating a 'vocal resonance' through poetic language. The concept of 'resonance' derives from the way that both poets talk about 'voice' as a vibration not just of the vocal chords, but also of words and language. Both poets contend with the various resonances that are established between different senses, sounds, meanings and sensations created by words, but there is a marked shift in Mallarmé's work which begins, seemingly, to place a greater emphasis on the sensation of language. The aesthetic implications of this are significant. Of course, for Baudelaire and Mallarmé, who are both indebted to Poe's *Philosophy of Composition*, the notion of 'aesthetics' implies a supposedly 'scientific' approach towards the concept of Beauty.[2] The origins of the word 'aesthetics' from the Greek 'aisthêtikos' also imply that this 'science' is predominantly a science of sensation. Baudelaire's defining use of the word 'esthétique' in his collected art criticism of the 'Curiosités esthétiques' embodies both these meanings: what strategies should be used in order to create beauty in art, and how do they affect us? I shall suggest that the 'science' of creating beautiful sensations uncovers some significant new developments at the hands of Baudelaire and Mallarmé.

In particular, after Baudelaire's 'correspondances', Mallarmé shifts the focus towards the 'sensation' of poetic language as a particular defining feature of

---

[2]   Edgar Allan Poe, 'The Philosophy of Composition', *Essays and Reviews* (New York: The Library of America, 1984).

aesthetic experience. In order to create a 'sensation' through poetic language, a certain set of conditions is required. Mallarmé is careful to prepare the way for a particular process of vibration which suspends meaning in order to concentrate on the wider range of effects or responses that can emanate from particular patternings of language. It was Margaret Miner who first coined the term 'resonant gaps', and this seems to be precisely what is at stake for Mallarmé as he seeks to enable language to resonate within the interstices between possible meanings or interpretations.[3] The implication of this, as I shall propose, is that a particularly demanding kind of 'resonance' begins to emerge from poetic language, one which suggests that the human voice will only be profoundly active and memorable if the whole body is involved in a particular process of vibration.

Exchange

Perceiving 'voice' as a process of vibration raises questions about the stability of 'voice' as a concept. What emerges from the writings of both poets is that this instability is a necessary feature of their aesthetic agenda. Such a shifting concept of 'voice' enables them to exploit the potentially negative aspects of using 'voice' in poetry, including those that derive from misunderstandings or conflicting opinions. I develop this in my fourth chapter by exploring the ways in which Baudelaire and Mallarmé deal with the process of 'voice' as it becomes an exchange of different voices, particularly in the context of conversation. My analysis of particular textual traits which designate voice (or, in the case of Mallarmé, deliberately try to avoid designating a specific voice) leads me to explore the extent to which the process of exchanging voices is central to our understanding of the aesthetic effects of using 'voice' in poetry. On a basic level, a process of exchange implies a reciprocal giving and taking; in the context of exchanging voices, this suggests that in order to be able to take on different voices, each poet (and, indeed his reader) must be prepared to give up his own individual voice. In fact, I shall suggest that the very concept of an 'individual voice' is an inherently unstable feature of language which both poets exploit to the full in their poetic texts. In order to establish that yearned-for resonant sensation, it seems that the poets must avoid those voices which are overtly subjective. My analysis will demonstrate that as a result, it becomes increasingly difficult for anyone to accept responsibility for a particular voice. The poets begin, then, to favour voices which are strange, abstract or difficult to identify.

In the case of both Baudelaire and Mallarmé, adopting the quality of strangeness demonstrates an acceptance of the fact that there is always ample scope for misunderstandings within the context of conversational exchanges. As I explore in my fifth chapter, misunderstandings do not, however, necessarily result

---

[3] Margaret Miner, *Resonant Gaps between Baudelaire and Wagner* (Athens, GA: University of Georgia Press, 1995).

in a failure to elicit a resonant response. In Baudelaire's prose poem 'L'Étranger', for example, a mysterious stranger seems persistently to misunderstand his interlocutor's intentions:[4]

> 'Qu'aimes-tu le mieux, homme énigmatique, dis? ton père, ta mère, ta sœur ou ton frère?
> – Je n'ai ni père, ni mère, ni sœur, ni frère.
> – Tes amis?
> – Vous vous servez là d'une parole dont le sens m'est resté jusqu'à ce jour inconnu.'

> ['Tell me, enigmatic man, who do you like best? Your father, your mother, your sister or your brother?'
> 'I have no father, no mother, no sister and no brother.'
> 'Your friends?'
> 'You are using a word whose meaning, up until today, has remained unknown to me.']

The initial interlocutor uses words that the 'extraordinaire étranger' ['extraordinary foreigner'] seems not to understand; the 'étranger' himself concludes the conversation with an enigmatic and perplexing response, emphasised by the use of ellipsis: 'J'aime les nuages...' ['I like the clouds...'].[5] In Mallarmé's aesthetic, meanwhile, the advantage of misunderstanding is that it prevents the conversational interlocutor (and also the reader) from approaching the poetic conversation with too many preconceptions or clichéd interpretations. The quality of strangeness instead leads the reader to re-read, to re-voice, and to re-act in a different way each time the poetic text is brought to voice.

---

[4]   Charles Baudelaire, *Œuvres complètes,* ed. by Claude Pichois, Bibliothèque de la Pléiade, 2 vols (Paris: Gallimard, 1975–1976), I, p.277. All subsequent references will be designated by the abbreviation B.*OC*.

[5]   Steve Murphy explores this impossible conversation in his analysis 'Six réponses de *L'Étranger* ou l'art de tuer la conversation', highlighting that 'Les tirets qui ponctuent la plupart des débuts de ligne de *L'Étranger* marquent avec insistance un échange de voix' ['The dashes which punctuate most of the beginnings of lines in *L'Étranger* insistently signal an exchange of voices']. Steve Murphy, *Logiques du dernier Baudelaire: Lectures du Spleen de Paris* (Paris: Champion, 2003), pp.161–177.

Music

It is perhaps not surprising that music becomes such an important feature of both poets' attitudes towards the notion of 'voice'.[6] Music has the advantageous property of being able to communicate and create a resonance even though its voices may be incomprehensible, foreign, strange or abstract. My final chapter broaches the issue of music in relation to the process of using 'voice' in poetry, and reconsiders initial hypotheses put forward in my opening chapter on poetic principles, where I acknowledge the profound influence of musical criteria on poetic composition during the nineteenth century. The slippage between the status of verbal and non-verbal uses of voice becomes an important conundrum for each poet's output. It is for this reason, I suggest, that neither the model of vocal music nor the model of instrumental music is specifically privileged by either poet. Poetry instead becomes idealised as a 'chant-instrument', different from vocal music, different from instrumental music, different from music altogether, and yet still beholden to it. Music, after all, has voices which interact and converse in strange and mysterious ways – and this is inherent to the aesthetic ideal for poetic composition that Baudelaire and Mallarmé seem to yearn for. I focus in particular on the ways in which each poet exploits the precarious balance between music and poetry by acknowledging the ways in which both arts continue to borrow from one another. This persistent borrowing of poetry by music and music by poetry – particularly, though not exclusively, through repetitive traits such as refrains – further elucidates the process of exchanging voices that I explore in earlier chapters, since it suggests that the process of exchange is not simply one of conversation or dialogue between particular voices, but also one which results in the loss of certain voices as others (such as those of music) take precedence.

I supplement my analysis of the interaction between poetic and musical voices by considering a particular form which seemingly unites them both, that is to say, the song setting. Whilst I do not attempt to do a full analysis of all the Baudelaire or Mallarmé poems set to music (since this would go far beyond the intended scope of the present study), I shall focus briefly on a small number of examples which demonstrate the ways in which the exchange between poetry and music is always complicated by disruptions, irregular patternings and disappearances. The process of give-and-take between poetry and music enacts the process of exchanging voices in a particularly profound way (since poetry hankers after music's abstraction and emotive force, and music hankers after poetry's meanings). Exchanging both poetic

---

[6]   Clive Scott's 'État présent' focusing on French verse analysis notes that recent critical attention has begun to explore the important relationship between voice and music in poetic composition. See *French Studies*, 60:3 (2006), 369–376. My own approach seeks not to privilege 'voice' over 'music', or 'orality' over 'musicality' (or indeed vice versa), but to understand how 'voice' cannot be dissociated from 'music' in the poetry and poetics of Baudelaire and Mallarmé, drawing, where relevant, from contemporary song settings of their poems.

and musical voices inevitably results in moments where the exchange falters, is disrupted, or distorted; and I shall conclude by suggesting that it is precisely these moments that Baudelaire and Mallarmé are at pains to exploit in order to elicit a particular aesthetic response. So my initial question – what is the difference, if any, between reading poetry out loud and reading it internally? – takes on an entirely different colour in the context of the song setting. The differences in interpretation and reading that arise from different settings of a poem will remind us that the relationship between music and poetry is a productive one because the aesthetic response that is able to emerge actively engages with lingering vestiges of different voices which gradually lose themselves in a process of exchange.

Voice, Conversation and Music

By taking an overarching approach which acknowledges important relationships between voice, conversation and music, this study aims to offer a more comprehensive analysis than that which has been carried out thus far by other scholars in the field. Research into Baudelairean voices has frequently privileged particular issues such as duality or gender. Barbara Johnson, for example, has focused on the duality of Baudelaire's voice and 'la structure dialogique de la plupart des *Fleurs du Mal*' ['the dialogic structure of the majority of *Les Fleurs du Mal*']; my own approach acknowledges the importance of dialogue in Baudelaire's writings, but rather than placing emphasis on the duality of the 'je' and 'tu' personae inscribed therein, I take an aesthetic standpoint which privileges a more abstract process of exchange.[7] Rosemary Lloyd has addressed the issue of gendered voices in *Les Fleurs du Mal*, suggesting that 'Baudelaire's poems seduce us into setting aside the gender-specific mask of the hypocrite reader, and living instead through that plethora of personae that mill about in his destabilizing and therefore liberating world'; I accept this interchangeability of gendered voices as an inherent feature of an aesthetic approach to 'voice', particularly during an era of poetry where any direct relationship between 'voice' and subject becomes increasingly destabilised.[8] Such destabilisation is further exacerbated by issues of temporality and death, and Elissa Marder's work on the relationship between conversational speech and consciousness of time, offers an important springboard for my project.[9] Concerning Mallarméan voices, critical research has already touched on issues such as dynamics and the relationship between voice and text. Roger Pearson, for example, has addressed Mallarmé's predilection for quieter

---

[7]   Barbara Johnson, *Défigurations du langage poétique: la seconde révolution baudelairienne* (Paris: Flammarion, 1979), p.60.

[8]   Rosemary Lloyd, 'Hypocrite Brother, Hypocrite Sister: Exchanging Genders in *Les Fleurs du Mal*', *French Studies*, 53:2 (1999), 167–175 (p.174).

[9]   Elissa Marder, *Dead Time: Temporal Disorders in the Wake of Modernity (Baudelaire and Flaubert)* (Stanford: Stanford University Press, 2001), p.18.

dynamic volumes in his circumstantial poetry, such as reading 'sotto voce'; I elaborate on this concept in relation to the wider corpus of Mallarmé's writings.[10] Bertrand Marchal has analysed the way in which Mallarmé converts writing into voice in 'Hérodiade', and metaphorises the notion of 'voice' by comparing it to that most evocative of symbolist images, the setting sun; I seek to break down the distinction between 'voice' and writing and aim to avoid metaphorical readings of 'voice' in my analysis since my approach addresses 'voice' as a dynamic process rather than a symbolic image.[11] The most encompassing approach to the notion of 'voice' in relation to nineteenth-century poetry to date is Clive Scott's work which focuses on the context of reading and translating poetry. Scott's work provides invaluable refinement of the issues surrounding this slippery concept; I shall draw from Scott's analyses in order to develop these in more detail within the context of Baudelaire and Mallarmé in particular.[12]

Fundamentally, 'voice' is an area of study which is burdened with numerous critical preconceptions, which derive principally from fields outside of poetry and from developments in twentieth-century literary criticism in particular. Of particular relevance to this study is the work of Roland Barthes, Gérard Genette and Jacques Rancière but it is important to acknowledge the extent to which scholars in fields as diverse as philosophy of language, linguistics, poststructuralism, phenomenology and deconstructionism have all broached the concept of 'voice', frequently in widely conflicting ways. Since classical antiquity, 'voice' has typically been dubbed the 'source' of language, as its originary – and therefore ideal – state which is to be privileged over writing. In France such perceptions persisted throughout the centuries, with a notable exponent of this idea being Rousseau who believed the voice to be an organ of the soul.[13] According to this theory, the originary state of voice is not speech but thought, which is considered to be a pre-utterance prior to either speech or writing. Such considerations about the origins of voice, and specifically about the relationship between thought and speech, have undergone important critical reinterpretations throughout the twentieth century. The voice

---

[10] See Roger Pearson, *Mallarmé and Circumstance: The Translation of Silence* (Oxford: OUP, 2004).

[11] See Bertrand Marchal, *La Religion de Mallarmé: poésie, mythologie et religion* (Paris: José Corti, 1988); 'une forme de lecture, immanente au poème ... convertit l'écriture en voix' ['a form of reading, immanent to the poem ... converts writing into voice'], p.55 and 'Cette phrase ... mime le mouvement solaire de la voix, mouvement d'élévation puis de symétrique retombée' ['This phrase ... mimics the solar movement of the voice, a movement of elevation and then of falling back down again'], p.67.

[12] See Clive Scott, *Channel Crossings: French and English Poetry in Dialogue 1550–2000* (Oxford: Legenda, 2002) and *The Poetics of French Verse: Studies in Reading* (Oxford: Clarendon, 1998).

[13] See Jean-Jacques Rousseau, *Essai sur l'origine des langues* (Paris: Aubier Montaigne, 1974), p.119. See also Lydia Goehr, *The Quest for Voice: On Music, Politics, and the Limits of Philosophy* (Oxford: Clarendon, 1998), p.104.

of thought is considered to be what constitutes a subject, and language itself. But the placing of language at the root of being would, according to poststructuralist thought, therefore imply that speaking or writing subjects are dislocated from their originary source.[14] However, definitions of what this 'originary source' might be are conflicting: for Barthes, the 'grain de la voix' ['the grain of the voice'] is the individual or unique (emotive) quality underlying each person's voice; for Kristeva individual phonemes are what constitute the workings of voice; for Derrida, who critiques long-held beliefs in 'logocentrism', meaning or truth behind voice is to be found in writing, not speaking; for Agamben the originary source is an incoherent cry or scream that has not yet been actualised into meaning.[15] Although the voice has an identifiable materiality within the human body, it is also bears aesthetic properties through language, as my own analysis will explore, since this has important ramifications for working with poetry.

The very instability of 'voice', which can appear and emerge in so many different guises in the context of poetry, is inherent to the developing symbolist aesthetic of the late nineteenth century in France. During the same period, writers in other fields, and in particular novelists, were beginning to explore the possibility of 'reproducing' the voice of 'le peuple'. Zola began to experiment with this idea in *L'Assommoir* in particular, and the Goncourt brothers endeavoured to convey particular qualities of the working-class voice in their work by using non-standard French. For these novelists, direct speech or dialogue became an important area of focus. Yet where novelists sought to reproduce as far as possible, poets instead sought to exploit a more dynamic interaction between different voices that goes beyond textual techniques of reproduction. Where 'voice' becomes interesting in poetry, I suggest, is at those moments where it is put into action

---

[14]   For further analysis of these perspectives see, for example, Christina Howells, *Derrida: Deconstruction from Phenomenology to Ethics* (Cambridge: Polity Press, 1998), pp.45–75; or Carolyn Abbate, *Unsung Voices: Opera and Musical Narrative in the Nineteenth Century* (Princeton: Princeton University Press, 1991).

[15]   See Roland Barthes, 'Le Grain de la voix' in *Œuvres complètes,* ed. by Éric Marty, 3 vols (Paris: Seuil, 1994), II; Julia Kristeva, *Polylogue* (Paris: Seuil, 1977) and *La Révolution du langage poétique* (Paris: Seuil, 1974); Jacques Derrida, *La Voix et le phénomène: introduction au problème du signe dans la phénoménologie de Husserl* (Paris: PUF, 1989), *Ulysse gramophone* (Paris: Galilée, 1987) and *De la Grammatologie* (Paris: Minuit, 1967); Giorgio Agamben, *Language and Death: the Place of Negativity* (Minneapolis: University of Minnesota Press, 1991). For a summary of different critical arguments pertaining to the concept of 'voice', see also Paul Zumthor, *Performance, réception, lecture* (Longueuil: Éditions du Préambule, 1990). Clive Scott's analysis of voice or 'vocal presence' in fin-de-siècle French and English verse specifically privileges the Barthes–Kristeva model of the 'géno-texte' which he defines as 'a play of signifiers where meaning is always in the process of being made, unmade and re-made' and which is opposed to the expressive voice of the 'phéno-texte' where meanings are already articulated. See *Channel Crossings*, p.181. Whilst I shall refer later to Barthes' essay on 'Le Grain de la voix', my own approach draws from an aesthetic argument rather than a semiotic one.

(even subconsciously) under conditions that are strained, challenging, or even artificial. There are inevitable moments of crisis and confusion, there are inevitable moments of impotence and silence; but these are also counterbalanced by moments of confidence and clarity. It is easy to lament the fact that poetry is no longer read out loud, and that people (students or otherwise) simply no longer know how to read poetry. However, since reading poetry is complicated by the fact that so many different vocal decisions need to be made, I shall call into question the extent to which either Baudelaire or Mallarmé intended their poetry to be read out loud, and address whether the effects produced by reading out loud are necessarily to be privileged over an internal reading. As the contemporary poet Yves Bonnefoy has suggested, a distinction between reading out loud and reading internally is difficult to maintain.[16] The nuances that I shall explore in the varying dynamics of voice, as they are exploited by each poet, will allow me to break down distinctions between reading out loud and reading internally.

In my exploration of different possible performance scenarios for poetry, theories of 'performativity', particularly those which explore the dynamic properties of performance, will influence my analysis of how 'voice' can be both internal and external, and both written and spoken.[17] Each poet is aware of the wider scope of performance possibilities for his poetry, which might remain in the privacy of a fireside armchair, or may encroach upon more public domains of music and theatre. John E. Jackson suggests that Mallarmé's poetry has a more interior and oblique addressee than Baudelaire's:

> Baudelaire parle, il fait de son poème le théâtre d'une parole qui, le plus souvent, est orientée vers un destinataire clairement identifié. Ainsi l'oralité devient-elle, plus qu'un caractéristique relative, le registre naturel de sa poésie. À l'opposé du rêve mallarméen d'une écriture se réfléchissant seule dans l'espace nocturne et

---

[16] 'Y aurait-il quelque différence, pour un auteur, entre lire son œuvre (avec ses yeux, sur la page) et prononcer à voix haute un texte déjà écrit? Cette distinction ne tient pas' ['is there a difference of some sort, for an author, between reading his work (with his eyes, on the page) and speaking a text already written out loud? This distinction does not stand up']. Yves Bonnefoy, *La Poésie à voix haute* (Condeixa-a-Nova: Ligne d'ombre, 2007), p.31.

[17] J.L. Austin's speech-act theory remains the dominant work in this area. See *How to Do Things with Words* (Oxford: Clarendon, 1962). The critical concept of 'performance' was popular in the late 1980s and early 1990s. With specific reference to Baudelaire and Mallarmé, see Marie Maclean, *Narrative as Performance: The Baudelairean Experiment* (London and New York: Routledge, 1988) and Mary Lewis Shaw, *Performance in the Texts of Mallarmé: The Passage from Art to Ritual* (Pennsylvania: Pennsylvania State University Press, 1993). More recently, Joseph Acquisto has further nuanced the issue of performativity in relation to symbolist poetry and music, referring to recent work by Jonathan Culler, and suggesting that 'a performative approach to criticism infuses repetition with dynamism; it is an open-ended view of texts as unstable and perpetually tending to reinvention by acts of reading and writing'. Joseph Acquisto, *French Symbolist Poetry and the Idea of Music* (Aldershot: Ashgate, 2006), p.5.

désolé d'une chambre déserte, la poésie des *Fleurs du Mal* ne cesse de s'incarner dans une voix à laquelle elle finit par s'identifier.[18]

[Baudelaire speaks, he makes his poem the theatre of the spoken word which, more often that not, is directed towards a clearly identified addressee. In this way, orality becomes more than a relative characteristic of his poetry, and becomes its natural register. In contrast to the Mallarméan dream of writing which reflects itself alone in the nocturnal and desolate space of a deserted room, the poetry of *Les Fleurs du Mal* never ceases to be embodied in the voice with which it ends up identifying itself.]

However, Patrick McGuinness highlights how Mallarmé in fact considered reading to be a process linked to theatre and performance:

reading for Mallarmé and the Symbolists is often couched in terms of theatrical metaphors, while performance (including, perhaps especially, that which does not occur within the confines of theatre) is frequently associated with an idealized experience of reading.[19]

Whilst it is evident that Mallarmé privileged theatrical dialogue in such poems as 'Hérodiade' and 'L'Après-midi d'un faune', theatrical performance is not the only way in which he intended his poetry to be read. In fact, as Roger Pearson makes clear in his analysis of Mallarmé's lecture on Villiers de l'Isle-Adam, for Mallarmé using language entails close attention to what it means to use one's voice:

[There is] an important theme in Mallarmé's 'Message': that 'writing', or the fashioning of language, is an oral as well as a manual activity, the writer both a speaker and the source of a manuscript, someone to be heard as well as read.[20]

---

[18]   John E. Jackson, 'Le Jeu des voix: de l'interpellation et de quelques autres formes énonciatives dans *Les Fleurs du Mal*' in *L'Année Baudelaire*, 6, ed. by John E. Jackson, Claude Pichois and Jean-Paul Avice (Paris: Champion, 2002), p.69.

[19]   Patrick McGuinness, 'Mallarmé reading theatre', in *The Process of Art: Essays on Nineteenth-Century French Literature, Music and Painting in Honour of Alan Raitt*, ed. by Mike Freeman et al. (Oxford: Clarendon, 1998), p.85.

[20]   Roger Pearson, 'Mallarmé's Homage to Villiers de L'Isle-Adam', in *The Process of Art*, ed. by Mike Freeman et al., p.136. This viewpoint is also confirmed in McGuinness' earlier article on symbolist theatre. Even the theatrical text reveals uncertainties over reading and performance. McGuinness writes: 'The Symbolists ... conceive of performance not as a slick and adequate transposition from one medium to another, from page to stage, but as a veritable battleground, where each component, written word, spoken word, gesture and so on fights for a place in a hierarchy which is never a priori assured.' Patrick McGuinness, 'From Page to Stage and Back: Mallarmé and Symbolist Theatre', *Romance Studies*, 26 (1995), 23–40 (p.34).

Of course, Mallarmé's lecture on Villiers is, in Pearson's words, a 'printed version of an oral event' which is quite distinct from his poetry. It becomes clear from the way in which Mallarmé uses voices in both his verse and prose poetry that this blurring of distinctions between speaking and writing, between possible performances and vocal enactments, is one of the central tenets of his attitude towards the notion of 'voice'.

Each potential vocal enactment is nuanced by decisions pertaining to punctuation, metrical accents and syntactical structures, and these affect the way in which 'voice' can be put into action through poetry. A lack of punctuation or a disruption in metre or syntax, for example, can cause the reader to question where to breathe or pause when reading a verse line. Focusing on such small-scale elements in the context of a particular aesthetic agenda should lead us to a more detailed understanding of what using 'voice' means for each poet. As we shall see, neither Baudelaire nor Mallarmé is prescriptive about how his poetry is to be read; even though they are both aware of the differences between speaking (or reading) out loud and speaking (or reading) internally, and between speaking and writing, they do not privilege one particular vocal enactment over another. This, I shall suggest, is primarily because both poets are so profoundly preoccupied with the ways in which poetry relates to music and musical performance. Having spent many an evening in concert halls listening to recitals or operas, or indeed performing songs in front of an audience, I have long toyed with questions such as: how much does it matter whether an audience can hear the words? How much does it matter whether an audience can understand the words? How important are programmes with texts and translations? To what extent does the singer communicate the sentiment of the text, even though the audience may not understand the words? To what extent does the composer himself make this sentiment part and parcel of his composition? Although finding the answers to all these much broader questions would go far beyond the confines of this current study, my analysis seeks to explore what it means to bring poetry to voice in terms of the shifting poetic rules, ideals and value systems that pervade the symbolist aesthetic.

PART I
Rhetoric

Chapter 1
Poetic Principles:
Rhetoric, Prosody and Music

Then read from the treasured volume
The poem of thy choice,
And lend to the rhyme of the poet
The beauty of thy voice.

Henry Wadsworth Longfellow, 'The day is done', v.37–40[1]

One way of approaching the concept of 'voice' in the writings of Baudelaire and Mallarmé is to consider what kind of principles or conventions underpin their use of language, and the extent to which these principles contribute to a definition of voice as something which is both active and memorable. A particular concern for Baudelaire and Mallarmé, who were writing during a period of increased uncertainty regarding the status of poetry, was the question: how might each poet ensure that his reader will be attuned to the poet's own aesthetic? This question is one which stems from the age-old rhetorical idea that an orator or poet must know his audience in order to achieve his intended outcomes. Since the advent of the printing press, however, knowing one's audience was no longer a possible given, and poets have had to rely instead on certain literary conventions in order to ensure that their poetry is well-received by their audience. This 'literisation' of literature, to borrow Gérard Genette's term, meant that attention was increasingly focused on rhetorical figures or tropes known as the 'elocutio' element of rhetorical practice:

> c'est apparemment dès le début du Moyen Age que commence de se défaire l'équilibre propre à la rhétorique ancienne. … la rhétorique du *trivium*, écrasée entre grammaire et dialectique, se voit rapidement confinée dans l'étude de l'*elocutio*, des ornements du discours, *colores rhetorici*. L'époque classique … et plus particulièrement encore au XVIIIe siècle, hérite de cette situation.[2]

> [it seems to be that from the beginning of the Middle Ages the equilibrium of ancient rhetoric starts to come undone. … the rhetoric of the *trivium*, squashed between grammar and logic, finds itself rapidly confined to the study of the

---

[1]   *The Complete Poetical Works of Longfellow* (Boston: The Riverside Press, 1922), pp.64–65.

[2]   Gérard Genette, *Figures III* (Paris: Seuil, 1972), p.22.

elocutio, of the embellishments of discourse, *colores rhetorici*. The classical era
… and most especially the eighteenth century, inherits this situation.]

By the middle of the nineteenth century, however, we find with Baudelaire, and
later Mallarmé, an increasing lack of conviction in the belief that such figurative
devices will secure an effective poetic response. Rather like Flaubert's ironising
of particular 'idées reçues' ['commonplaces'], Baudelaire and Mallarmé begin to
ironise accepted conventions, and to forge innovative ways of writing poetry that
place a renewed emphasis on the voice of both the poet and his reader; instead of
relying on particular tropes or devices to ensure a particular effect, the poets begin
to rely on particular ways of using voices to ensure a more active and immediate
relationship between the poet and his reader.

Clive Scott has suggested that Baudelaire in particular privileges an immediacy
of response:

> the Baudelairean … aesthetic … finds value in immediacy of response, in
> unmediated impulsivity, in the ability to profit from chance and to cultivate
> coincidence.[3]

Scott goes on to suggest, following Benjamin, that Baudelaire's aesthetics of
immediacy therefore negate, or at least fundamentally devalue, the role of memory.
I shall argue, on the other hand, that it is precisely because of the perceived
immediacy of 'voice' in poetry that the memory begins to play a more active role.
In this chapter, I shall propose a re-evaluation of the ancient rhetorical model
so that the focus is no longer purely on just one element of poetic composition,
which Genette highlights as the 'elocutio' element, but also on the role of the
'actio' element (which privileges voice and immediacy of effect) and the role
of the 'memoria' element (which privileges memory and longevity of effect).[4]
It is not simply a question of a particular poet 'speaking' to a particular reader
through his poetry. At the active, immediate moment of using one's voice (whether
in the context of writing, reading, speaking or performing), the effects created
resonate with memories of numerous other voices. Such effects, however, are only
achieved by careful manipulation of accepted conventions which seek to establish
a relationship between the poet and his reader.

---

[3]   Clive Scott, *Channel Crossings: French and English Poetry in Dialogue 1550–2000*
(Oxford: Legenda, 2002), p.181.

[4]   The five processes of rhetorical composition were the 'inventio' (defining the subject
matter), the 'dispositio' (organising the argument), the 'elocutio' (the embellishment of the
argument through metaphors, similes or other rhetorical tropes), the 'actio' (pronunciation
and gesture) and the 'memoria' (strategies for committing to memory). Rhetorical treatises
traditionally emphasised the importance of coherence, whereby each of the five processes
of composition would necessarily influence the other four parts.

Innovative, questioning poets such as Baudelaire and Mallarmé make the uncertainty of poeticity a necessary and integral feature of their writing; they recognise that any endeavour to codify or classify poetic language, with the specific aim of guaranteeing a particular response, is erroneous. Yet they do not do away with poetic principles altogether. By analysing the status of rhetoric in nineteenth-century France, together with accepted rules of prosody and developments in both these areas, I shall demonstrate that the uncertainty of these poetic principles drives Baudelaire and Mallarmé towards a concept of 'voice' which is both active and memorable. In order to safeguard both the immediacy and longevity of effects created by poetic language, the poets also begin to rely on a particular important ally. That ally is music. Music offers an approach which helps to evaluate what is pleasing to the ear, with the implication that the effects created by music will be more immediate than those created by language alone. As a result, musical principles begin to feature with greater prevalence in poetic treatises written during the later stages of the century. I suggest that the traditional principles underlying poetry are increasingly re-moulded by Baudelaire and Mallarmé according to an aesthetic sensitivity which places an important emphasis on sounding out active and memorable effects of poetry.

By proposing to re-evaluate the rhetorical principles of 'actio' and 'memoria', I am of course aware that these stem from an outmoded paradigm. Roland Barthes, for example, in his seminar on rhetorical practices given at the 'École pratique des hautes études' in December 1970, chooses to eliminate from his discussion the 'actio' and the 'memoria' elements, claiming that they were no longer relevant once the printed text began to take over from spoken discourse:

> Les deux dernières (*Actio* et *Memoria*) ont été très vite sacrifiées, dès lors que la rhétorique n'a plus seulement porté sur les discours parlés (déclamés) d'avocats ou d'hommes politiques, ou de 'conférenciers' ... mais aussi, puis à peu près exclusivement, sur des 'œuvres' (écrites). ... Mais, comme ces deux dernières opérations sont absentes de l'œuvre (opposé à l'*oratio*) et comme, même chez les Anciens, elles n'ont donné lieu à aucun classement (mais seulement à de brefs commentaires), on les éliminera, ici, de la machine rhétorique.[5]

> [The last two (*Actio* and *Memoria*) were very quickly sacrified as soon as rhetoric no longer only governed speeches (declamations) by lawyers or politicians, or 'orators' ... but also, and then more or less exclusively, (written) 'works'. ... But, since these last two processes are absent from the work (as opposed to the *oratio*) and since, even in Antiquity, they did not give rise to any classification (but only to brief commentaries), we shall eliminate them from the rhetorical machine.]

---

[5]   'L'ancienne rhétorique' in *Œuvres complètes,* ed. by Éric Marty, 3 vols (Paris: Seuil, 1994), II, pp.929–930.

This follows suggestions by other twentieth-century rhetorical theorists such as Genette and later Paul Zumthor who claim that the advent of the printed text instigated not only a more individual interaction between a work and its audience, but also a process of 'silencing':

> la rencontre de l'œuvre et de son lecteur est par nature strictement individuelle, même s'il y a pluralité de lecteurs dans l'espace et le temps. Cette personalisation de la lecture a été fortement accentuée, il est vrai, depuis qu'au cours des XVe, XVIe, XVIIe siècles, s'en est répandue une pratique purement visuelle et muette.[6]

> [the encounter between the work and its reader is by its very nature strictly individual, even if there is a plurality of readers in space and time. This personalisation of reading, became particularly evident, in fact, when purely visual and silent reading practices became widespread during the course of the fifteenth, sixteenth, and seventeenth centuries.]

In fact, I shall suggest that the aesthetics of voice in the context of Baudelaire's and Mallarmé's poetic practices counter these claims that the written or printed text spelt the demise of what could be called 'vocal' practices or performances of poetry. I propose, furthermore, that the rhetorical model which sees the 'actio' and the 'memoria' elements as integral to the way in which a particular work is formulated also remains an integral part of Baudelaire's and Mallarmé's writings. The issue that Barthes, Genette and Zumthor sought to explain during the latter half of the twentieth century – that of the demise of rhetorical practices which relate particularly to the process of reading (out loud or otherwise) and remembering – is brought into sharper focus in the context of my approach to Baudelaire's and Mallarmé's poetry.

There are, of course, no viable technical manuals available which explain 'how to read Baudelaire' or 'how to read Mallarmé'. The present-day reader must inevitably face potential risks of anachrony, misinterpretation, or misreading poetry. But it is not only the present-day reader who is faced with the question of how to read late nineteenth-century French verse. Already Gossart had proclaimed in his 1859 treatise that 'peu de personnes déclament bien' ['few people declaim well'], where 'déclamer' means 'la manière de lire ou de réciter les vers' ['the way of reading or reciting verse'].[7] For Baudelaire in particular, who suffered the pains of his 1857 trial, the fact that so few people know how to read verse effectively is a problem that needs to be addressed. Baudelaire's self-reflective 'Épigraphe pour un livre condamné' is the only poem, besides 'Au lecteur', which explicitly

---

[6] Paul Zumthor, *Performance, réception, lecture* (Québec: Editions du Préambule, 1990), p.59.

[7] Alexandre Gossart, *Traité complet de la versification française* (Paris: Maire-Nyon, [1859?]), p.130.

deals with the art of reading. By contrast, Mallarmé's liminal sonnet 'Salut' can scarcely be said to offer explicit instructions on the art of reading poetry. That both Baudelaire and Mallarmé avoid long prefaces or explanatory texts suggests, however, that the poets' way of addressing this thorny issue was expressed through their poetic compositions themselves. In order to establish the aesthetic framework for the poets' attitudes towards the concept of 'voice' in poetry, I shall analyse their writings in the context of important nineteenth-century principles, conventions and expectations.

Finding Guarantees in the Wake of Change

To whom shall I speak, what shall I say, and how shall I say it? Such self-conscious reflections inform Baudelaire's liminal 'Au lecteur' and pervade both his *Fleurs du Mal* and his prose poems. Particularly in the wake of the 1857 trial over the purportedly immoral content of the first edition of the *Fleurs du Mal*, Baudelaire is preoccupied with the question of how his poetry might be read. His vitriol towards those who brought him to trial is expressed most explicitly in a poem entitled 'Épigraphe pour un Livre condamné' (B.*OC*.I, p.137) published in the *Revue européenne* in 1861, and which some critics consider to have been intended as a preface to the second edition of the *Fleurs:*

> Lecteur paisible et bucolique,
> Sobre et naïf homme de bien
> Jette ce livre saturnien,
> Orgiaque et mélancolique.
>
> Si tu n'as fait ta rhétorique
> Chez Satan, le rusé doyen,
> Jette! tu n'y comprendrais rien,
> Ou tu me croirais hystérique.
>
> Mais si, sans se laisser charmer,
> Ton œil sait plonger dans les gouffres,
> Lis-moi, pour apprendre à m'aimer;
>
> Âme curieuse qui souffres
> Et vas cherchant ton paradis,
> Plains-moi! ... Sinon, je te maudis!
>
> [Quiet and bucolic reader,
> Sober and innocent upstanding man,
> Throw away this book which is saturnine,
> Orgiastic and melancholy.

If you have not studied rhetoric
Under Satan, the cunning master,
Throw it away! because you would understand nothing,
Or you would think me hysterical.

But if, without succumbing to any charms,
Your eye knows how to plunge down into the gulf,
Read me, to learn to love me;

Curious soul who suffers
And go on looking for your paradise,
Pity me! ... Otherwise, I curse you!]

The contrast that this octosyllabic sonnet establishes with 'Au lecteur' is apparent in the first line. Where in the final line of 'Au lecteur', Baudelaire addresses a reader who is 'hypocrite' ['hypocritical'] and his 'semblable' ['double'] and 'frère' ['brother'], here in the 'Épigraphe' he disdains the 'Lecteur paisible et bucolique' (v.1). Baudelaire establishes an idea of the kind of reader he wishes to address, aware that what he endeavours to say in his poetry may be misunderstood by a reader who is not attuned to his aesthetic ('tu n'y comprendrais rien' v.7). In order to ensure a mutual understanding between poet and reader, Baudelaire invokes a devilish rhetoric ('Si tu n'as fait ta rhétorique / Chez Satan ...' v.5–6). Rhetoric – the art of organising a discourse effectively, and a subject which Baudelaire studied formally at school – is subverted and distorted by the invocation to the devil. Does this recourse to a devilish rhetoric imply a complete rejection of the traditional rules and mores that would typically govern poetic production? Is Baudelaire suggesting that the art of rhetoric is undermined altogether by his own poetic endeavour?

The figure of the devil in the *Fleurs du Mal* offers a nuanced answer to these questions. Baudelaire's references to 'Satan' or 'Le Diable' offer more than simply a personification of the spirit of evil or decadence: his identification with Satan is due in part to the notion that the alliance between the devil and the domain of hell (as is made particularly explicit in 'Au lecteur') serves to strengthen Baudelaire's own position as a poet through the resonances that this sparks with the important poet figures of Dante's *Inferno*. In the fourth stanza of 'Au lecteur' (B.*OC*.I, p.5), Baudelaire writes:

C'est le Diable qui tient les fils qui nous remuent!
Aux objets répugnants nous trouvons des appas;
Chaque jour vers l'Enfer nous descendons d'un pas,
Sans horreur, à travers des ténèbres qui puent. (v.13–16)

[It is the Devil who holds the puppet strings which make us move!
We find charms to counter the repugnant objects;
Each day towards Hell we descend step by step,
Without being horrified, across the shadows which stink.]

The 'nous' persona that permeates the stanza (and indeed the whole of 'Au lecteur') unites the poetic 'je' not only to the kind of reader hypothesised in the tercets of the 'Épigraphe' cited above and designated as 'hypocrite' in the final line of 'Au lecteur', but also to the figures of Dante and his poet-guide Virgil. The descent into hell which Baudelaire describes in line 15 as 'Chaque jour vers l'Enfer nous descendons d'un pas', echoing Virgil's words to Dante "'Or discendiam qua giù nel cieco mondo"',[8] grants Baudelaire's devilish rhetoric a sense of authority and heritage.

This authority is further reinforced in the prose poem 'Le Joueur généreux' (B.*OC*.I, pp.325–328) where Baudelaire converses with a devilish figure who tells him of a famous devilish orator who claimed that "'la plus belle des ruses du diable est de vous persuader qu'il n'existe pas!'" ["'the most brilliant ruse of the devil is to convince you that he doesn't exist!'"]. Baudelaire then goes on to write that:

Le souvenir de ce célèbre orateur nous conduisit naturellement vers le sujet des académies, et mon étrange convive m'affirma qu'il ne dédaignait pas, en beaucoup de cas, d'inspirer la plume, la parole et la conscience des pédagogues; et qu'il assistait presque toujours en personne, quoique invisible, à toutes les séances académiques.

[The memory of this celebrated orator naturally brought us to the subject of academies, and my strange guest told me that he did not despise, in many cases, inspiring the quill, the spoken word and the conscience of pedagogues; and that he was almost always present in person, although invisible, at all academy meetings.]

Whilst the allusion to the 'académie' is probably an ironic jibe on Baudelaire's part as a result of his failed candidature for the Académie française in 1861–1862 (early drafts of the prose poem suggest that it was composed between 1861–1864), Baudelaire's suggestion that the devil infiltrates even the rhetoric of esteemed authorities such as the Académie française indicates that he is aware of the changes taking place in nineteenth-century French rhetorical practices, including in pedagogical circles. Baudelaire's rejection of those readers who have not followed this path into a hellish domain inhabited by 'la ménagerie infâme de nos vices' ('Au lecteur' v.32) suggests that he abhors those who seek too naïve or sedate a

---

[8]   Dante, *Inferno*, ed. and trans. by Robert Durling (Oxford: OUP, 1996), pp.70–71; (Canto IV, v.13), "'Now let us descend down here into the blind world'".

poetry (hence the claim in the 'Épigraphe' that this kind of reader is a 'Sobre et naïf homme de bien' v.2). Baudelaire's devilish rhetoric does not, then, imply an outright rejection of conventional practices, but rather a more sophisticated and challenging perspective of what it means to write poetry, and of what it means to communicate that poetry to a reader.[9]

What Baudelaire's 'Épigraphe' reveals is that one of the central concerns of rhetoric – to know your audience and to construct your argument accordingly – is a concern for Baudelaire. But knowing his audience is a problematic endeavour.[10] That Baudelaire rejects simplistic or naïve ways of constructing his poetic argument is symptomatic of the changes that poetry undergoes during the nineteenth century in France. Victor Hugo had famously declared 'Guerre à la rhétorique' ['War on rhetoric!'] in his poem 'Réponse à un acte d'accusation' of January 1834. The rhetoric that Hugo repudiated was one that rigidly upheld formal and standardised uses of rhetorical tropes and figures and of metrical rules. The overt parallel that Hugo draws between traditional rhetorical practice and the '*ancien régime*' reveals a political agenda which Hugo exploits as a metaphor whose purpose is to distinguish between an outmoded formal rhetoric and a new rhetorical practice.[11] Hugo's recognition, in the 1830s, that the rhetorical basis for poetry needed a new lease of life, is compared to a revolutionary movement. Hugo writes in the closing stages of the 'Réponse à un acte d'accusation':

> Le mouvement complète ainsi son action.
> Grâce à toi, progrès saint, la Révolution
> Vibre aujourd'hui dans l'air, dans la voix, dans le livre.
> Dans le mot palpitant le lecteur la sent vivre.[12]

> [Thus the movement completes its action.
> Thanks to you, sacred progress, the Revolution

---

[9]   Whilst not referring specifically to nineteenth-century France, Rice and Schofer comment: 'Whereas ancient rhetoric taught speakers of public address, modern rhetorical practice has created a new literature which asks the reader to participate constantly in the construction of texts, and to discover in texts themselves the rules for reading and understanding them.' Donald Rice and Peter Schofer, *Rhetorical Poetics: Theory and Practice of Figural and Symbolic Reading in Modern French Literature* (Madison: University of Wisconsin Press, 1983), p.xiv. Although Baudelaire does not take it to such an extent, he recognises that developments in rhetorical practices place greater emphasis on the reader.

[10]   This does not mean, however, that is impossible, as Lawrence Porter has suggested: 'Baudelaire found that to make contact with his audience was impossible, or worse yet, pointless.' Lawrence Porter, *The Crisis of French Symbolism* (Ithaca and London: Cornell University Press, 1990), p.x.

[11]   Victor Hugo, 'Les Contemplations' in *Œuvres poétiques*, ed. by Pierre Albouy, Bibliothèque de la Pléiade, 2 vols (Paris: Gallimard, 1967), II, p.497.

[12]   'Les Contemplations', p.499.

Still vibrates today in the air, in the voice, in the book.
In the beating word the reader feels it is alive.]

Notwithstanding the disparagingly ironic tone that permeates most of the poem, these lines show Hugo's belief in the idea that rhetoric and poetry are undergoing a palpable renaissance. The words 'dans l'air, dans la voix, dans le livre' suggest that this process of renewal finds its validation in the relationship between hearing, speaking and reading – and that its effectiveness depends on the vibrancy of poetic language.

Hugo's positive diction describing this revolution and change finds itself rephrased, in Baudelaire's 'Épigraphe' about 30 years later, in more subversive language. Baudelaire is no longer certain that the vibrancy of poetic language will be sufficient to guarantee a particular response from his reader. Baudelaire's need to call upon the devil, upon hell, and even upon Dante and Virgil, to serve as guarantors for rhetorical effectiveness suggests that the war on rhetoric that Hugo had declared has not resulted in a glorious victory which sees rhetoric eliminated altogether. In fact Hugo followed his poetic declaration of 'Guerre à la rhétorique' in the second hemistich with the words 'et paix à la syntaxe' ['and peace to syntax'].[13] By raising the status of syntax to one that replaces rhetoric as a means of guaranteeing effectiveness, Hugo sets in motion a certain degree of slippage between rhetoric and syntax. Both imply a set of rules and strictures for organising language, with rhetoric theoretically posing as a larger-scale strategy, and syntax as a smaller-scale device concerned with individual phrase units. But Hugo's focus on grammatical syntax as a supposedly more sure method for guaranteeing an effective use of language is in fact just as problematic as the method of rhetoric which he eschews. That Mallarmé, in the closing stages of the nineteenth century, reiterates Hugo's call to rely on syntax – even though Mallarmé himself employs the most extravagant and complex syntax in his own poetry – shows how Mallarmé's own approach to syntax implies a more challenging use of language. Mallarmé writes in 'Le Mystère dans les lettres' (published in *La Revue blanche*, 1 September 1896):

> Quel pivot, j'entends, dans ces contrastes, à l'intelligibilité? il faut une garantie –
> La Syntaxe – [14]

> [What linchpin, I hear, in these contrasts, for intelligibility? a guarantee is needed –
> Syntax –]

The ensuing ellipsis, however, is provocatively ambiguous. Similarly, Baudelaire's provocative approach to rhetoric (rather than an outright refusal of it) is expressed

---

[13]   'Les Contemplations', p.497.

[14]   Stéphane Mallarmé, *Œuvres complètes*, ed. by Bertrand Marchal, Bibliothèque de la Pléiade, 2 vols (Paris: Gallimard, 1998–2003), II, pp.232–233. All subsequent references

in his reference to the cleverness of the 'rusé doyen' ('Épigraphe' v.6). From Hugo in the 1830s, to Baudelaire in the 1860s, right through to Mallarmé in the 1890s, the question of finding a guarantee for making oneself understood by others pervades poets' minds, and finds no ultimate resolution beyond the suggestion that the accepted rules and conventions need to be challenged.

Rhetoric and Prosody in nineteenth-century France

The poetic changes that swept through France in the wake of Hugo are felt in the new uses of poetic language that begin to dissolve entrenched stylistic traits in order to take on a renewed vibrancy. The political analogy that Hugo employs – which sees various regimes cast aside only to be reinstated briefly before being swept away again – is one which expresses the instability of the status of rhetoric during the nineteenth century in France. In order to understand these changes it is necessary to take into account the context in which they are taking place. In particular, educational practices fuelled poets' knowledge of rhetoric, and the way in which it relates to poetic production. It is perhaps not surprising that Françoise Douay-Soublin, in her study on nineteenth-century rhetoric, also uses, like Hugo, a politically-charged vocabulary. With her main focus on formal rhetoric in terms of educational practices and political usages, she identifies three distinct phases which are outlined as follows in Table 1.1.[15]

Table 1.1   Phases of rhetoric in nineteenth-century France

Date	Phase	Description
1800–1820	restoration	rise in favourable opinion which is badly organised
1820–1850/1860	renaissance	favourable opinion and institutions start working together (in particular the oral exam for the baccalauréat)
1860–1890	reappraisal	the institution persists as opinion starts turning negative

The focus of Douay-Soublin's study does not directly address poetic output during the period, but her analysis does however draw attention to the fact that rhetorical practices underwent a turbulent phase. This, in turn, confirms the attitudes of poets such as Hugo, Baudelaire and Mallarmé towards rhetoric: it is recognised as an important strategy for organising language, and yet its validity is called into question.

---

will be designated by the abbreviation M.*OC*.

[15]   Françoise Douay-Soublin, 'La rhétorique en France au XIXe siècle à travers ses pratiques et ses institutions', in *Histoire de la rhétorique dans l'Europe moderne 1450–1950*, ed. by Marc Fumaroli (Paris: PUF, 1999), p.1201.

During Baudelaire's and Mallarmé's formative years, rhetoric remained an important part of the educational system. Although it is difficult to ascertain precisely which school textbooks on rhetoric either Baudelaire or Mallarmé used, Joëlle Gardes-Tamine reminds us, for example, that Baudelaire attended the Collège Louis-le-Grand where the 'proviseur', Jules-Amable Pierrot-Deseilligny, published various textbooks on rhetoric which were used relatively widely in the education system.[16] What emerges from studies on nineteenth-century rhetorical practices is that rhetorical training focused primarily on three main areas:

1. stylistic imitation of Latin or Greek prose or poetry
2. uses of figures and tropes, and
3. rules of French versification or prosody.

To give an exhaustive analysis of nineteenth-century French rhetorical or prosodic treatises would not only be of questionable value, but also fall outside the scope of this study. A sample selection, however, of the kind of works being published during the period indicates that there is an increasing lack of distinction between definitions of terms such as 'rhetoric', 'prosody', 'eloquence' and 'versification'. Furthermore, the distinctions between genres (whether rhetorical genres such as the 'genus nobile' or the 'genus humile' or literary genres such as narrative, poetry or theatre) is increasingly blurred.[17] This is due, in part, to an intensification in the belief that language is inherently 'musical' and should be governed, therefore, by rules pertaining to aural perception. This is the increasing trend which can be identified from a study of a sample selection of treatises published during the course of the century. In my selection outlined in Table 1.2 below, I have deliberately chosen works which were widely used in the education system, and treatises on prosody which are either prefaced by poets (in particular Hugo and Mallarmé) or written by poets themselves (such as those by Banville and Ghil).[18]

---

[16]   Joëlle Gardes-Tamine, 'Rhétoriques et prosodies', in *Lectures des 'Fleurs du Mal'*, ed. by Steve Murphy (Rennes: Presses Universitaires de Rennes, 2002), p.183.

[17]   Banville, for example, even goes so far as to liken poetry's nobility to a direct access to the soul and God. Whilst Banville's suggestion is somewhat tongue-in-cheek, it nonetheless reminds us of the classical view of poetry in which it is divinely inspired by the god Apollo and communicated to the poet through the Muses: 'La Poésie doit toujours être noble, c'est-à-dire intense, exquise et achevée dans la forme, puisqu'elle s'adresse à ce qu'il y a de plus noble en nous, à l'Âme, qui peut directement être en contact avec Dieu' ['Poetry must always be noble, that is to say, intense, exquisite, and complete in its form, since it appeals to the most noble part of us, to the Soul, which can be in direct contact with God']. Théodore de Banville, *Petit Traité de poésie française* (Paris: Librairie de l'Écho de la Sorbonne, [1872?]), p.8.

[18]   I have not included in my list treatises on Latin prosody which were common in the education system such as the *Traité d'élégance et de versification latine* and other *prosodies latines* based primarily on an eighteenth-century treatise by Le Chevalier. Many of the

Table 1.2   Rhetorical treatises and prosodies published in nineteenth-century
             France

Date	Author	Treatise
1820–1822	Jules-Amable	*Cours d'éloquence française*
1836	Pierrot-Deseilligny	*Choix de compositions françaises et latines ...* *des meilleurs élèves de l'université moderne,* *avec les matières et les arguments*
1827–1830	Pierre Fontanier	*Figures du discours* (based on Dumarsais' 1730 *Traité des Tropes*)
1839–1882	Louis Quicherat	*Petit Traité de versification française* (with authorisation from the Ministre de l'Instruction publique: 'l'usage de cet ouvrage est autorisé pour les classes d'humanités dans les collèges' – numerous editions throughout the century)
1844	Wilhem Ténint	*Prosodie de l'école moderne* (with 'Lettre Avant-propos' by Victor Hugo and 'Préface' by Émile Deschamps)
1859	Alexandre Gossart	*Traité complet de la versification française* *renfermant une nouvelle théorie de la rime,* *la prosodie, la déclamation, les gestes, des* *observations sur la mise en musique de la* *poéise, une description de toutes espèces de* *poèmes, un précis historique*
1872	Théodore de Banville	*Petit Traité de poésie française*
1879	Louis Becq de Fouquières	*Traité général de versification française*
1885–1904	René Ghil	*Traité du Verbe* (with 'Avant-dire' by Mallarmé in 1886 edition)

What emerges from an analysis of these treatises is that in the earlier phase
of the century, the broader view of rhetorical practice was of primary importance
(this is evidenced in both Pierrot-Deseilligny's and Fontanier's texts which
were widely used in the education system). Towards the middle of the century,
a greater number of treatises on versification emerge which are concerned with
the validity of certain poetic forms and metres (such as treatises by Quicherat,
Ténint and Gossart). Gossart's treatise also signals a marked change which sees a
specific emphasis being placed on the 'performance' and 'musicality' which was

---

treatises outlined in Table 1.2, however, were modelled on Latin prosodies such as those
by two influential treatise writers of the eighteenth century (Dumarsais and La Harpe) who
translated from Latin works. We also know, for example, that Baudelaire composed verse
in Latin not simply as part of his schoolboy exercises but also for inclusion in *Les Fleurs
du Mal* with 'Franciscæ meæ laudes' (B.*OC*.I, pp.61–62). My decision to focus solely on
French treatises is due to the fact that French theorists were endeavouring to validate the
rules governing the style and usage of French language in the literary domain.

to characterise treatises published in the later stages of the century (such as those by Banville, Becq de Fouquières and Ghil).

A common trait that runs throughout these works, however, is a concern for validation through a sense of literary heritage or authority. Many of these treatises frequently cite classical authors such as Boileau, Corneille, Molière or Racine, or eighteenth-century authors such as Rousseau or Voltaire.[19] The recourse to examples from a more stable era of literary rules suggests that the changes in the status of literary 'legislation' during the nineteenth century in France complicates the way in which poets can put particular theories into practice. Baudelaire, as we have seen above in the 'Épigraphe', sought to validate his rhetorical practices by recourse to an ancient poetic heritage in the form of Dante and Virgil. The questions surrounding poetic heritage during the nineteenth century are, I suggest, fuelled by doubt and uncertainty concerning poetry's status, as rhetorical principles become increasingly undermined and as music begins to play an increasingly important role in the compositional process.

Versification, Manipulation and Explanation

What, however, is the value of rhetorical or prosodic theories, and how do they relate to poetic practice? The response, I suggest, is twofold. In the first instance, rhetorical treatises and prosodies offer a justification for poetic language which poets seek in order to validate their own work. For example, many theories of versification, including those outlined above, seek to locate the root or origin of French verse. There is a marked tendency to refer back to the twelfth-century roots of the hallowed dodecasyllabic line. Some treatise-writers – and even Baudelaire and Mallarmé themselves – resort to an anthropological view, claiming that the rules of versification (and in particular the alexandrine) arose as a natural result of the innate rhythms and harmonies of the French language itself. In the second instance, the work of treatise-writers offers an explanation of the possible strategies available to would-be poets; significantly, however, it is on this level that theory and practice begin to diverge.

---

[19] Banville contests the notion that the seventeenth and eighteenth centuries serve as suitable eras for ensuring poetry's heritage, and opens his *Petit Traité* with the words: 'Presque tous les traités de poésie ont été écrits au dix-septième et au dix-huitième siècle, c'est-à-dire aux époques où l'on a le plus mal connu et le plus mal su l'art de la Poésie' ['Almost all the treatises on poetry were written during the seventeenth and eighteenth centuries, that is to say during the periods in which the art of Poetry was the least understood and known']. He goes on to qualify this statement, however, by explaining that he nevertheless recognises the genius of Corneille, Racine, Molière and La Fontaine (and indeed he uses numerous examples from the works of each of these authors throughout his treatise). Furthermore, he still has recourse to a literary past as validation for the poetic endeavour, and identifies the sixteenth century as the most important model. Banville, *Petit Traité*, pp.1–2.

Baudelaire's poetic practice serves as an important indication of the kind of developments taking place not only with regard to rhetorical and prosodic theories themselves, but also with regard to their perceived value for poets and their audience. During the middle phase of treatise-writing in nineteenth-century France, significant attention is dedicated to permissible line lengths and verse forms, and numerous examples are offered which reinforce the supposed historical longevity of certain forms and metres. A particular concern expressed in each of the treatises is the pronunciation of the *e muet* and how this affects not only the scansion of French verse, but also the rule of alternation between masculine and feminine rhymes (an issue which becomes central to the debate over the 'musicality' of verse). In his influential treatise Wilhem Ténint claimed that 'La rime est le seul générateur du vers français' ['Rhyme is the sole generator of French verse'].[20] As Graham Robb reminds us, for example, Mallarmé was known to have sketched out his rhyme scheme before filling in the rest of the verse line.[21] Mallarmé was, however, later to accuse this prosodic trait of favouring rhyme above all else as one of the main reasons why French verse underwent a crisis of faith. He writes in 'Crise de vers':

> Accordez que la poésie française, en raison de la primauté dans l'enchantement donnée à la rime, pendant l'évolution jusqu'à nous, s'atteste intermittente. (M.*OC*.II, p.205)

> [We must agree that French poetry, because of the importance of the enchantment granted to rhyme, during its evolution up to the present day, proves to be intermittent.]

A cynical conclusion could be drawn from this example: that poets largely ignored any of the theories of versification being expounded by treatise-writers, and that literary rules are only formed in order to be broken. In fact the situation in nineteenth-century France is more complex than this (especially since Banville, for example, was both poet and theorist, albeit a theorist whose writings are laced with irony). Each treatise-writer inevitably had his own particular agenda to propound. Some predicate greater liberty with verse strictures, others proclaim the inadmissibility of enjambement, for example;[22] and yet, by and large, rules of

---

[20]   Wilhem Ténint, *Prosodie de l'école moderne* (Paris: Didier, 1844), p.101.

[21]   'The table [of possible rhymes] confirms what we already know from other sources – René Ghil, Paul Valéry and Mallarmé himself: he liked to write his poems with the rhymes already in place.' Graham Robb, *Unlocking Mallarmé* (New Haven and London: Yale University Press, 1996), p.58.

[22]   Robb, for example, writes of Banville: 'le *Petit Traité* n'est pas un catalogue objectif des richesses de la prosodie française; il témoigne d'un effort pour imposer des points de vue dont quelques-uns sont particuliers à Banville' ['the *Petit Traité* is not an objective catalogue of the richness of French prosody; it demonstrates an attempt to impose certain

versification remained relatively constant throughout the century. It is perhaps not surprising, therefore, that Baudelaire's and Mallarmé's own verse reveals a clear respect for traditional prosodic legislation in terms of metre, rhyme and form, whilst also beginning to experiment at various points in their careers with the possibility of transgressing or manipulating the rules, since this was beginning to become accepted practice throughout the century.[23]

Hugo's rather insipid 'Lettre Avant-propos' to Ténint's *Prosodie de l'école moderne* praises the theorist for his analysis of the burgeoning 'vers brisé' and newly developing liberties in versificatory practices. Later Banville, in his own *Petit Traité*, acknowledges Ténint's exploration of the possibility of placing the cæsura at any point within the alexandrine line:

> Dans sa remarquable prosodie, publiée en 1844, M. Wilhem Ténint établit que
> le vers alexandrin admet douze combinaisons différentes, en partant du vers qui
> a sa césure après la première syllabe pour arriver au vers qui a sa césure après la
> onzième syllabe. Cela revient à dire qu'en réalité la césure peut être placée après
> n'importe quelle syllabe du vers alexandrin.[24]

> [In his remarkable prosody, published in 1844, M. Wilhem Ténint establishes
> that the alexandrine line permits twelve different combinations, starting with the
> verse whose caesura falls after the first syllable, and ending with the verse whose
> caesura falls after the eleventh syllable. This effectively means that in reality the
> caesura can be placed after any syllable within the alexandrine line.]

Banville then goes on to conclude that total freedom with the hallowed alexandrine line should be permitted but he is careful to qualify his statement:

> Faisons plus: osons proclamer la liberté complète et dire qu'en ces questions
> complexes l'oreille décide seule.[25]

> [Let's go further: let's go so far as to proclaim total freedom and to say that when
> it comes to these complex issues, it is the ear alone which is able to decide.]

So Banville declares that it is only by listening to poetry that its effectiveness and validity can be discerned; the rules themselves are irrelevant. This of course

---

points of view, some of which are particular to Banville himself']. Graham Robb, *La poésie de Baudelaire et la poésie française 1838–1852* (Paris: Aubier, 1993), p.223.

[23] For a detailed analysis – based on Cornulier's system of 'métricométrie' – of each poet's metrical irregularities over the course of their careers, see David Evans, *Rhythm, Illusion and the Poetic Idea: Baudelaire, Rimbaud, Mallarmé* (Amsterdam and New York: Rodopi, 2004).

[24] Banville, *Petit Traité*, pp.96–97.

[25] Banville, *Petit Traité*, p.97.

recalls Hugo's earlier claim in the 'Réponse à un acte d'accusation' that it is only through listening out for the vibrations of poetic language that a renewed poetic vibrancy can take place. So prescriptive legislation surrounding poetic endeavours is not done away with altogether, but the emphasis shifts so that a new aesthetic criteria, the art of listening to poetry, takes centre stage in the debate over poetic validity and status. The willingness on the part of nineteenth-century poets and prosodists to explore new developments in verse form is perhaps best revealed through Baudelaire's and Mallarmé's own experimentations with the prose poem form. Whilst I am not suggesting that this means that all poetry therefore becomes a reflexive experimentation with its own self (although many critics have delighted in reading nineteenth-century poetry in this way), it is evident that poetry comes to be defined in terms of how it affects the reader, and – to borrow a term from Banville – in terms of whether or not it is able to 'charmer l'oreille, enchanter l'esprit' ['charm the ear, enchant the mind'].

In order to sound out poetry's effects, poets increasingly turn away from prosodic legislation itself and look instead towards different art forms for confirmation or validation of their poetic endeavours. Treatises by Gossart, Becq de Fouquières and Ghil seem to mark a further shift in emphasis which specifically privileges the relationship between poetry and music, a relationship which was to become so central to the aesthetic of both Baudelaire and Mallarmé. The recourse to other art forms has both aesthetic and theoretical ramifications. As Ténint proclaimed: 'Or, tout est analogie dans les arts; tout se tient' ['Everything is analogy in the arts; everything is tied in together'][26] – a doctrine which points towards Baudelaire's important theory of 'correspondances' – and Banville writes:

> La Poésie ... est à la fois Musique, Statuaire, Peinture, Éloquence; elle doit charmer l'oreille, enchanter l'esprit, représenter les sons, imiter les couleurs, rendre les objets visibles, et exciter en nous les mouvements qu'il lui plaît d'y produire.[27]

> [Poetry ... is at the same time Music, Sculpture, Painting, Eloquence; it must charm the ear, enchant the mind, represent sounds, imitate colours, make objects visible, and excite within us the movements which it enjoys creating within itself.]

The analogy with other art forms is not only based on the idea of aesthetic correspondence, but also on the effects that experimentation with the rules of an art can produce. If stagnation and poetic sterility are to be avoided, and if poetic vibrance and resonance are to be achieved, then the rules of prosody must develop and be manipulated by the poets.

---

[26]   Ténint, *Prosodie de l'école moderne*, p.85.
[27]   Banville, *Petit Traité*, p.8.

So Baudelaire's devilish rhetoric referred to in the second stanza of the 'Épigraphe' begins to take on a new light: 'faire sa rhétorique chez Satan' is all about being a 'rusé doyen'. A devilish rhetoric means cunning manipulation of the venerable art of poetry. Baudelaire is, for example, renowned for being one of the greatest manipulators of sonnet form. In the 'Épigraphe', Baudelaire eschews the alexandrine metre, which according to traditional prosodic strictures would have been the appropriate verse metre for the sonnet form that he has chosen. He opts instead for the octosyllabic line, which although an accepted traditional French metre, was considered inappropriate to the sonnet form. Writing in the mid-nineteenth century, Quicherat makes it clear that the octosyllabic line is not appropriate for this type of poem:

> Le vers de *huit* syllabes ... est un de nos plus anciens mètres. ... Il se prête à tous les tons: il sert à l'épître (sérieuse ou badine), à la poésie descriptive, à l'ode, aux stances, à l'élégie, au conte, à la chanson, à l'épigramme, au rondeau. Il semble moins convenir à la ballade et au sonnet.[28]

> [Le verse of *eight* syllables ... is one of our most ancient metres. ... It lends itself to all tones: it works for the epistle (whether serious or playful), for descriptive poetry, for the ode, for lyric stanzas, for the elegy, for the short story, for the 'chanson', for the epigram, for the rondo. It seems less well suited for the ballad or for the sonnet.]

Banville, however, proclaims 30 years later:

> Le Sonnet peut être écrit en vers de toutes les mesures.[29]

> [The Sonnet can be written in all possible verse lengths.]

Banville would nevertheless decree that Baudelaire's 'Épigraphe' is an irregular sonnet because it does not follow what he defines as the only admissible 'regular' rhyme scheme for a sonnet (ABBA ABBA CCD EDE, where Baudelaire here uses ABBA ABBA CDC DEE). These discrepancies between the definition of the sonnet form by prosodists, whether in terms of metre or rhyme scheme, and Baudelaire's own manipulative practices indicate that Baudelaire's aesthetic agenda had begun to search for new forms of validation outside of traditional strictures. Yet Baudelaire does not do away with the rules altogether. For example in the 'Épigraphe' he maintains the 'volta' between the quatrains and the tercets, clearly signalled by the insertion of 'Mais' at the beginning of the first tercet. The final line also retains the kind of rhetorical force typically required of sonnet

---

[28]   Quicherat, *Petit Traité de versification française*, 8th edn (Paris: Librairie Hachette, 1882), p.101.

[29]   Banville, *Petit Traité*, p.171.

form with its virulent 'Sinon, je te maudis!'. The two imperatives that Baudelaire inserts at the beginning of the last line of each of the tercets ('Lis-moi', 'Plains-moi') also add an extra layer of rhetorical force, by implying that the process of reading must also be a process of compassionate understanding (the traditional rhetorical 'captatio benevolentiæ'). The hinted anaphora with the imperatives of the tercets ('Lis-moi', 'Plains-moi') is also reinforced by the anaphoric imperative 'Jette' at the third line of each of the quatrains: in this way the contrast between two different types of reader is firmly established. Baudelaire favours the type of reader who has studied rhetoric with the devil and who is therefore able to discern the effects of Baudelaire's subtle manipulations.

These rhetorical manipulations are further reinforced by the rhyme words. The richness of the A-rhyme words in particular ('bucolique', 'mélancolique', 'rhétorique', 'hystérique') sets up a patterning of contrasts and analogies: 'bucolique' is posited as the calm opposite of 'mélancolique', 'rhétorique' as the ordered opposite of 'hystérique', but the couplet over the stanzaic break which allies 'mélancolique' and 'rhétorique' reinforces the Baudelairean attitude to rhetorical techniques. Rhetorical practices for Baudelaire are far from simple and unproblematic. The other particularly rich rhyme in the poem of 'gouffres' and 'souffres' in the tercets reinforces this attitude and Baudelaire thereby requires his preferred reader to enter with him into the uncertainty of the abyss of poetic language. He turns away from any rhetorical poetics that would simply be 'paisible', 'bucolique', 'sobre' or 'naïf', and takes on a more questioning stance. The curiosity addressed in the first line of the final tercet ('Âme curieuse') also implies a rhetorical curiosity which goes beyond simplistic interpretation of traditional rules and will find its rich rewards in the yearned-for 'paradis' that closes the line. Baudelaire recognises that unless he and his reader are able to challenge what it means to employ rhetoric within poetry, little reward or satisfaction will be gained from reading it. The 'Épigraphe' confirms the idea that rhetoric's primary aim – to persuade the reader – will only be effective if Baudelaire can establish a sophisticated rapport with his reader.

This, in turn, reaffirms the status of rhetoric in Baudelaire's aesthetic. Although he is careful to manipulate rhetorical strategies to his own end, he understands that rhetorical and prosodic systems are essential and ingrained within human language. In the 'Salon de 1859', Baudelaire makes it clear that he perceives both rhetoric and prosody to be inherent to the human condition:

> il est évident que les rhétoriques et les prosodies ne sont pas des tyrannies inventées arbitrairement, mais une collection de règles réclamées par l'organisation même de l'être spirituel. (B.*OC*.II, pp.626–627)

> [It is clear that rhetorics and prosodies are not arbitrarily invented tyrannies, but a set of rules required by the very make-up of the spiritual being.]

The political metaphor, already seen in Hugo's attitude towards rhetoric, is used by Baudelaire to contest the notion that rhetoric or prosody might be an arbitrarily dictated tyranny. For him, the rules are innate and necessary. Moreover, as Baudelaire goes on to say in the 'Salon de 1859', the rules which govern artistic production do not stifle originality but have the opposite effect. This recalls the view expressed by the dedicatee of *Les Fleurs du Mal* in the opening stanza of his poem 'L'Art', published in the same year as the *Fleurs:*

> Oui, l'œuvre sort plus belle
> D'une forme au travail
> Rebelle,
> Vers, marbre, onyx, émail.[30]

> [Yes, the work of art emerges most beautifully
> From a material which is
> Rebellious,
> Verse, marble, onyx, enamel.]

Gautier's poem allies content with form. By choosing a difficult verse structure which is metrically concise (three of the four lines of each quatrain tantalisingly hint at the alexandrine by using hexametres, and the third line of each stanza consists of only two syllables), Gautier puts his theory into practice. Baudelaire's attraction to the notion that adhering to formal constraints will serve rhetorical effect is confirmed in his oft-cited letter to Armand Fraisse, dated 18 February 1860, in which he expresses in a maxim-like turn of phrase the same notion that Gautier expresses in 'L'Art':

> Parce que la forme est contraignante, l'idée jaillit plus intense. Tout va bien au Sonnet, la bouffonnerie, la galanterie, la passion, la rêverie, la méditation philosophique.[31]

> [Because the form is restrictive, the idea bursts forth more intensely. Everything suits the Sonnet: farce, flattery, passion, reverie, philosophical meditation.]

---

[30]   Théophile Gautier, 'Émaux et Camées', in *Poésies complètes*, ed. by René Jasinski, 3 vols (Paris: Nizet, 1970), III, p.128. Gautier's diction of precious stones in 'L'Art' not only refers back to the title of his collection, but also – by including 'vers' in the list – reinforces the poetic commonplace of using precious stones to designate rhymes. See also Graham Robb's analysis of the use of 'onyx' in Mallarmé's 'sonnet en *yx*' in *Unlocking Mallarmé*, p.64.

[31]   Charles Baudelaire, *Correspondance*, ed. by Claude Pichois, Bibliothèque de la Pléiade, 2 vols (Paris: Gallimard, 1966–1973), I, p.676. All subsequent references will be designated by the abbreviation B.*Corr.*

This belief that the greater the constraint, the more intense the poetic idea, is qualified, however, by the notion already expressed in the 'Salon de 1859': prosodic constraints are not arbitrary rules but result from a need for organisation by the human condition. Manipulation of these innate rules is not a contradiction of them, but a more sophisticated development of them. As Gautier warned in the fifth line of 'L'Art': 'Point de contraintes fausses!' ['No false constraints!']. Gautier's warning is heeded by Baudelaire who recognises the distinction between unnatural or false rules and the rules of prosody whose roots he believes 'plongent plus avant dans l'âme humaine que ne l'indique aucune théorie classique' ['are to be found far deeper within the human soul than any classical theory suggests'] (B.*OC*.I, p.183). He then goes on to state that:

> la poésie française possède une prosodie mystérieuse et méconnue (B.*OC*.I, p.183)

[French poetry has a mysterious and undervalued prosody]

If French prosody is 'mystérieuse et méconnue', it is not through want of analysis and study that it remains thus (as the plethora of treatises on French prosody testifies). It is a necessary condition of prosodic rules to be 'mystérieuse et méconnue', because this is a mark of their sophistication. If prosody were self-explanatory, poetry would simply enter the domain of banal technical display, whereby every response would be entirely predictable, confirming expectations in an entirely dissatisfactory way.[32]

It is for this reason that Baudelaire rejects, in his fourth 'projet de préface', the notion that he should explain his art:

> Mon éditeur prétend qu'il y aurait quelque utilité ... à expliquer pourquoi et comment j'ai fait ce livre, quels ont été mon but et mes moyens, mon dessein et ma méthode. Un tel travail de critique aurait sans doute quelques chances d'amuser les esprits amoureux de la rhétorique profonde ... Mais ... ne paraît-il pas évident que ce serait là une besogne tout à fait superflue, pour les uns comme pour les autres, puisque les uns savent ou devinent, et que les autres ne comprendront jamais? (B.*OC*.I, p.185)

[My editor claims that it would be in some way useful ... if I explained why and how I have written this book, and what my aims and my means, my design and my method, were. Such critical reflection would no doubt be of some interest to those who enjoy profound rhetoric ... But ... surely it is obvious that it would

---

[32]   As Baudelaire writes in his first 'projet de préface': 'le rythme et la rime répondent dans l'homme aux immortels besoins de monotonie, de symétrie et de surprise' ['rhythm and rhyme meet man's immortal needs for monotony, symmetry and surprise'] (B.*OC*.I, p.182).

be an entirely superfluous requirement, of no use to anyone, since some simply know or imagine it, whereas others will just never understand it?]

Baudelaire also makes a distinction in this passage between rhetoric per se and a 'rhétorique profonde', which reaffirms the Baudelairean distinction made in the 'Épigraphe' between those who will comprehend the complexities of his 'devilish' rhetoric and those who will not. This passage also elaborates the notion that poetic language must remain 'mystérieuse et méconnue' precisely because it comes from the unfathomable, immense and painful depths of human experience. This recalls in turn the rhyme which allies the 'gouffres' and the verb 'souffres' in the tercets of the 'Épigraphe', for example.

The diction which permeates Baudelaire's writings on rhetoric and prosody increasingly exploits the unknown and the unknowable in poetry. Baudelaire seeks to envelop himself in this unknown in the closing lines of the final poem of *Les Fleurs du Mal*, 'Le Voyage' (B.*OC*.I, p.134):

> Nous voulons, tant ce feu nous brûle le cerveau,
> Plonger au fond du gouffre, Enfer ou Ciel qu'importe?
> Au fond de l'Inconnu pour trouver du *nouveau!* (v.142–144)

> [Since this fire burns in our minds, we want
> To plunge to the bottom of the gulf, Hell or Heaven, what does it matter?
> To the bottom of the Unknown in order to find something *new!*]

The frequent alliance that Baudelaire makes between the idea of 'mystère', the 'méconnu' or the 'inconnu' and the verb 'plonger' confirms his view of a 'rhétorique profonde' as part of a natural, innate feature of the human condition that is too profound and too subtle to be explained. This is reiterated in his article on Gautier:

> Je ne puis certainement pas faire ici un cours complet de poétique et de prosodie. S'il existe dans notre langue des termes assez nombreux, assez subtils, pour expliquer une certaine poésie, saurais-je les trouver? Il en est des vers comme de quelques belles femmes en qui se sont fondues l'originalité et la correction; on ne les définit pas, on les *aime*. (B.*OC*.II, p.125)

> [I cannot of course give a complete course in poetics and prosody here. If there are enough terms in our language which are subtle enough to explain a particular type of poetry, would I be able to find them? The same goes for verse as for certain beautiful women in whom both originality and propriety are intermingled; we don't define them, we *love* them.]

This dual reluctance to define or explain poetry and to define or explain a woman's beauty also emerges in the poem 'Tout entière' (B.*OC*.I, p.42). The poetic 'je' is goaded by the devil who asks him to explain and analyse a woman's beauty. Baudelaire's familiarity with the devil's ruses, however – since of course he has studied rhetoric under him – means that although the 'Démon' who entered Baudelaire's bedroom had hoped to '[l]e prendre en faute' ['catch him in flagrante'] (v.3), Baudelaire is wise to this, and instead retorts, in the penultimate stanza of the poem, that any analysis is impotent in the face of the woman's beauty:

> Et l'harmonie est trop exquise,
> Qui gouverne tout son beau corps,
> Pour que l'impuissante analyse
> En note les nombreux accords. (v.17–20)

> [And the harmony which governs
> The whole of her beautiful body is too exquisite,
> For impotent analysis to be able
> To note down its numerous accords.]

Nor is the analogy of the beautiful woman in the context of poetry itself an arbitrary one. The terms used to describe the woman's beauty are frequently used to describe the notion of poetics: 'harmonie', 'gouverne', 'analyse', 'nombre' are all terms that occur again and again in prosodic treatises in relation to the poetic art. Baudelaire makes it clear that he will not take on the role of prosodic theorist; this is not because he feels he is unqualified to do so, but because he recognises that explaining poetics will not bring him or his reader any closer to an understanding of poetry and its effects.

The Poet's Privilege: Hearing Voices

So not only does Baudelaire refuse to try to explain the rules of prosody, but as the 'projets de préface' and the 'Épigraphe' indicate, he recognises that not everyone is in the privileged position of being able to accept that true 'rhétorique' is necessarily 'profonde' and that 'prosodie' is necessarily 'mystérieuse et méconnue'. Baudelaire does accept, however, that there might be some possibility of attaining a deeper understanding of the rules and methods behind a person's art, but he believes that it is solely the wise and subtle poet – the 'rusé doyen' of the 'Épigraphe' perhaps – who will be able to comprehend the complexities underlying literary rules, and, more importantly, who will know how to employ them effectively. This view is put forward in his article on Wagner, where he contests a prevailing view amongst contemporary critics that a true artist will be driven purely by his 'génie' and will not resort to any sense of 'rationalité' in explaining or theorising his art. Although Baudelaire refuses to explain his own poetry, he perceives his role as poet as one which puts him in the best position for evaluating and explaining Wagner's art. His disdain for critics who believe that Wagner cannot be a musician, a poet and a critic all at once, leads Baudelaire to a conclusion that justifies his own position as critic:

> Le lecteur ne sera donc pas étonné que je considère le poète comme le meilleur de tous les critiques. (B.*OC*.II, p.793)

> [The reader will not be surprised therefore that I consider the poet to be the best of all critics.]

Leaving aside the tinges of irony and self-justification that underlie this statement, this standpoint serves as an important qualification of Baudelaire's refusal to explain or rationalise art through rigid theoretical formulations. As Rosemary Lloyd has demonstrated, the critic who is also a creative writer 'has no need to shield himself with dogma'.[33] For Baudelaire, history offers incontrovertible proof of the fact that poetry comes first, and that rules arise as a necessary result of poetic practice:

> La poésie a existé, s'est affirmée, et elle a engendré l'étude des règles. Telle est l'histoire incontestée du travail humain. (B.*OC*.II, p.793)

> [Poetry existed, it affirmed itself, and it gave birth to the study of rules. This is the uncontested history of human endeavour.]

Baudelaire's argument up to this point in the Wagner article has followed a somewhat circuitous route, contrasting 'incomplete' poets with 'great' poets, and comparing these with 'great' artists who are also critics. He establishes a chronology for critical analysis of 'les lois obscures' ['obscure laws'] underlying poetry (B.*OC*.II, p.793) in terms of a necessarily post-facto rationalisation. Fundamentally, Baudelaire stresses that if anyone is going to analyse 'les lois obscures' of poetry – which are necessarily 'mystérieuses et méconnues' since rhetoric is 'profonde' and innate to human language – then this must be done only by someone who is already skilled in the art.

The implications of this are significant. As the 'Épigraphe' and 'Au lecteur' poems confirm, even if someone does analyse or explain their art, only a skilled reader or audience will be able to understand what is at stake. The relationship between the poet and his audience, therefore, is predicated on a devilish, cunning, subtly manipulated rhetoric which is exclusively targeted at those who are sensitive to the poet's art (with the implication that only those who are poets themselves will be able to truly analyse Baudelaire's endeavours). Profoundly

---

[33] Rosemary Lloyd, *Baudelaire's Literary Criticism* (Cambridge: CUP, 1981), p.271.

influenced by Poe's *Philosophy of Composition* of 1846, he writes in his fourth 'projet de préface':[34]

> Montre-t-on au public affolé aujourd'hui, indifférent demain, le mécanisme des trucs? Lui explique-t-on les retouches et les variantes improvisées aux répétitions, et jusqu'à quelle dose l'instinct et la sincérité sont mêlés aux rubriques et au charlatanisme indispensable dans l'amalgame de l'œuvre? Lui révèle-t-on toutes ... les horreurs qui composent le sanctuaire de l'art? (B.*OC*.I, p.185)

> [Does one show to the public who are panic-stricken today, and indifferent tomorrow, the mechanism behind tricks? Does one explain to them the alterations and the variations improvised upon repetition, and to what extent instinct and sincerity are intermingled with the rubrics and charlatanism which are indispensable to the amalgam of the work of art? Does one reveal to them ... all the horrors which make up the sanctuary of art?]

The fickleness of the general public in the face of art means that they will be the least disposed to comprehend, or even to enter into, the convoluted and mysterious world of poetic composition. The poet's refusal to explain his art does not denigrate the value of rhetorical and prosodic theories themselves, but offers a more sophisticated reaction towards such theories that, in turn, means that more sophisticated demands are made of his reader. Sophistication, I suggest, means an aesthetic attentiveness which derives from a careful reading of poetry. The kind of reading or performance practices associated with the poetry of Baudelaire and Mallarmé will be analysed in greater detail in the following chapter, but it is sufficient at this stage to state that the poets themselves considered a careful reader to be one who listens attentively to the subtleties of the poetic line.

Like Baudelaire, Mallarmé is uneasy about explaining poetic techniques to the public. This is evident towards the end of his career in a draft for an article on verse, published posthumously. Mallarmé believes that a writer should not be expected to explain his art:

---

[34]   'Most writers – poets in especial – prefer having it understood that they compose by a species of fine frenzy – an ecstatic intuition – and would positively shudder at letting the public take a peep behind the scenes, at the elaborate and vacillating crudities of thought – at the true purposes seized only at the last moment – at the innumerable glimpses of idea that arrived not at the maturity of full view – at the fully-matured fancies discarded in despair as unmanageable – at the cautious selections and rejections – at the painful erasures and interpolations – in a word, at the wheels and pinions – the tackle for scene-shifting – the step-ladders, and demon-traps – the cock's feathers, the red paint and the black patches, which, in ninety-nine cases out of a hundred, constitute the properties of the literary *histrio*'. Edgar Allan Poe, 'The Philosophy of Composition', *Essays and Reviews* (New York: The Library of America, 1984), p.14.

Je détonne … qu'il y a toujours, pour l'écrivain, à discourir au public, même réduit à des confrères, encore que cela se fasse couramment, sur la technique. A peine si ces dissertations sont de mise, un instant, de vive voix, entre camarades. (M.*OC*.II, p.475)

[I disagree … that it is always necessary, for a writer, to talk in public, even only amongst fellow writers, even though it is very common, about techniques. These detailed examinations are only barely appropriate, briefly, in person, between close friends.]

Mallarmé's disquiet is based on a question of register and formality. He eschews lengthy dissertations on literary techniques, but he is willing to accept the possibility of a brief exchange on the matter between close friends; this notion of a brief, fleeting, transient exchange about poetic language will become one of the central tenets of his aesthetics of voice, as will be explored in subsequent chapters. Mallarmé's distaste for talking about literary techniques might suggest that he is not in favour of rhetorical or prosodic rules at all. In fact what is apparent elsewhere in his writings, and indeed what is upheld by his poetic practices, is that, like Baudelaire, he maintains a reverence towards prosodic strictures. Even in his most questioning text concerning the status of poetry, the 'Crise de vers' text of the late 1880s and the early 1890s, he affirms – and welcomes – the necessity of such strictures:

Cette prosodie, règles si brèves, intraitable d'autant: elle notifie tel acte de prudence, dont l'hémistiche, et statue du moindre effort pour simuler la versification, à la manière des codes selon quoi s'abstenir de voler est la condition par exemple de droiture. (M.*OC*.II, p.206)

[This prosody, such brief rules, inflexible at that: it officially gives notification of such an act of prudence as the hemistich, and gives a ruling on even the smallest attempt at simulating versification, in the style of those codes according to which, for example, refraining from stealing is the condition of honesty.]

The legislative vocabulary in this passage ('notifie', 'statue', 'droiture', 's'abstenir de voler') implies a negative stance – but the negativity is addressed towards those whose attitudes concerning the application of versificatory rules are intransigent. He contrasts the negative legislative vocabulary of those who adhere to prosodic rules simply as an 'acte de prudence' to those who, in the ensuing paragraph, remain 'fidèles à l'alexandrin' ['faithful to the alexandrine'] (amongst whose number Mallarmé would count himself). According to Mallarmé, if the alexandrine is placed in unsuitable hands, it will result in a negative, 'puéril' verse line which does little more than 'simuler la versification': therefore it cannot be true poetry. Mallarmé introduces as his guideline for effective poetry a criterion which is paradoxically primordial and yet subjective:

> Les fidèles à l'alexandrin, notre hexamètre, desserrent intérieurement ce mécanisme rigide et puéril de sa mesure; l'oreille, affranchie d'un compteur factice, connaît une jouissance à discerner, seule, toutes les combinaisons possibles, entre eux, de douze timbres. (M.*OC*.II, p.206)

> [Those who are faithful to the alexandrine, our hexametre, undo this rigid and childish mechanism of its metre from within; the ear, freed from a contrived counter, recognises a certain joyful pleasure in discerning, of its own accord, all the possible combinations between the twelve timbres.]

By turning to the 'oreille', and to the 'jouissance' that can be experienced by listening to the poetic line, Mallarmé privileges a use of the alexandrine line which imaginatively moves away from the traditional division into two clearly defined hemistichs of six syllables each. The use of the verb 'desserrer' in this context not only implies the sense of undoing, but also of making the verse line speak to itself (as in the turn of phrase 'desserrer les dents' in order to speak). This is how the 'oreille' is able to hear the new resonances and combinations made possible by the verse line itself. In this respect, Mallarmé is evidently very close to the theories of both Banville and Ténint who, as explained above, explore all the different possible combinations of the alexandrine verse line.

So Mallarmé is not proclaiming anything new, but rather is affirming what had become accepted practice in France amongst the more innovative poets of the latter stages of the nineteenth century. When he then goes on to say:

> envisageons la dissolution maintenant du nombre officiel, en ce qu'on veut, à l'infini, pourvu qu'un plaisir s'y réitère. (M.*OC*.II, p.207)

> [let us go so far as to envisage the dissolution of the official number into whatever we want, infinitely, provided that a pleasure is reiterated in it.]

he echoes what Banville writes in his treatise about declaring the need for total freedom with the alexandrine line, as long as it can 'charmer l'oreille, enchanter l'esprit' ['charm the ear, enchant the mind'].[35] The influence of Banville's prosodic theories on Mallarmé is made clear by his recognition that Banville provides an ideal example of how the alexandrine line can open itself up to greater flexibility, whilst not yet requiring a total dissolution of prosodic rules. In the Huret interview of 1891, Mallarmé reiterates this view by designating Banville as a 'maître':

> avec la merveilleuse science du vers, l'art suprême des coupes, que possèdent des maîtres comme Banville, l'alexandrin peut arriver à une variété infinie, suivre tous les mouvements de passion possible. (M.*OC*.II, p.699)

---

[35]   Banville, *Petit Traité*, p.8.

[with the remarkable science of verse, the supreme art of 'coupes', which masters like Banville possess, the alexandrin can attain an infinite variety, and follow all the possible movements of passion.]

The diction that Mallarmé employs to justify this stance is one which persistently has recourse to human passions (which is itself a rather Aristotelian point of view). Here he explicitly uses the word 'passion'; elsewhere, as we have seen, he refers to the 'jouissance' or 'plaisir' that the verse line should elicit. But this passionate engagement with the traditional French verse line is not without careful nuance. He declares in 'Solennité' that:

> tout poème composé autrement qu'en vue d'obéir au vieux génie du vers, n'en est pas un. (M.*OC*.II, p.199)

> [any poem composed other than with a view to obeying the ancient genius of verse, is not one.]

This declaration is qualified by the suggestion in 'Crise de vers', that an adherence to traditional verse strictures is a haunting requirement:

> la réminiscence du vers strict hante ces jeux à côté et leur confère un profit. (M.*OC*.II, p.207)

> [the reminiscence of strict verse haunts these games on the sidelines and grants them a profit.]

That this haunting presence allows for a positive outcome in the form of 'profit' implies that Mallarmé's relationship with prosodic strictures thrives on a dual strategy that privileges both the 'oreille' (and its concomitant possibility for 'jouissance' or 'plaisir' elicited from the way language speaks and is heard) and 'réminiscence' (and its possibility for generating a productive 'profit'). It is not simply by coincidence that the ear and memory are allied in the closing lines of 'Crise de vers':

> Le vers qui de plusieurs vocables refait un mot total, neuf, étranger à la langue et comme incantatoire, achève cet isolement de la parole ... et vous cause cette surprise de n'avoir ouï jamais tel fragment ordinaire d'élocution, en même temps que la réminiscence de l'objet nommé baigne dans une neuve atmosphère. (M.*OC*.II, p.213)

> [The verse which out of several terms recreates a whole new word, foreign to its language and as if incantatory, achieves this isolation of the spoken word ... and causes you the surprise of never having heard such an ordinary fragment of

speech, at the same time as the reminiscence of the named object basks in a new atmosphere.]

The alliance between 'parole' / 'élocution' / 'oreille' and a sense of 'réminiscence' is one of the founding bases for Mallarmé's poetic endeavours. Rather like his hint at the importance of quasi-Aristotelian 'passions' in the composition of poetry, this alliance hints at the rhetorical practice which considers the importance of the 'actio' and the 'memoria' elements of rhetorical discourse; the 'actio' element is concerned with speaking and listening to language, and the 'memoria' element is concerned with ways of remembering. Mallarmé's suggestion here in 'Crise de vers' is that by speaking and listening to poetic language in such a way as to privilege the effects that individual phonemes can create, new, surprising mental impressions can be elicited which draw from past experiences of language. This attitude, which evidently draws heavily not only from Baudelaire's attitude towards manipulation of poetic language but also from prosodists' developing theories, suggests that a new poetic aesthetic is coming to light which places particular emphasis on the ways in which poetry can be brought to voice both actively and memorably.

Music to the Ear and 'l'écriture à haute voix'

Baudelaire's and Mallarmé's concern with the governing principle of the 'oreille' is not only closely related to the rhetorical and prosodic practices of the later stages of the nineteenth century in France but is also profoundly influenced by an increasing preoccupation with music. Baudelaire goes so far as to claim that prosody is what ultimately conjoins poetry and music, writing in his third 'Projet de préface' of:

> comment la poésie touche à la musique par une prosodie dont les racines plongent plus avant dans l'âme humaine que ne l'indique aucune théorie classique (B.*OC*. I, p.183)

> [how poetry touches music through a prosody whose roots are to be found far deeper within the human soul than any classical theory suggests]

This recalls Baudelaire's belief that prosodic rules are a fundamental feature of human existence, but he stresses that this essential quality also directly affects music. The ideal of music suffuses the poetry of both Baudelaire and Mallarmé, and becomes an artistic commonplace throughout the century. Reaffirming his admiration for Banville, and for his adherence to the alexandrine line, Mallarmé corroborates Baudelaire's view of the relationship between prosody and music. In his musically-titled 'Symphonie Littéraire' (published in *L'Artiste*, 1 February 1865) Mallarmé writes:

C'est que cet homme [Banville] représente en nos temps le poète, l'éternel et le classique poète, fidèle à la déesse, et vivant parmi la gloire oubliée des héros et des dieux. Sa parole est, sans fin, un chant d'enthousiasme, d'où s'élance la musique et le cri de l'âme ivre de toute la gloire. (M.*OC*.II, p.284)

[It is the fact that this man [Banville] represents in our time the poet, the eternal and classical poet, who is faithful to the goddess, and living amongst the forgotten glory of heros and gods. His word is, unendingly, a song of enthusiasm, from which music takes off and the cry of the soul drunk on all this glory.]

By describing Banville's poetic voice as one which sings out with enthusiasm, Mallarmé does what is typical of the era: he talks of poetry as song and music, re-emphasising its oral and aural properties.

Theoretical formulations about the relationship between poetry and music abounded during the latter decades of the nineteenth century. Writing in the late 1870s, for example, Louis Becq de Fouquières endeavours in his treatise to write out verse rhythms in musical notation. He claims that 'composer un vers, c'est construire une phrase musicale' ['to compose a verse is to construct a musical phrase'].[36] René Ghil, on the other hand, seeks to establish a direct relationship between vowels, colours and instruments.[37] That the closing paragraphs of Mallarmé's 'Crise de vers' initially served as the 'Avant-dire' to Ghil's 1886 *Traité du verbe* confirms Mallarmé's close interest in the relationship between poetry and music (even if, ultimately, he distanced himself from Ghil's concepts).[38] Music became a means of validating poetry, and operated alongside carefully manipulated rhetorical and prosodic practices to develop an audience's poetico-musical ear and so attune it to new ways of approaching poetry. Music has the supposed advantage of being an art form which is intended to be heard, played or sung, rather than 'simply' being read. By bringing music back into such close contact with poetry on an aesthetic level, and by granting it the same authoritative status as rhetoric or prosody for 'governing' the poetic art, Baudelaire and Mallarmé undermine any assumption that the reading of poetry can be a purely individual and silent activity.[39]

---

[36] Louis Becq de Fouquières, *Traité général de versification française* (Paris: Charpentier, 1879), p.182.

[37] I shall explore this in more detail in Chapter 6. See, for example, Table 6.2.

[38] Joseph Acquisto, for example, has explored how Ghil's work intersects with Mallarmé's at certain moments, suggesting that 'the common ground that they share in the defining moments of the mid-1880s is established not *by* any one text but rather *between* [a] network of texts'. Joseph Acquisto, *French Symbolist Poetry and the Idea of Music* (Aldershot: Ashgate, 2006), p.114.

[39] As I explore in Chapter 6, Mallarmé's famous description of a 'musicienne du silence' ['musician of silence'] in 'Sainte' (M.*OC*.I, p.27) calls into question the status of silence in relation to music.

In fact, the significance of the idea of music in relation to the principles underlying poetry is determined by the ways in which both arts actively and memorably affect the body. In response to the voices of Wagner's music, for example, Baudelaire commented: 'toute chair qui se souvient se met à trembler' ['all flesh which remembers begins to tremble'] (B.*OC*.II, p.795). He discerns a close rapport between the action of trembling and the creation of a memorable response within the body. The governing principle for an aesthetics of voice, then, is to be found not in treatises or prosodic strictures, but in the relationship between voice and text as it affects the body. In the closing pages of *Le Plaisir du texte*, published in 1973, Barthes begins to mull over the importance of the rhetorical principle of 'actio' in particular. He proposes a notion of 'écriture à haute voix' ['writing out loud'] as a linguistic ideal which may be unattainable but which – he believes – twentieth-century writers such as Sollers and Artaud have nevertheless attempted to achieve. Barthes writes:

> Dans l'Antiquité, la rhétorique comprenait une partie oubliée, censurée par les commentateurs classiques: l'*actio*, ensemble de recettes propres à permettre l'extériorisation corporelle du discours: il s'agissait d'un théâtre de l'expression, l'orateur-comédien 'exprimant' son indignation, sa compassion, etc.[40]

> [In Antiquity, rhetoric comprised a forgotten part, omitted by classical commentators: the *actio*, a collection of formulae designed to enable the bodily exteriorisation of a speech: it was a question of a theatre of expression, the orator-actor 'expressing' his indignation, his compassion, etc.]

Barthes contrasts this expression of the passions to the very physical expression of what he terms 'l'écriture à haute voix' and reiterates terminologies from a 1972 article published in *Musique en jeu* entitled 'Le Grain de la voix' by emphasising:

> le grain du gosier, la patine des consonnes, la volupté des voyelles, toute une stéréophonie de la chair profonde: l'articulation du corps, de la langue, non celle du sens, du langage.[41]

> [the grain of the throat, the patina of consonants, the voluptuousness of vowels, a complete stereophonics of the whole body: the articulation of the body, of the tongue, not of meaning, of language.]

For readers of Mallarmé in particular, Barthes' argument here sparks resonances. After all, did not Mallarmé write of his famous 'Sonnet en *yx*', in a letter to his friend Henri Cazalis dated 18 July 1868:

---

[40] Barthes, *Œuvres complètes*, II, p.1528.
[41] Barthes, *Œuvres complètes*, II, p.1529.

J'extrais ce sonnet, auquel j'avais une fois songé cet été, d'une étude projetée sur *la Parole* : il est inverse et je veux dire que le sens, s'il en a un, (mais je me consolerais du contraire grâce à la dose de poësie qu'il renferme, ce me semble) est évoqué par un mirage interne des mots mêmes. En se laissant aller à le murmurer plusieurs fois on éprouve une sensation assez cabalistique. (M.*OC*.I, p.731)

[I extract this sonnet, which I first dreamt of this summer, from a planned study on the *Spoken word*: it is inverse and by that I mean that the meaning, if there is one, (but I would console myself of the contrary thanks to the dose of poetry it contains, it seems to me) is evoked by an internal mirage of the words themselves. By letting yourself murmur them several times, you feel a rather cabalistic sensation.]

For Mallarmé it is the sensation of the words rather than their meaning which seems to take precedence. This hints at an engagement with poetic language which is reliant on a physical murmuring through which it becomes possible to experience the effect of what Barthes describes as 'la patine des consonnes, la volupté des voyelles'.[42] Rimbaldian resonances are also pertinent here: Rimbaud's 'Voyelles' sonnet prefigures the possibility of a 'volupté des voyelles'. Mallarmé also specifically refers to the relationship between language and the human body in the late 1870s. In the second chapter of *Les Mots anglais*, in which he borrows from Max Müller's theories on philology (published in France in the late 1860s), he writes:

le Mot présente, dans ses voyelles et ses diphtongues, comme une chair; et, dans ses consonnes, comme une ossature délicate à disséquer. (M.*OC*.II, p.949)

[the Word presents, in its vowels and its diphthongs, like flesh; and, in its consonants, like a delicate bone structure to be dissected.]

That Mallarmé arrives at such a consideration – pre-Sollers, pre-Artaud, and very much pre-Barthes – suggests that the consideration of voice and reading practice in late nineteenth-century French poetry may be more reliant on some form of 'écriture à haute voix' than has previously been considered.

This casts a new light on what it might mean to read Mallarmé's poetry, and it is for this reason that I consider the pertinence of 'actio' and 'memoria' as critical models for the analysis of poetry in this period. Whilst neither Baudelaire nor Mallarmé specifically write about these particular elements of rhetorical practice, it is clear that they are profoundly influenced by an aesthetic agenda which places renewed emphasis on the 'music' of poetry, on the way it sounds or the way it is 'voiced', and on its ability to create a memorable response. Each poet respects

---

[42]   I explore Mallarmé's use of the term 'sensation' in Chapter 3.

prosodic strictures but must also manipulate them in order to revolutionise the poetic art which draws increasingly from musical concepts in order to develop a particular aesthetic experience which is both active and memorable. Translating Edgar Allan Poe's tale, 'The Power of Words', in 1854, Baudelaire wrote: 'Chaque parole n'est-elle pas un mouvement créé dans l'air?' [Is not every word an impulse on the air?']⁴³ The creation of a 'mouvement dans l'air' moves from voice to text and back again via a compositional process that is attentive to the properties and qualities of the human voice: it is this process, I suggest, that ensures both the immediacy and longevity of our response to poetic language. It seems, then, that Hugo was not so far off the mark when he talked of a revolution in poetry in terms of a vibration 'dans l'air, dans la voix, dans le livre':

> Le mouvement complète ainsi son action.
> Grâce à toi, progrès saint, la Révolution
> Vibre aujourd'hui dans l'air, dans la voix, dans le livre.
> Dans le mot palpitant le lecteur la sent vivre.⁴⁴

> [Thus the movement completes its action.
> Thanks to you, sacred progress, the Revolution
> Still vibrates today in the air, in the voice, in the book.
> In the beàting word the reader feels it is alive.]

---

43   Edgar Allan Poe, *The Penguin Complete Tales and Poems of Edgar Allan Poe* (London: Penguin, 1982), p.442; *Nouvelles histoires extraordinaires*, trans. by Charles Baudelaire (Paris: Gallimard, 1951–1974), p.281.

44   'Les Contemplations', p.499.

PART II
Body

Chapter 2

'La Voix humaine': The Dynamics of Voice

Longtemps, longtemps, la *voix humaine* fut base et condition de la *littérature*. …
Les qualités que l'on peut énoncer d'une voix humaine sont les mêmes que l'on doit
étudier et *donner* dans la poésie.

[For a very long time, the *human voice* was the basis and condition of literature.
… The qualities that can be expressed about a human voice are the same ones that
should be studied and given in poetry.]

Paul Valéry, 'Tel Quel – Littérature'[1]

The Hugolian 'mot palpitant' implies a sense of regularity, a pulsation, an
oscillation, albeit in a heightened state of emotional intensity. The Barthesian
model of 'le grain de la voix' ['the grain of the voice'] sensed through 'l'écriture
à haute voix' ['writing out loud'] also implies a heightened state of emotional
intensity, but does not imply any sense of a regular pulsation of language as such.
I would suggest that Baudelaire's and Mallarmé's use of poetic language resides
not only chronologically between the Hugolian and the Barthesian models, but
also aesthetically. Both poets exploit the potential for emotional intensity elicited
by the use of the human voice in poetic language, but neither is confident about
the regularity of its effects, and neither requires that their poetry be specifically
read aloud in order to produce these effects. This is due, in part, to the decline in
the belief that poetry is designed solely either to be sung or recited out loud. Yet
neither poet can forget poetry's heritage as an oral art. In writing and publishing
their poetry, they remained aware that their poetry might be read silently, it might
be read out loud, or it might even be set to music and sung: the possibilities for
vocal enactments are numerous (and indeed their poetry continues to be read,
recited and sung today in many different ways). My purpose is not to suggest
that the poetry of Baudelaire and Mallarmé is an oral poetry, but nor do I wish to
suggest that it is *not* an oral poetry. This is because of the particular way in which
each poet inscribes his awareness of the importance of the human voice within his
poetic texts.

In this chapter, I will explore possibilities for vocal enactments, and will seek
to address in particular how to avoid the problems of talking about 'internal'
or 'external' uses of 'voice' in the context of poetry. Remembering that neither
Baudelaire nor Mallarmé were prescriptive about how their poetry was to be

---

[1]   Paul Valéry, *Œuvres*, ed. by Jean Hytier, Bibliothèque de la Pléiade, 2 vols (Paris:
Gallimard, 1957–1960), II, pp.549–550.

read, and drawing briefly from two treatises on the art of reading published in the nineteenth century (by Dubroca and Gossart), I shall demonstrate that it is necessary to break down this distinction because the human voice itself implies too varied a set of parameters and qualities. An analysis of the various properties of the human voice that Baudelaire and Mallarmé exploit will also confirm this point. Some reported anecdotes written by friends of each of the poets describe instances in which they read their own poetry out loud, and these serve as a reminder that there is no unique way to read poetry. The different attributes of voice that they explore in their poetry span a dynamic range from silence to a whispering or a murmuring, through to qualities such as 'douce' ['soft'] (B.*OC*.I, p.41) or 'terne' ['dull'] (M.*OC*.I, p.6), or towards a further extreme 'rauque' ['raucous'] (B.*OC*. I, p.350), and through to non-verbal attributes such as a 'rire' ['laughter'] or 'cri' ['shout' / 'cry'] (which I analyse below). The varying dynamics of voice implicate both changes in volume and movement, through a gradation of air flow. As Poe expressed in 'The Power of Words', translated by Baudelaire, using one's voice requires a 'mouvement dans l'air' ['movement in the air'] which, in turn, determines volume and quality of tone. I shall suggest that it is when this 'mouvement dans l'air' does not actually physically take place, and instead is sensed or imagined 'internally', that the human attributes of voice become particularly interesting for Baudelaire and Mallarmé.

In my analysis of the varying dynamic attributes of the human voice in differing poetic contexts, I seek to address ways in which different textual practices affect decisions about pronunciation and scansion. I shall suggest that the poets exploit the infinitely variable qualities of the human voice in order to create particularly memorable effects. Since both Baudelaire and Mallarmé are as renowned for their prose poetry as they are for their verse poetry, I also consider what conventions or topoi each poet exploits within the context of prose poetry in order to explore the dynamic properties of 'voice'. I shall inevitably turn my attention to that most remarkable of poetic experiments, Mallarmé's 'Un Coup de dés', since this is a text which poses the most significant conundrums in relation to using one's voice in the context of poetry; conventions seem to be totally thwarted and uncertainties about how to put 'voice' into action prevail. However, I suggest that the unusual nature of 'Un Coup de dés' is rooted in a particular attitude towards vocal practices which I explore below.

Vocal Enactments

There are no instances in the writings of either Baudelaire or Mallarmé where they directly specify that their poetry is to be read out loud. This leaves the reader with a whole gamut of options, and the different performance scenarios for poetry can be broadly categorised under the following headings:

reading to oneself internally
reading to oneself out loud
↯ reading to others out loud (recitation)
✱ singing a song setting
listening to others reading out loud / singing

Whilst these scenarios do not take into account other factors such as age, gender, language, culture, historical background or setting, they provide the main framework for evaluating poetic performance. Since my analysis will specifically emphasise the inherent differences between voices, I do not propose to address each individual factor in turn, but to accept such differences as a necessary feature of human language. A reader of Baudelaire or Mallarmé, for my analysis, is one who is already sufficiently familiar with the French language, and sufficiently versed in the prosodic norms of French poetry, and sufficiently sensitive to the chronological distance that separates us from the nineteenth century. In other words, I, like Baudelaire and Mallarmé themselves, am not concerned with a naïve reader who encounters Baudelaire or Mallarmé with no tools at his or her disposal to grasp the subtle complexities of the text. Of course Mallarmé himself famously declared that he was only concerned with 'intelligent' readers,[2] and Baudelaire declared post-trial in an 1857 letter addressed to the Ministre d'État that 'ce livre ne s'addressait qu'à un petit nombre de lecteurs' ['this book was only addressed to a small number of readers'] (B.Corr.I, p.416). What these comments express is that both poets – although they may have eschewed being prescriptive about how their poetry should be read – were concerned with finding a suitable reader for their poetic texts. Since Baudelaire was charged with offending the public moral order, and Mallarmé faced the charge of obscurity or difficulty, both authors had problematic rapports with their reading public. This is due not only to the fact that the majority of readers are insensitive readers, but also to the fact that each person's voice is unique yet multi-faceted.

Even in the first century, the influential rhetorician Quintilian in his *Institutio oratoria* effectively shrugged his shoulders at the prospect of trying to prescribe how to use one's voice in public-speaking, making an analogy with the infinite range of facial expressions that each individual is capable of, and likening this to the infinite range of expressions latent within each person's voice:

> utendi voce multiplex ratio. nam praeter illam differentiam quae est tripertita, acutae gravis flexae, tum intentis tum remissis, tum elatis tum inferioribus

---

2 See for example the 'Enquête Huret': 'si un être d'une intelligence moyenne, et d'une préparation littéraire insuffisante, ouvre par hasard un livre ainsi fait et prétend en jouir, il y a un malentendu, il faut remettre les choses à leur place' ['if someone of average intelligence, and insufficient literary preparation, opens by chance a book like this and claims to get pleasure from it, there is a misunderstanding, things must be put back in their place'] (M.OC.II, p.700).

modis opus est, spatiis quoque lentioribus aut citatioribus. Sed his ipsis media interiacent multa, et ut facies, quamquam ex pacissimis constat, infinitam habet differentiam, ita vox, etsi paucas quae nominari possint continet species, propia cuique est, et non haec minus auribus quam oculis illa dinoscitur.[3]

[There are many reasons for using the voice. For, notwithstanding that division which is tripartite (that is high, low, modulating) there is the need for tones which are now stretching and now relaxed, now higher and now lower, and also for tempi which are slower or quicker. But amongst these things there lie many intermediary levels; just as a face, although it comprises very few components, possesses infinite diversity, thus the voice, even though it comprises only a few parts which can be named, is peculiar to each individual, and is recognised by the ears in the same way as the face is discerned by the eyes.]

Quintilian goes on to state that many people simply do not possess the appropriate physical qualities necessary for using the voice effectively. In turn, nineteenth-century treatise writers reiterated this concern, suggesting that few people are adept at reciting poetry. In the very early stages of the nineteenth century, Louis Dubroca, referring to Aristotle's *Poetics*, comments that there are 'trois propriétés essentielles' of the human voice when it is used out loud: 'la *résonnance*, l'*intonation* et le *mouvement*'.[4] He goes on to remark that on the whole, the performance of French verse in the early stages of the nineteenth century in France is unsatisfactory:

Des erreurs graves se sont introduites … dans l'énonciation publique. Les uns croient prosodier en faisant longues toutes les syllabes, et alors ils ne marchent plus, ils se traînent, et ils accablent les auditeurs du poids de leur lecture. D'autres, par une prononciation rapide, où nulle prosodie n'est marquée, donnent à leur débit un caractère de sécheresse et d'aridité capable de glacer l'attention la plus marquée.[5]

[Serious errors have begun to affect … public recitation. Some think they are being poetic by making all syllables long, but then it doesn't flow any more, they drag, and they overwhelm their audience by the heaviness of their reading. Others, by using a rapid pronunciation, in which none of the prosodic elements are observed, render their recitation so dry that they make even the most committed listener glaze over.]

---

[3]   Quintilian, *Institutio oratoria*, 2 vols (Oxford: Clarendon, 1970), II, p.657 (Book 11, Chapter 3.17–18).

[4]   Louis Dubroca, *Traité de prononciation des consonnes finales des mots français* (Paris: Dubroca, 1808), p.3.

[5]   Dubroca, *Traité de prononciation*, p.22.

The two extremes of reading style that Dubroca outlines – on the one hand, placing too strong an emphasis on granting each syllable of the verse line the same weight, and on the other, granting too little weight to the syllabic structure of the line – lead him to conclude that a good performance would consist of a 'mélange' ['mixture'] or 'combinaison' ['combination'] of different syllabic weightings. This conclusion is not particularly innovative, but it does reinforce the problematic outlined, which is that prescribing how poetry should be read is an impossible task. Another elocutionary theorist, Alexandre Gossart, writing in the late 1850s, claims that most people simply do not possess the right physical make-up in order to be able to read poetry out loud effectively:

> Peu de personnes déclament bien, parce qu'il faut pour cela une attention soutenue, une perception rapide, un organe agréable, assez flexible pour prendre les intonations diverses que le sujet exige, et assez puissant pour donner au ton plus ou moins de force suivant la nécessité: on trouve rarement toutes ces conditions réunies.[6]

> [Few people declaim well, because in order to do so you need sustained attention, rapid perception, a pleasing voice, which is flexible enough to take on all the different intonations that the subject matter requires, and which is powerful enough to give more or less power to the tone depending on what is necessary: rarely does one find all of these conditions together in the one person.]

For Gossart, the human voice needs to be both 'agréable', 'flexible' and 'puissant' – suitably nebulous terms which once again fail to overcome the fundamental conundrum: that the human voice is not only unique but also infinitely varied, so much so that few people can be called 'good' readers of poetry (in the sense of being adept at reading out loud, although this also has implications for the reader's interpretative abilities). Whilst the purpose of the treatises written by Dubroca and Gossart was to serve as an elocutionary training system, their work reinforces the notion that reading out loud does not necessarily do a better service to poetry than reading silently.

Impulses on the Air

So how does this truism affect Baudelaire's or Mallarmé's poetic output? Where Dubroca and Gossart were concerned with reciting poetry out loud, neither Baudelaire nor Mallarmé make this their primary concern. Is there a correlation between being inept at reciting poetry and reading solely for oneself? The intervention of the written, published text evidently plays a role in answering this

---

[6] Gossart, *Traité complet de la versification française* (Paris: Maire-Nyon, [1859?]), p.131. Indeed Quintilian had already made the same claim in his *Institutio oratoria*.

question, but more significantly, so too does the level of familiarity with a given poetic language. It has often been stated that in order to read Mallarmé, one must persistently re-read, going over lines and words already encountered in order to derive various possible interpretations and responses, whereas Baudelaire's poetry is more easily understood on a first reading. The difference between the poets' use of language is due, in part, to the differing ways in which they inscribe their own voice within their poetic texts. Endeavouring to make a critical distinction between reading out loud and reading internally falters because each poet exploits, at different moments within their poetry, differing dynamic properties of the human voice. This suggests that they are aware of the kind of difficulties that Quintilian, Dubroca and Gossart outlined in their treatises in relation to prescribing how to use one's voice in poetry. Baudelaire even specifically accepts freedom on the reader's part, writing in the 'Dédicace à Arsène Houssaye' which opens his prose poem collection: 'Nous pouvons couper où nous voulons, moi ma rêverie, vous le manuscrit, le lecteur sa lecture' ['We can break off wherever we want, me my reverie, you the manuscript, the reader his reading'] (B.*OC*.I, p.275). The way in which a text is read or performed cannot be controlled precisely because the range of possible factors influencing a performance are so numerous and manifold. As Peter Dayan suggests in his analysis of the siren voices in Baudelaire's 'Le Voyage':

> if the voices of these sirens are not comprehensible, on the other hand they are perfectly audible. They are heard every time a poem is read. Heard in translation, perhaps; translated, or transposed, into the voice of whoever reads them (especially, of whoever reads them out); it is not, one might say the original *voice* (did it ever exist?) that we hear; but the words, at least, are there for our ears.[7]

The transposition of textual voices into the voice of the reader at the point of performance (even if it is difficult to uphold, as Dayan does, the importance of specifically reading out loud) opens up the idea that voices in poetry are not silent or static but expose readers to a particular type of sonorous movement.

It is the power of the words themselves which profoundly influences attitudes towards the aesthetic effects of poetic language. Poe's tale 'The Power of Words' sets up a dialogue between two protagonists, Oinos and Agathos. The conversation leads towards Agathos' revelation to Oinos that everything is made up of 'impulses upon the air', and this motion, in turn, is 'the great medium of creation'. As the dialogue reaches its conclusion, Agathos addresses a rhetorical question towards Oinos: 'And while I thus spoke, did there not cross your mind some thought of the *physical power of words? Is not every word an impulse on the air?*'[8] The conclusion

---

    [7]   Peter Dayan, *Music Writing Literature, from Sand via Debussy to Derrida* (Aldershot: Ashgate, 2006), p.38.

    [8]   Edgar Allan Poe, *The Penguin Complete Tales and Poems of Edgar Allan Poe* (London: Penguin, 1994), p.442.

that is reached is that planets, worlds, flowers, stars are all created by the power of words themselves – instigated by, as Baudelaire would translate it, a 'mouvement créé dans l'air' ['movement created in the air'].[9] This 'mouvement dans l'air' emphasises the dynamic nature of words. The aesthetic stance of Baudelaire and Mallarmé privileges the human voice in action by exploring its range of dynamic possibilities. I use the term 'dynamics of voice' in both its musical sense meaning 'volume' and in its more scientific sense designating 'movement' or 'action' (the two meanings, of course, being clearly interlinked). It is precisely because the human voice is able to take on so many varied intonations, timbres and emotive properties – both internally and externally – that Baudelaire and Mallarmé place a renewed emphasis on the human voice as the founding basis of a poetic aesthetic which seeks to create lasting and memorable effects.

Baudelaire and Mallarmé Reading their own Poetry

The first instances of either Baudelaire or Mallarmé bringing their poetry to voice took place in the form of reading their own poetry to themselves and to friends. Various anecdotal accounts, written by friends of the poets at a later date, offer a personal angle on the way that Baudelaire and Mallarmé used their own voices. The friends who provide the few short accounts that remain are often poets themselves. Of Baudelaire, Théodore de Banville writes that:

> des fois chez Joissans j'ai entendu … Baudelaire dire de sa belle voix charmeresse les poèmes inédits des *Fleurs du Mal*.[10]

> [on occasions at Joissans's I heard … Baudelaire reciting unpublished poems from his *Fleurs du Mal* in his beautiful charming voice.]

and Théophile Gautier writes:

> Baudelaire s'exprimait souvent d'une façon solennelle et sentencieuse, appuyant sur chaque terme pour lui donner plus d'importance.[11]

> [Baudelaire often expressed himself very solemnly and sententiously, putting emphasis on each term in order to give it more importance.]

---

[9]   Edgar Allan Poe, *Nouvelles histoires extraordinaires*, trans. by Charles Baudelaire (Paris: Gallimard, 1951–1974), p.281.

[10]   Théodore de Banville, *Souvenirs*, cited in Charles Baudelaire, *Curiosités esthétiques, L'Art romantique et autres Œuvres critiques*, ed. by Henri Lemaitre (Paris: Bordas, 1990), p.565.

[11]   Théophile Gautier, *Baudelaire*, ed. by Jean-Luc Steinmetz (Bordeaux: Le Castor Astral, 1991), p.114.

The adjectives that Banville and Gautier use – the old-fashioned 'charmeresse' instead of 'charmeuse', and 'solennelle' and 'sentencieuse' – imply that Baudelaire's public reading style was a formal and considered one. Even the Goncourt brothers agree with this – even though their opinion of Baudelaire is slightly less favourable than that of his fellow poets Banville and Gautier. Describing an evening in which they hear Baudelaire rigorously defending his *Fleurs du Mal* which had just been taken to trial in 1857, they write:

> Baudelaire soupe à côté, sans cravate, le col nu, la tête rasée, en vraie toilette de guillotiné. Une seule recherche: de petites mains lavées, écurées, mégissées. La tête d'un fou, la voix nette comme une lame. Une élocution pédantesque … Se défend, assez obstinément et avec une certaine passion rêche, d'avoir outragé les mœurs dans ses vers.[12]

> [Baudelaire dines apart, without a tie, with a bare neck, his head shaved, looking like someone about to be guillotined. Just one meticulous detail: small hands which are washed, spotlessly clean, tanned. The head of a madman, voice as sharp as a blade. A pedantic way of speaking … He defends himself, somewhat obstinately and with a certain degree of raw passion, from the charge of having offended the public moral order in his poetry.]

The Goncourts' description of Baudelaire's 'élocution pédantesque' confirms Gautier's opinion of his voice being 'solennelle et sentencieuse'. Although these latter two descriptions by Gautier and the Goncourts do not speak specifically of Baudelaire reading poetry, they at least grant some indication as to the kind of way in which Baudelaire used his voice in public.[13]

---

[12]   Edmond and Jules de Goncourt, *Journal: Mémoires de la vie littéraire*, 3 vols (Paris: Flammarion, 1956–1989), I, p.301 (dated Paris, October 1857).

[13]   Graham Robb gives two further examples of Baudelaire reading his own verse which further corroborate the descriptions of Baudelaire's voice provided by Banville, Gautier and the Goncourts: 'On imagine ce rythme accentué par la voix de Baudelaire: "Il nous récitait", écrit Jules Levallois, "d'une voix précieuse, douce, flûtée, onctueuse, et cependant mordante, une énormité quelconque, *Le Vin de l'assassin* ou *la Charogne*. Le contraste était réellement saisissant entre la violence des images et la placidité affectée, l'accentuation suave et pointue du débit." Le même contraste a été remarqué par Charles Cousin: Baudelaire "psalmodiait ses vers d'une voix monotone, mais impérieuse"' ['One can imagine this rhythm accentuated by the voice of Baudelaire himself: "He recited something of great significance to us", writes Jules Levallois, "in an elegant, sweet, singing, smooth, and nonetheless caustic voice; *Le Vin de l'assassin* or *la Charogne* perhaps. The contrast between the violence of the imagery and the affected placidness, between the mellifuous and the shrill tones of the recitation, was extremely striking." The same contrast was noticed by Charles Cousin: Baudelaire "chanted his poetry in a monotone but imperious voice"']. *La poésie de Baudelaire et la poésie française 1838–1852* (Paris: Aubier, 1993), p.272.

Of Mallarmé, on the other hand, Valéry famously commented on the private reading of 'Un Coup de dés' that:

> il se mit à lire d'une voix basse, égale, sans le moindre 'effet', presque à soi-même.[14]

> [he started reading in a low voice, on an even tone, without even the slightest 'effect', almost as if reading to himself.]

Valéry's description of Mallarmé's reading style in this instance, written in February 1920 to the director of the journal *Marges*, is one which specifically takes on a defensive tone, and is intermingled with Valéry's own preferences and inclinations. In the following paragraph, he continues:

> J'aime cette absence d'artifices. La voix humaine me semble si belle intérieurement, et prise au plus près de sa source, que les diseurs de profession presque toujours me sont insupportables, qui prétendent *faire valoir, interpréter*, quand ils surchargent, débauchent les intentions, altèrent les harmonies d'un texte; et qu'ils substituent leur lyrisme au chant propre des mots combinés.[15]

> [I like this absence of artifice. I find the human voice so beautiful in itself, taken from so close to its source, that I almost always find professional speakers intolerable; those who think that they *lend great weight, interpret*, when in fact they overburden, distort intentions, and alter the harmonies of a text; and in the place of the true song of the combination of words, they substitute their own lyricism.]

Valéry's reflections confirm not only his own position, but also the issue highlighted above that not everyone is adept at reading poetry effectively, and that, significantly, 'trained' performing voices are also not necessarily the most effective. Mallarmé's reportedly quiet, introspective reading style – which is in direct contrast to the descriptions of Baudelaire's more solemn declamatory style – is no doubt due in part to the fact that the reading of 'Un Coup de dés' took place in the privacy of Mallarmé's own home, directed only towards Valéry himself. But Valéry was particularly affected by Mallarmé's soft approach to reading poetry, and even composed a free-verse poem in 1912 entitled 'Psaume sur une voix' which serves as a homage to Mallarmé's understated voice:

---

[14] Valéry, *Œuvres*, I, p.623.
[15] Valéry, *Œuvres*, I, pp.623–624.

A demi voix,
D'une voix douce et faible disant de grandes choses:
D'importantes, étonnantes, de profondes et justes choses,
D'une voix douce et faible.
La menace du tonnerre, la présence d'absolus
Dans une voix de rouge-gorge,
Dans le détail fin d'une flûte, et la délicatesse du son pur.
Tout le soleil suggéré
Au moyen d'un demi-sourire.
(Ô demi-voix),
Et d'une sorte de murmure
En français infiniment pur.
Qui n'eût saisi les mots, qui l'eût ouï à quelque distance,
Aurait cru qu'il disait des riens.
Et c'étaient des riens pour l'oreille
Rassurée.
Mais ce contraste et cette musique,
Cette voix ridant l'air à peine,
Cette puissance chuchotée,
Ces perspectives, ces découvertes,
Ces abîmes et ces manœuvres devinés,

Ce sourire congédiant l'univers!...

Je songe aussi pour finir
Au bruit de soie seul et discret
D'un feu qui se consume en créant toute la chambre,
Et qui se parle.
Ou qui me parle
Presque pour soi.

[With half a voice,
With a sweet and faint voice saying great things:
Important, surprising, profound and apt things,
With a sweet and faint voice.
The menace of thunder, the presence of absolutes
In the voice of a robin,
In the fine detail of a flute, and the delicateness of pure sound.
The whole sun suggested
By a half-smile
(O half-voice),
And with a sort of murmur
In an infinitely pure French.
Whoever could not catch the words, whoever heard it from some distance,

Would have thought that he was saying nothing.
And they were nothings for the ear
Reassured.
But this contrast and this music,
This voice barely making the air ripple,
This whispered power,
These perspectives, these discoveries,
These depths and these operations all imagined,

This smile dismissing the universe!...

Finally, I am dreaming also
Of the sound of silk alone and quiet
Of a fire which burns whilst creating the whole room,
And which talks to itself.
Or which talks to me.
As if to itself.]

The 'puissance chuchotée' of Mallarmé's voice for Valéry indicates both the creative and emotional force that Valéry discerned in Mallarmé's voice. As Christine Crow has emphasised:

> we find in this passage the emotion of the living voice as a creative principle in its own right.[16]

Whilst it must be remembered that Valéry's interpretation of Mallarmé's voice is strongly coloured by his own reverent admiration of the elder poet, it is nonetheless tempting, however, to draw the conclusion that where Baudelaire tended towards a more forceful use of his voice in reading poetry, Mallarmé preferred a more reticent dynamic. The conclusion is, of course, somewhat lacking in sufficient evidence, but it nevertheless seems to confirm the different vocal aesthetics of each poet based on the dynamic range explored in their poetic output. Baudelaire, as will be seen, presents vocal scenarios in a much more clearly designated way than Mallarmé. In Mallarmé, a vocal scenario is often harder to discern – and this, it seems, is a deliberate decision which clearly distinguishes Baudelaire's aesthetic from Mallarmé's, as attitudes towards the effects created by the voice develop over the course of the century.

Dynamics

The dynamic range of the human voice – from the half-whispered murmurings favoured by Mallarmé, through to the more melodramatic tones favoured by

---

[16]   Christine Crow, *Paul Valéry and the Poetry of Voice* (Cambridge: CUP, 1982), p.37.

Baudelaire – is expressed through various textual designations of voice. Distinct from the performance scenarios outlined above, a series of differing vocal enactments can be discerned within the poetic texts of Baudelaire and Mallarmé, which I schematise according to three different dynamic levels in Table 2.1.

Table 2.1   Textual designations of vocal enactments

most clearly designated	• direct speech signalled by quotation marks or other typographic indications • imperatives • descriptive passages recounting a speaking or singing voice
less clearly designated	• use of personal pronouns in order to address addressee ('tu', 'vous') • as if speaking rhetorical questions • apostrophe and personification
least clearly designated	• enjambement, shifted caesura, synaeresis, diaeresis, homophony, phonemic patternings and other small-scale technical traits which require attentive reading or decision-making upon reading / speaking / singing

At times, a combination of these vocal enactments are used within poems, and each poet favours different strategies over others (Mallarmé, for example, uses very little direct speech in comparison to Baudelaire who employs the technique quite freely, as will be discussed in greater detail in later chapters).

A clear example of how these differing designations of vocal enactments are employed poetically can be found in the first poem of *Les Fleurs du Mal*, 'Bénédiction' (B.*OC*.I, pp.7–9). Not only are there extended instances of direct speech enclosed in quotation marks (of the 19 quatrains in the poem, only seven are not enclosed within speech marks, while those that are span three different instances of direct speech: the poet's mother addresses God, the poet's mistress 'va criant sur les places publiques' ['goes out shouting in public squares'] (v.37), and the poet himself then addresses God), but these instances of direct speech also use imperatives ('Soyez béni', v.57). The narratorial voice of the poem also recounts how the poet figure 'cause avec le nuage' ['chats with the cloud'] (v.25) and goes on to describe how the poet figure 's'enivre en chantant du chemin de la croix' ['becomes intoxicated by singing the stations of the cross'] (v.26).[17] The

---

[17]   These two turns of phrase have wider connotations with which the attuned reader of Baudelaire will be familiar. The relationship between the poet and the clouds is reiterated in the prose poems 'Le Confiteor de l'artiste' and 'La Soupe et les Nuages'. The implication is that the clouds comprehend the poet's vocalised reflections better than those around him. The three words 'de la croix' of the second citation inevitably point towards a latent reference to the painter Eugène Delacroix whose work Baudelaire admired greatly, although other art

verbs used to describe the poet as a young boy are verbs which bear a specifically vocal quality ('causer', 'chanter' ['to chat', 'to sing']), and these also serve to set up the final instance of direct speech within the poem where the (now grown-up) poet himself addresses God. The conceit that Baudelaire sets up in this poem is one which exploits the traditional image of the poet as a divinely-inspired bard. Baudelaire subverts this tradition, not only by claiming a prophetic place for himself as a poet who is able to create verse without the need for divine intervention, but also by employing his voice in a way which profoundly ironises the oral tradition of poetry. In the final five stanzas of the poem (enclosed in speech marks), instead of considering God to be omnipotent, the poet assumes an omnipotence of his own, through the repeated anaphora at the beginning of stanzas 16 and 17 'Je sais que …' ['I know that …']. The diadem that the poet prepares is specifically his own: 'ma couronne mystique' ['my mystical crown'] (v.67), and he confidently expresses that he shall crown himself with a poetic crown which is no longer formed from the old-fashioned verse conceits (in the intransigent forms of 'bijoux', 'métaux', 'perles' ['jewels', 'metals', 'pearls'] v.69–70) which claim their power from divine intervention ('Par votre main montés' ['Set by your hand'] v.71), but which is formed out of a much more intangible material ('de pure lumière' ['of pure light'] v.73). It is this intangibility – rather like the impossible ephemerality of conversing with clouds – that Baudelaire seeks to capture. By placing this poem at the very beginning of Les Fleurs du Mal, Baudelaire immediately challenges not only the notion of poetry as a divinely-inspired oral tradition, but also questions what kind of vocal enactments poetry is able to exploit.

The different vocal enactments within 'Bénédiction' correlate to different dynamic ranges. The furious raging of the mother's direct address to God is loud and outspoken, the description of the poet speaking and singing is hushed, the direct speech of the poet's mistress is cried out boldly in public, and the poet's own direct address to God is a serene outpouring. These differing dynamic designations, signalled by different vocal enactments, not only serve the narrative drama of the poem but also draw attention to the ways in which the human voice can be exploited in poetic language. This is a poem in which the human voice is put into action in so many diverse ways that it prompts the reader to become more aware of his or her own voice, and of how the human voice can be manipulated to create different effects. Although there are three clear instances of three different human voices in this poem (designated by the direct speech of the mother, the mistress, and the poet figure himself), it is precisely because these instances are textual instances that the dynamics of voice begins to take on a more pertinent significance. Baudelaire is, to a certain extent, using the textual strategy of direct speech to mimic the action of speaking out loud, but he does not require that the poem itself should be spoken out loud. The dissolution of the distinction between

---

critics were quick to denigrate his work. If the reference to Delacroix is indeed implied, it strengthens the notion that the figure of the poet in 'Bénédiction' is, like Delacroix, a figure whose artistic genius is misunderstood.

the external and the internal voices of the poem's protagonists and of its potential reader allows for an aesthetics of voice which exploits the dynamic range of the human voice as it is heard by the reader of a poem – whether that reading be internal or aloud.

Impulses on the Body

In some respects, my analytical endeavour to break down the dichotomy between internal and external uses of the human voice does little more than to reveal a commonplace – we are all so familiar with the practice of putting on different voices, of hearing different tones, timbres, intonations both in human speech, in mental imagination and in reading texts which require different voices in the form of different protagonists. Yet this commonplace has a more fundamental grounding that is often ignored. Deirdre Reynolds' work on kinesthetics (particularly in relation to dance and representations of movement) outlines an important neuroscientific approach. Modern neuroscientists maintain that in order to instigate a movement of the body, the brain primes the necessary muscles for action, even though the actual action may not necessarily take place:

> 'Virtual' (anticipated or imagined) movement is itself a physical event. ... 'Pre-movement' [is] the process where a set of muscles contracts in anticipation of a movement to be performed by a different part of the body [and] ... originates in the brain, triggered by the formation of the intention to move.

> It has been shown that neural pathways are 'excited' (primed for action by the transmission of electrical impulses to the muscles) as a result of simply forming an intention to move, without any contraction of the muscles taking place.[18]

If this same process takes place when someone imagines a speaking voice without actually speaking, then the distinction between internal and external uses of the human voice cannot be maintained. The 'dynamics of voice' that I suggest, then, becomes not simply an issue of volume (how loud might a voice be), but also an issue of movement or action, even if that movement is in essence a 'pre-movement'. Poe's claim that there is a physical power of words, in that they create 'impulses on the air' may not, therefore, be so far removed from the physiological truth. The stars, flowers and volcanoes that, according to Poe, are created by the physical power of words themselves are indeed 'created' within the mind, which has been primed for movement by the words. That Baudelaire, as I have mentioned, translates the title of Poe's tale as 'La Puissance de la Parole', thereby specifically relating 'words' to the spoken word (rather than, for example, choosing the word 'mot'), and that he

---

[18]   Deirdre Reynolds, *Rhythmic Subjects: Uses of Energy in the Dances of Mary Wigman, Martha Graham and Merce Cunningham* (Alton: Dance Books, 2007), p.14.

renders this in the singular 'parole' rather than 'paroles', grants an importance to the way that bringing language to voice through poetry hovers between the states of pre-movement and movement. The flowers that Baudelaire creates through the poetic language of *Les Fleurs du Mal* have been brought into being by the physical power of words themselves, enacted by the impulses on the body. And Mallarmé's own speaking of the word 'fleur' in 'Crise de vers' (M.*OC*.I, p.213) leads him towards a more fundamental understanding of the purity of language as a creative force which is brought to life through careful use of the human voice.

The creative force of the voice in Mallarmé's poetry is expressed through an attentive attitude to the power of words in action. The gentle 'mouvement dans l'air' of the 'brise' ['breeze'] in the tercets of Mallarmé's sonnet 'Dans le jardin' (M.*OC*.I, p.66), dated August 1871, carries with it not only the aroma of the flowers but also the whispering of the name of the wife of the Irish poet William Charles Bonaparte-Wyse, to whom the poem is dedicated:

> Voilà pourquoi les fleurs profondes de la terre
> L'aiment avec silence et savoir et mystère,
> Tandis que dans leur cœur songe le pur pollen:
>
> Et lui, lorsque la brise, ivre de ces délices,
> Suspend encore un nom qui ravit les calices,
> À voix faible, parfois, appelle bas: 'Ellen!' (v.9–14)
>
> [This is why the profound flowers of the earth
> Love her with silence and knowledge and mystery,
> Whilst within their hearts pure pollen dreams:
>
> And he, whilst the breeze, drunk on these delights,
> Still suspends a name which delights the calyxes,
> In a faint voice, sometimes, calls softly: 'Ellen!']

In another 'Sonnet' from the 1870s which begins 'Sur les bois oubliés' (M.*OC*.I, p.67), the voice of a dead wife (this time Mallarmé's friend Ettie Yapp) forms the entirety of the poem which, unusually for Mallarmé, is expressed as direct speech enclosed within speech marks. In the final tercet, the dead female figure asks that her name be murmured in order that she may be brought back to life:

> Âme au si clair foyer tremblante de m'asseoir,
> Pour revivre il suffit qu'à tes lèvres j'emprunte
> Le souffle de mon nom murmuré tout un soir. (v.12–14)
>
> [Soul trembling to sit down in such a bright home,
> In order to revive all I need is to borrow from your lips
> The breath of my name murmured throughout an evening.]

In these two sonnets, the typical Mallarméan trait of speaking softly or whispering is explicitly privileged. This soft dynamic volume, coupled with the thematics of the 'brise' or the 'souffle', seems to allow Mallarmé not only to breathe poetic protagonists into life through naming, but also to breathe poetic language itself into life through the subtlety of his diction. In the final line of 'Dans le jardin', the visual patterning of the 'elle' of 'appelle' which is picked up in the name 'Ellen' is able to resonate because Mallarmé explicitly requires the volume to be 'bas'. In the final line of 'Sonnet', it is because he specifies a quietude ('murmuré') that the soft 'm' and 'n' sounds of the pallendromic 'mon nom' are able to create a lingering effect required by the thematics of the line. Even though readers might not necessarily read these poems out loud, the dynamic markings which qualify the human voices represented in 'Dans le jardin' and 'Sonnet' are acknowledged by the mental 'pre-action' process that allows the reader to genuinely sense the soft dynamic without it actually necessarily taking place.

The gentle dynamic of the 'souffle' or the 'brise' lends a certain imperceptibility to poetic language, which pushes aside any too-pervasive intervention by a cacophonous human voice which would mask the attempt to breathe poetry into life. This is rather like the refusal on Baudelaire's part in 'Tout entière' (B.*OC*.I, p.42) to analyse what particular feature of his mistress' body is the most attractive. The concluding lines of the poem declare that:

> Son haleine fait la musique
> Comme sa voix fait le parfum! (v.23–24)

> [Her breath makes music
> As her voice makes perfume!]

The mistress' breath and voice create a music and perfume which, in Baudelaire's aesthetic, are correspondent qualities of poetic language (expressed in the first two lines of the same quatrain as 'O métamorphose mystique / De tous mes sens fondus en un!' ['O mystical metamorphosis / Of all my sense melted into one!']). The creative properties of the human voice are precisely what animates poetry for Baudelaire and Mallarmé: without the human voice, poetry falters because there is no one to bring it to life. As the critic Kibédi-Varga puts it:

> Un poème est un texte le plus souvent écrit, parfois oral, qui existe, à l'état virtuel, dans un livre, dans une revue ou au fond de la mémoire. Pour que le poème devienne vivant, existe vraiment, bref pour qu'il s'actualise, il faut aussi un être humain qui sache le lire, en silence ou à haute voix, ou le réciter.[19]

---

[19]   Aron Kibédi-Varga, *Les Constantes du poème: à la recherche d'une poétique dialectique* (The Hague: Van Goor Zonen, 1963), p.10.

[A poem is a text most often written, sometimes oral, which exists, in a virtual state, in a book, a magazine or in the depths of memory. For a poem to come alive, to truly exist, in short, for it to actualise itself, it is necessary that there also be a human being who knows how to read it, in silence or out loud, or to recite it.]

This relationship between the human voice who 'activates' a poetic text and the role of the human voice as represented within poems by Baudelaire and Mallarmé is founded on an important aesthetic concern for both poets: in order for their own voices to succeed through their poetry, they are absolutely reliant on the voices of others. The interaction of perfume and music in 'Tout entière' is also symbolic of the interaction between voices that the poets require. In the final tercet of Baudelaire's 'Parfum exotique' (B.*OC*.I, pp.25–26), this interaction of perfume and music, and its correlation with an interaction between voices is made explicit:

> Pendant que le parfum des verts tamariniers,
> Qui circule dans l'air et m'enfle la narine,
> Se mêle dans mon âme au chant des mariniers. (v.12–14)

> [Whilst the fragrance of the green tamarind trees,
> Which circulates in the air and swells my nostrils,
> Mixes with the song of the sailors in my soul.]

The fragrance of the tamarind tree, like the aroma of the flowers carried by the 'brise' in Mallarmé's sonnet 'Dans le jardin', is carried through the air and intermingles with the singing voices of the sailors. Like the final line of Mallarmé's 'Sonnet' cited above, the prevalence of the labial phoneme 'm' in this final line of 'Parfum exotique' emphasises the role of the reader's voice upon reading. It requires the reader either to bring his or her lips together or to 'pre-action' that movement, and to do this so repeatedly that his or her own voice should begin to intermingle with the sailor's song as it is expressed through the poet's own voice.

In fact this same image of the sound of sailors singing, which sets in motion an interaction between other human voices, is employed by Mallarmé as a means to overcome poetic impotence. In 'Brise marine' (M.*OC*.I, p.15), the extent of patternings on the same 'm' phoneme is significant because it is built primarily on the cluster of repetitions – under various linguistic guises – of the same root word 'mât' ['mast'] ('ta mâture' v.9, 'les mâts' v.13, 'sans mâts, sans mâts' v.15). When the culminating word of the poem comes as 'des matelots' ['of the sailors'] (v.16), although it does not stem from the same root, the sound patterning has already been established. Moreover, in order to confirm the syllabic count of the alexandrine line, the middle 'e' of the word is pronounced (where ordinarily it would be clipped). So the call to listen to the sailors' song that is made in the final line ('Mais, ô mon cœur, entends le chant des matelots!' ['But, oh my heart, listen to the song of the sailors!']) carries a whole swathe of resonances. This is done through the internal build-up of the labial 'm' patternings, through the prosodic requirement of forcing the clipped 'e' of 'matelots' to be pronounced, and through the external resonances with Baudelaire's own call to listen to the sailors' song of 'Parfum exotique'. Mallarmé has thereby constructed the narrative of 'Brise marine' in such a way as to exploit the human voice through the possibility of intermingling with other human voices, in order to overcome the tired relationship between body and text that he laments in the opening line of the poem: 'La chair est triste, hélas! et j'ai lu tous les livres' ['My flesh is sad, alas!, and I've read every book'] (v.1). The 'brise' referred to by the title has resonances with the 'crise' or breaking point of poetic development that Mallarmé experienced at the time of composition in the mid 1860s, which is reinforced by the stark image of the 'vide papier' ['empty paper'] (v.7). By re-invigorating the 'triste chair' through a poetic text that posits the possibility of an 'exotique nature' (v.10) in the way it hints at less regular versificatory designs (such as the caesural conundrums and enjambement of lines 2–3), Mallarmé reinstates the role of the human voice within the text as a way of revivifying poetry.

'Le rire'

Textual representations of the human voice in the poetry of Baudelaire and Mallarmé have far more to do with uncovering new possibilities for putting the voice into action through the intermingling with other voices, and the infinite poetic possibilities and iterations that this entails, than trying to capture an originary vocal enactment. If there is any mimetic representation of the human voice in the poetry of Baudelaire or Mallarmé it is in order to highlight the necessary artifice of poetic language. Mallarmé makes this explicit in the octosyllabic sonnet 'Feuillet d'album' (M.*OC*.I, pp.31–32) which follows the Shakespearean sonnet form, concluding with a rhyming couplet. The same 'mouvement dans l'air' image is exploited in this poem through the conceit of his Faun-like flute-playing ('Mademoiselle qui voulûtes / Ouïr se révéler un peu / Le bois de mes diverses flûtes' ['Mademoiselle who wishes / To hear some manifestation / Of the wood of my various flutes'] v.2–4) which he later describes as a 'vain souffle' ['vain breath'] (v.9). The 'souffle' of the poem itself is unpunctuated: the sonnet has no punctuation other than the pauses created by the verse line breaks, as if this serves to mask the fact that the 'souffle' of the poem is taking place at all. In order to praise the child to whom the poem is addressed, the poetic voice devalues itself before the face of the child ('Pour vous regarder au visage' ['To look you in the face'] v.8). The contrast between the 'vain souffle' of the poem and the child's own 'mouvement dans l'air' comes in the final couplet of the sonnet, as it becomes clear that Mallarmé is at pains to avoid trying to imitate the laughter of the child which emanates from the face that he is admiring poetically:

Oui ce vain souffle que j'exclus
Jusqu'à la dernière limite
Selon mes quelques doigts perclus
Manque de moyens s'il imite

Votre très naturel et clair
Rire d'enfant qui charme l'air. (v.9–14)

[Yes this vain breath which I suspend
Right up to the final moment
Depending on my few crippled fingers
Lacks the means if it imitates

Your very natural and clear
Child's laughter which charms the air.]

In other words, the artifice of Mallarmé's own verse poetry does not in any way try to imitate the natural simplicity of the child's laughter. The vocal enactments proposed by poetic language cannot live up to the child's laughter not only because the laughter comes out naturally, where poetic language requires the persistent trying-out and experimentation of an 'essai' ['test' / 'attempt'] (v.5), but also because the child's laughter is devoid of words, whereas poetic language is all too concerned with the words themselves.

Baudelaire perceives laughter as something painful. Paraphrasing from a *Conte normand* by Philippe de Chennevières, he expresses this in his study on caricature, 'De l'essence du rire':

Le rire et la douleur s'expriment par ... les yeux et la bouche. Dans le paradis terrestre ... la joie n'était pas dans le rire. ... Le rire et les larmes ne peuvent pas se faire voir dans le paradis de délices. Ils sont également les enfants de la peine, et ils sont venus parce que le corps de l'homme énervé manquait de force pour les contraindre. (B.*OC*.II, p.528)

[Laughter and pain are expressed through the eyes and the mouth. In the earthly paradise ... joy was not to be found in laughter. ... Laughter and tears cannot be found in the pleasures of paradise. They are also the children of pain, and came into existence because the aggravated human body lacked the strength to restrain them.]

For Baudelaire, a 'rire enfantin' ['childish laughter'] actively gets in the way of being able to write poetry (which he describes as a 'mensonge', or artifice). In 'Semper eadem' (B.*OC*.I, p.41), Baudelaire begs his mistress to be silent because her 'rire enfantin' is so at odds with poetic composition. In response to her question in the direct speech of the opening two lines of the sonnet:

'D'où vous vient, disiez-vous, cette tristesse étrange,
Montant comme la mer sur le roc noir et nu?' (v.1–2)

['From whence comes, you said, this strange sadness,
Rising up like the sea onto the black and bare rock?']

the Baudelairean poetic voice tries to silence her. The fact that Baudelaire makes his plea across the 'volta' of the sonnet reinforces the notion that her voice is obstructing his poetic endeavour:

Et, bien que votre voix soit douce, taisez-vous!

Taisez-vous, ignorante! âme toujours ravie!
Bouche au rire enfantin! (v.8–10)

[And, although your voice may be sweet, be quiet!

Be quiet, ignorant lady! soul always enraptured!
Mouth with a childish laughter!]

As Elissa Marder has suggested, this exclamation is 'highly unpoetic' because we hear the poet's 'prosaic scream'.[20] However, Baudelaire exploits poetic techniques here in an attempt to safeguard his poetic voice. The repetitive anadiplosis of the imperative 'taisez-vous' is mirrored in the repetitive 'Laissez, laissez mon cœur s'enivrer d'un *mensonge*' ['Let, oh let my heart become drunk on a *lie*'] of line 12. These repetitions offer a way for the poet to reinforce his own voice above the noise of the mistress' voice whose joyful laughter hampers the possibility for the necessary artifice that is constructed through poetic language. Furthermore, 'Semper eadem' is a sonnet which raises some prosodic issues concerning the scansion of certain lines. In line 11, the reader is pulled up short by questions of pronunciation and scansion, revolving around the question of synaeresis or diaeresis of the [jɛ̃] sound. The verb 'tient' and the noun 'liens' should have the same syllabic weighting, but within the verse line, 'tient' is granted only one syllable, where 'liens' is extended to two: 'La Mort nous tient souvent par des liens subtils' ['Death often holds onto us with subtle bonds']. This disturbs the perceived sonorous symmetry of the line, and emphasises the poetic voice's distress in this poem as a result of his mistress' laughter trying to take precedence over his poetic artifice. The struggle between the poetic voice, the mistress' voice, and what is required of the reader reveals the complexity of involvement of the human voice required by this poem as it moves carefully and imperceptibly between the natural and the artificial.

---

[20]   Elissa Marder, *Dead Time: Temporal Disorders in the Wake of Modernity (Baudelaire and Flaubert)* (Stanford: Stanford University Press, 2001), p.18.

The aesthetics of voice put forward by these two poets seeks to explore the multiplicity of human vocal enactments, and to put to the test aspects which are at once natural and artificial, internal and external. They exploit this multiplicity in an attempt to uncover the power of poetic language itself. The ability to recognise and use a range of dynamics of the human voice involves a profound corporeal action which also entails a pre-action and a reaction. Where the 'pre-action' element of bringing a poem to voice incorporates being able to hear and use different voices without actually creating that 'mouvement dans l'air' by speaking out loud, the 'reaction' element of bringing a poem to voice comes in the form of re-reading and testing out different possibilities of pronunciation or scansion (and this becomes increasingly the case in the poetry of Mallarmé).

Prose Poem Conventions

One of the greatest poetic tests that Baudelaire and Mallarmé carried out has very little to do with the minutiae of pronunciation or scansion of a verse line. The prose poem form offered a different approach to the dynamics of voice because it was no longer beholden to a prosodic rigour. Whereas for Baudelaire, the prose poem was a departure from his career as a verse poet, a departure which he undertook in the latter stages of his career, Mallarmé wrote prose poetry throughout the course of his career, alongside his verse poetry. On the face of it, Baudelaire's prose poems seem to favour commonplace representations of voice; in fact Baudelaire introduces certain strategies which exploit the dynamic capabilities of the human voice, strategies which seem to influence Mallarmé's attitudes towards using voices in prose poetry. A comparison of Baudelaire's 'La Soupe et les Nuages' and the ensuing prose poem 'Le Tir et le Cimetière' reveals two key descriptions of the human voice which exploit traditional commonplaces. In 'Le Tir et le Cimetière' (B.*OC*.I, p.351), it is the voice of a dead soul who speaks to the 'promeneur' protagonist of the prose poem against the backdrop of the cemetery. Rather conventionally, Baudelaire describes the voice of the dead soul as a whispering voice: 'il entendit une voix chuchoter sous la tombe où il s'était assis' ['he heard a voice whispering beneath the tomb upon which he was sitting']. This conventional topos of a mysterious whispering voice of a dead soul is situated at the lower end of the dynamic register, and is in direct contrast to the rather extraordinary complaint that the voice makes against the noise of the shooting practice that is taking place nearby. In fact, the description of the dead soul's voice as a whispering voice turns out to be contradictory to the fierce vehemence of its rage against the noise:

> 'Maudites soient vos cibles et vos carabines, turbulents vivants, qui vous souciez si peu des défunts et de leur divin repos! Maudites soient vos ambitions, maudits soient vos calculs, mortels impatients, qui venez étudier l'art de tuer auprès du sanctuaire de la Mort!'

['Damn your targets and your rifles, living disturbers of the peace, who care so little for the dead and their divine repose! Damn your ambitions, damn your calculations, impatient mortals, who come to study the art of killing at the sanctuary of Death!']

The thrice-repeated anaphora on 'maudit(e)s soient' reinforces the vehemence of the dead soul's voice, which is at odds with its purported dynamic volume.

The preceding poem of the *Spleen de Paris* prose poem collection, however, presents a different vehement voice which, whilst once again following a conventional topos, is at least more in line dynamically with the content. The short two-paragraph prose poem 'La Soupe et les Nuages' (B.*OC*.I, p.350) contains two instances of direct speech, signalled by quotation marks. One is an internal reflection on the part of the poetic voice ('Je me disais …' ['I said to myself …']), the other, which closes the prose poem, is the voice of the poetic voice's mistress. The mistress' voice is described as being under the influence of alcohol:

j'entendis une voix rauque et charmante, une voix hystérique et comme enrouée par l'eau-de-vie, la voix de ma chère petite bien-aimée, qui disait: ' – Allez-vous bientôt manger votre soupe, s... b... de marchand de nuages?'

[I heard a raucous and charming voice, a voice which was hysterical and as if hoarse from whisky, the voice of my dear little beloved, who was saying: 'Are you going to eat your soup soon, you b... s... cloud merchant?']

The oxymoronic coupling of 'rauque' with 'charmante', and of the hysteria with the affectionate description of his mistress, heightens the irony of the representation of the human voice in this context. Throughout the short prose poem, Baudelaire has built up a patterning on the description of his mistress, from 'Ma petite folle bien-aimée' ['My little mad beloved'] in the opening line, to 'ma belle bien-aimée' ['my beautiful beloved'] and 'la petite folle monstrueuse' ['the little mad monstrous one'] in the poetic voice's reflection enclosed in speech marks, to 'ma chère petite bien-aimée' ['my dear little beloved'] in the second paragraph already cited above. The slippage between 'ma' and 'la', between 'folle' and 'belle', between 'bien-aimée' and 'monstrueuse' which is set up by this patterning reinforces the oxymoronic irony of Baudelaire's representation of the voice of his mistress. Whereas in verse poetry, the reader is expected to read and re-read carefully in order to pay attention to prosodic issues, here, in the prose poetry, the reader is required to be even more attentive to the possibility of poetic techniques and patternings, since the rejection of verse form renders these inexplicit. The representation and intervention of the human voice, then, takes on a different approach – the 'pre-action', the 'action' and the 'reaction' elements of the reading process are potentially disjointed by the thwarted expectations of conventional poetic forms. It seems that in order to compensate, to a certain degree, for the lack of reference points in the prose poem form, Baudelaire has opted to exploit conventional topoi in representing the human voice in order to challenge the reader to discover how the human voice is able to function within the form of prose poetry. The gauntlet is explicitly thrown down in 'La Soupe et les Nuages' by the ironic ellipsis of the final reported speech of the mistress which encourages the reader to fill in, with his or her own voice, and no doubt with a wry smile, the vulgar implications of the mistress' voice which have been left unsaid.

'Le cri'

It is not only the reader whose voice is challenged by the prose poem form. In 'Le Confiteor de l'artiste' (B.*OC*.I, p.279), the artistic struggle that the poet endures results in the death of the artist – but not before he has cried out in the closing phases of the duel:

> L'étude du beau est un duel où l'artiste crie de frayeur avant d'être vaincu.

> [The study of beauty is a duel in which the artist cries out in fear just before being overcome.]

The 'cri de frayeur', forming the poet's troubled swan song before he dies, is a distressed crying-out for poetry itself which might get lost in the prose poem form. The artistic struggle that Baudelaire exposed in 'Semper eadem' here returns in a different form: the battle between voices risks becoming little more than an uncontrolled crying-out on the part of the poet before death takes over. Where in 'Semper eadem', he advised his mistress to be silent so that he might live out some of his poetic artifice before the certainty of death arrives, in 'Le Confiteor de l'artiste' it is as if death has already overcome the poet who can no longer put up the struggle to fight for poetry. But where for Baudelaire this battle is most prevalent in his prose poetry, for Mallarmé, the struggle primarily manifests itself in verse poetry. Mallarmé's 'cri', unlike Baudelaire's non-verbal calling out in 'Le Confiteor', becomes a means for the poet to bring his uncertainty about the status of poetry to voice through poetic language itself. In 'Toast funèbre' (M.*OC*. I, p.27), which was originally composed as part of a series of poems written by a number of different poets to commemorate the death of Théophile Gautier, the 'cri' that resounds throughout the poem consists of four troubled words: 'Je ne sais pas!' ['I do not know'] (v.31). Since this poem is concerned with the work of another poet who no longer lives, the idea of poetic longevity and of retaining life through poetry even in the face of death drives the thematic narrative. The 'cri' in Baudelaire's 'Confiteor' takes place before the poet dies; in 'Toast funèbre', the 'cri' rattles around the tomb even after the poet's death:

> Vaste gouffre apporté dans l'amas de la brume
> Par l'irascible vent des mots qu'il n'a pas dits,

Le néant à cet Homme aboli de jadis:
'Souvenir d'horizons, qu'est-ce, ô toi, que la Terre?'
Hurle ce songe; et, voix dont la clarté s'altère,
L'espace a pour jouet le cri: 'Je ne sais pas'! (v.26–31)

[Vast gulf carried within the density of the mist
By the irascible wind of words he did not say,
The emptiness, to this Man abolished of old:
'Memory of horizons, oh you, what is Earth?'
Howls this dream; and, voice whose clarity falters,
Space has for its toy the cry: 'I do not know'!]

Although this poem purportedly celebrates the life and work of Gautier, it also reveals a large part of Mallarmé's own poetic aesthetic. The obliqueness and impersonality of the pronoun 'il' in line 27, and of figures such as 'le néant' and 'cet Homme' (v.28), and also of the 'voix' two lines later, allow for different possible interpretations concerning who is speaking, who has not spoken, and who is uncertain about speaking.[21] The figures of Gautier, Mallarmé and 'cette foule hagarde' ['this wild crowd'] (v.18) intermingle throughout the text so that by the time the 'cri' is heard in line 31, it is uttered by an impersonal voice: it is 'l'espace' who utters the 'cri', but the voice itself is not easily comprehensible ('voix dont la clarté s'altère' v.30). The four words 'Je ne sais pas' (v.31) pose both as an unsatisfactory response to the question of line 29, and as a perplexed crying out about the status of poetry and the relationship between poet, text and the crowd. The poetic voices in this poem are troubled by the 'mouvement dans l'air' that creates poetic worlds: rather than the evocative 'brise' or 'souffle' that Mallarmé so favours, here the air is haunted by 'l'irascible vent' (v.27). That the 'vent' is a 'vent des mots qu'il n'a pas dits' suggests that Mallarmé is haunted by the possibility that the 'mouvement dans l'air' which grants power to poetic language might be infiltrated or contaminated by other voices, and it is this that leads him to the troubled conclusion that he cannot know what memories of poetic horizons ('Souvenir d'horizons' v.29) are able to persist.

The memory of Gautier reinspires Mallarmé in his belief that Gautier's voice, in its final swan song, has been able to give birth to the symbolic flowers of poetry by granting a necessary 'mystère' to 'la Rose et le Lys':

Le Maître, par un œil profond, a, sur ses pas,
Apaisé de l'éden l'inquiète merveille
Dont le frisson final, dans sa voix seule, éveille

---

[21]   As Marian Zwerling Sugano suggests, 'the speaker calls on Gautier *as if* he desired to enter into dialogue with him'. The uncertainty of the *as if* is what is at stake here. Marian Zwerling Sugano, *The Poetics of the Occasion: Mallarmé and the Poetry of Circumstance* (Stanford: Stanford University Press, 1992), p.48.

Pour la Rose et le Lys le mystère d'un nom.
Est-il de ce destin rien qui demeure, non? (v.32–36)

[The Master, with an all-seeing eye, has, as he goes,
Calmed the anxious wonder of Eden
Whose final trembling, in his voice alone, awakens
For the Rose and the Lily the mystery of a name.
Is there anything left of this destiny, or not?]

The disconcerted uncertainty ('l'inquiète merveille') of the preceding stanza is 'apaisé' (v.33) by the trembling voice of the poet in death. The rhetorical question concerning what remains after the poet's death is answered a few lines later, where the violence of 'l'irascible vent des mots' (v.27) is replaced by 'une agitation solennelle par l'air / De paroles' ['a solemn turbulence by the air / Of spoken words'] (v.43–44). This is what survives ('Survivre' v.42) of the poet's voice: the unspoken 'mots' have been replaced by the spoken 'paroles', even though Mallarmé no longer includes any direct speech marks to signal the possibility of the spoken word. Rather like in Poe's tale 'The Power of Words', Gautier's – and implicitly Mallarmé's – ability to create the poetic flowers comes from an 'agitation de l'air' of the spoken word. But the action of speaking does not necessarily take place: it is sufficient that the poetic action, in the form of writing poetry that will be brought to life as it is read, takes place.[22] The uncertainty over poetic longevity, the uncontrolled 'cri' that shouts out 'Je ne sais pas!', is calmed by the softer dynamic of the 'agitation solennelle par l'air de paroles' which allows the poet – and poetry – still to live on.

The 'cri' and the 'rire' in the poetry of Baudelaire and Mallarmé pose a potential danger to poetic production which both poets embrace. It is perhaps not without irony that the verb 'écrire' contains both a 'cri' and a 'rire'. These two important elements of the human voice, which hover at the louder end of the dynamic range, must be explored in order to understand what lies behind the 'puissance de la parole'. It is the power of words themselves, uttered through the textual dynamic of poetry, that Baudelaire and Mallarmé hanker after. Textual mimicry of the human voice does not function on a purely mimetic level for either poet: both introduce elements into their poetic language that require the reader to pay attention to the way that words are formed – both in physical terms by the mind and the mouth in the processes of 'pre-action', 'action' and 'reaction', and in textual terms by the structure of the poetic architecture, whether in verse or prose form. The complexities of the dynamic range and qualities of the human voice are what lead both poets to eschew being prescriptive about how their poetry is to be read. But this does not mean that they disregard these complexities themselves:

---

[22]   In this respect, it is difficult to concur with Sugano's detailed analysis of the performativity of this poem as one which reads the poem in terms of 'a number of attempted but unsuccessful speech acts'. Sugano, *The Poetics of the Occasion*, p.53.

their poetry is suffused with questions about the dynamics of vocal enactments, whatever the performance scenario.

The Special Case of 'Un Coup de dés'

In fact, the varied dynamic properties of the human voice lead Mallarmé to propose, with a not insignificant amount of irony, that readers should pay attention to dynamics upon reading his most extraordinary poem, 'Un Coup de dés'. It was not Mallarmé's orginal intention to provide any kind of 'performance manual' for the poem, but he was asked by the editor of the journal *Cosmopolis* in which the first, imperfect, version of the poem was published, to furnish a preface in order to assist the journal's readers. Mallarmé considers the implications of the poem's unusual traits in order to explain how this affects the reading process when reading 'Un Coup de dés' out loud, and writes in his 'Observation relative au poème':

> de cet emploi à nu de la pensée avec retraits, prolongements, fuites, ou son dessin même, résulte, pour qui veut lire à haute voix, une partition. La différence des caractères d'imprimerie entre le motif prépondérant, un secondaire et d'adjacents, dicte son importance à l'émission orale et la portée, moyenne, en haut, en bas de page, notera que monte ou descend l'intonation. (M.*OC*.I, pp.391–392)

> [from this exposed use of thought with retractions, extensions, escapes, or its whole layout, emerges, for whoever wishes to read out loud, a musical score. The difference in fonts between the predominant motif, the secondary and the adjacent ones, dictates the level of importance for vocal projection and the placement, in the middle, at the top, or at the bottom of the page, will indicate whether the intonation should rise or descend.]

Mallarmé's diction here avoids being prescriptive ('pour qui veut lire à haute voix'), which indicates, first of all, that he does not perceive a reading out loud to be imperative to the poem. It is the defensive Valéry, once again, who is quick to explain the implications of Mallarmé's comments here, claiming that the words 'pour qui veut …' cannot be interpreted too broadly:

> La liberté que l'auteur concède (dans le préface à l'édition très imparfaite de *Cosmopolis*) de *lire* à haute voix le *Coup de Dés* ne doit pas être mal entendue: elle ne veut que pour un lecteur déjà familiarisé avec le texte, et qui, les yeux sur le bel album d'imagerie abstraite, peut enfin de sa propre voix, animer ce spectacle idéographique d'une crise ou aventure intellectuelle.[23]

---

[23]   Valéry, *Œuvres*, I, p.627

[The freedom which the author grants (in the preface to the very imperfect *Cosmopolis* edition) to *read Un Coup de Dés* out loud should not be misunderstood: this freedom is only granted to a reader who is already familiar with the text, and who, with his eyes on the beautiful album of abstract imagery, can at last, with his own voice, animate this ideographic spectacle of an intellectual crisis or adventure.]

What is significant about Valéry's analysis of Mallarmé's comments is that he believes that 'Un Coup de dés' is a text which requires significant familiarisation on the part of the reader before it may be performed out loud effectively. Valéry's wariness about the possibility that an unaccustomed reader may fail to grasp the complexities of the poem shows an awareness of Mallarmé's original design. The text is so unusual typographically that the only way to begin to comprehend it is to approach it again and again, each time sounding out different possibilities of poetic resonances according to the positioning and size of the words distributed across its various pages. Even though no definitive version was published during his lifetime, Mallarmé went to great pains to specify typographical spacings, font sizes and styles, likening its layout, as he does in the preface cited above, to a musical score or 'partition' (and this is also reinforced by the use of the word 'portée', which in this context implies not only the positioning of words on the page, but also the notion of a musical stave). Valéry, on the other hand, turns the 'score' into a theatrical 'spectacle' which is to be animated by the human voice of the reader. The recourse that both Mallarmé and Valéry have to other art forms which specifically require an external performance in fact raises an important question: how should the reader try to sound out poetic resonances if a text does not specifically require that it be read out loud?

One potential answer to this question comes in a format that Mallarmé himself would hardly have imagined. A CD-ROM version of 'Un Coup de dés' was published in 2000 and offers a range of different possible readings (including in translation, which I shall not consider here).[24] It presents the full text of 'Un Coup de dés' in such a way as to maintain the pagination and spacing (even though the reader of the CD-ROM version no longer has the experience that Mallarmé cherished of turning the page, or sensing the fold in the middle of the page). It also

---

[24]   *Mallarmé on CD-ROM: Un Coup de dés jamais n'abolira le hasard*, ed. and trans. by Penny Florence (Oxford: Legenda, 2000). In the introductory booklet, Penny Florence asks: 'what happens when you put this one-hundred-year-old multimedia experiment onto CD-ROM? Transposing this poem into virtual space actually facilitates the kind of reading it formally demands, but which paper renders obscure and difficult to realise. The centrality of the page to the experience and meanings of reading is not lost, but is rather freed. Using a digitised version of the text is not a substitute for reading it in the original, but rather a kinetic dimension of reading which, while it may be experienced independently, is fully understood only in relation to its tradition and to the intervention it makes into that tradition'. 'Typography, New (Information) Technology', p.24.

presents an interactive version of the text, which effectively allows the reader to build a 'do-it-yourself' rendition of the poem. Another element of the CD-ROM allows the reader to 'read' 'Un Coup de dés' 'accompanied' by the third movement of Claude Debussy's 'La Mer' (entitled 'Dialogue du vent et de la mer'). This inter-art rendition of the poem does not allow the reader to read at his own pace, since the text appears and disappears according to the spacings defined by the producers of the CD-ROM (the excerpt from 'La Mer' lasts 7.56 minutes and the text is spaced accordingly). Another inter-art element is the inclusion of trial lithographs for 'Un Coup de dés' by Odilon Redon. Finally, there are two different recordings of the poem being read out loud, once by Nicole Ward Jouve, the other by Yves Bonnefoy. Quite apart from the natural differences in timbre between the female and the male voices, what is interesting is that each reader makes different decisions not only about pacing and volume, but also about how the text interlinks across the supposed 'fold' of the page.

Where Ward Jouve's reading of the poem tends to follow the directions that Mallarmé put forward in his preface – that is to say, she uses a louder volume for words in a larger typeface, and her overall dynamic diminishes as she reads from the top left to the bottom right of the double pages – Bonnefoy's reading is more like Valéry's description of Mallarmé's reading, on a more level tone. Bonnefoy also takes much less time over either the folds in the page or page turns, where Ward Jouve tends to exploit the space by a longer pause in her reading. Ward Jouve also employs a floatier timbre for the italicised text, thus making a distinction between the different types of vocal qualities that seem to be required by the text. Each reading, however, lasts about nine minutes (with Bonnefoy's being marginally shorter), notwithstanding the different pacings and pauses that each reader chooses. There are, however, three moments where the two readers diverge in their opinions as to the flow of the text – and each of these instances take place where the central fold of the page comes into play. These instances affect not only syntax but also interpretation and meaning.

On the second double-page of the poem, which begins with the words 'LE MAÎTRE' (M.*OC*.I, pp.372–373), Bonnefoy's reading moves down the right-hand page before moving back across to the left-hand page (‖ represents the central fold in the page, | represents a line break):

LE MAÎTRE ‖ hors d'anciens calculs | où la manœuvre avec l'âge oubliée | jadis
il empoignait la barre ‖ surgi | inférant | de cette conflagration

Bonnefoy's reading emphasises the notion of old-fashioned former times by bringing the word 'jadis' closer to 'l'âge' and 'anciens calculs' of the first two lines of the right-hand page. Ward Jouve, on the other hand, moves back across to the left-hand page earlier, following the vertical orientation of the text, inserting the elliptical asides of 'surgi' and 'inférant' before the 'jadis':

LE MAÎTRE ‖ hors d'anciens calculs | où la manœuvre avec l'âge oubliée ‖
surgi | inférant ‖ jadis il empoignait la barre ‖ de cette conflagration

Ward Jouve's reading also syntactically suggests that the 'conflagration' stems
from 'la barre', although the sense of this would be impossible. The different
emphases of each reading require the listener to return again to the text to seek
other possible combinations, and to understand which elements of the text can
validly be said to refer to or qualify another. The elliptical asides of 'surgi' and
'inférant', for example, with their masculine endings, only seem to be able to
apply to 'le maître'. Upon hearing the text, however, the listener who does not
have the text in front of himself, would not be able to be certain that 'surgi' does
not qualify either the preceding word of Bonnefoy's reading ('la barre') or that
of Ward Jouve's reading ('l'âge oubliée'), which are both feminine nouns. The
different possible readings reinforce the notion that there is no 'correct' reading
of Mallarmé's poem, and that this poem – which thematises chance – exploits the
chance encounters of language upon (different) readings.

On the sixth double-page, which begins with the word '*soucieux*' (M.*OC*.I,
pp.380–381), Bonnefoy's reading follows across the page break according to the
relevant vertical spacing of the text:

La lucide et seigneuriale aigrette ‖ de vertige ‖ au front invisible | scintille | puis
ombrage | une stature mignonne ténébreuse ‖ debout | en sa torsion de sirène ‖
le temps | de souffleter

where Ward Jouve follows down the left-hand page on a couple of instances before
breaching the fold in the page.

La lucide et seigneuriale aigrette | au front invisible ‖ de vertige ‖ scintille | puis
ombrage | une stature mignonne ténébreuse | en sa torsion de sirène ‖ debout | le
temps | de souffleter

Once again, elliptical qualifying words or phrases (in this instance 'de vertige' and
'debout') are applied in two different ways by each reader, allowing for different
possible interpretations. The temptation (and traditional habit) of most readers
would be to apply the qualifiers to the nearest possible noun. This time there is no
clear masculine or feminine designation which would enable certain combinations
to be excluded – whether there is an 'aigrette de vertige' (Bonnefoy) or a 'front
invisible de vertige' (Ward Jouve), or whether indeed the 'vertige' can be applied
to other elements of the page, is undecidable.

Finally, on the subsequent double-page (M.*OC*.I, pp.382–383), Ward Jouve
follows the flow of the phrase according to the font size (here a medium-sized font,
capitalised and italicised):

C'ÉTAIT ‖ LE NOMBRE

where Bonnefoy inserts the italicised aside (in a very small font) in the middle:

C'ÉTAIT | issu stellaire ‖ LE NOMBRE

The typographical decisions of this poem – font size, capitalisation or italicisation, as well as the positioning on the page – are relevant to the reading process not simply because Mallarmé was at such pains to ensure that the typography was exactly as he desired it to be, but also because they offer further parameters for selecting how words can be combined upon reading. Typographical layout must also take into account the fold in the page (and the gaps in reading that arise from turning over a page). The significance of the fold in the page, then, is not simply its immutable presence, but the fact that it can be bridged in different ways in order to allow for different possible readings to emerge.

Being able to listen again and again to other people's readings of this extraordinary poem reminds us that not only will each person's vocal qualities differ, but so too will interpretative combinations and possibilities.[25] Neither Bonnefoy's nor Ward Jouve's reading is a definitive reading (and nor, even, would Mallarmé's own reading of this poem to Valéry have been the 'definitive' reading). Just like a musical score, the text of the page itself does not prescribe one definitive rendition (and this is where Mallarmé's description of this poem as a 'partition' offers a useful parallel). A trained musician is able to 'read' a musical score and 'hear' the piece before him on the page even before it is performed out loud, but both an 'internal' performance and any potential 'external' performance will always be different on each rendition. What is important is that the reader is able to 'hear' the potential resonances of different combinations of words, phrases and sounds in order to exploit moments where elements of the text both conflict and concur. Of course this raises a further question – and it is a question that preoccupies both Baudelaire and Mallarmé – what happens if poetry fails to resonate at all?

---

[25]   Heather Williams' analysis of this text, for example, reminds us that 'Words not only *can* belong to more than one syntactic or phonetic sequence, but *must* do so, because "ordinary" linear reading is thwarted at every turn, forcing the reader to take account of its depth or space, and not only of its progress forward'. Heather Williams, *Mallarmé's Ideas in Language* (Bern: Peter Lang, 2004), p.94.

Chapter 3
Vocal Resonance

She smiled at him, making sure that the smile gathered up everything inside her and directed it toward him, making him a profound promise of herself for so little, for the beat of a response, the assurance of a complementary vibration in him.

F. Scott Fitzgerald, Tender is the Night[1]

Il m'a dit: 'Cette nuit, j'ai rêvé.
J'avais ta chevelure autour de mon cou.'
[He said to me: 'Last night I dreamt.
I had your hair around my neck.']

Pierre Louÿs, 'La Chevelure', v.1–2[2]

Je connais ta voix … Si, tu prends une voix méchante. … J'ai le fil autour de mon cou. J'ai ta voix autour de mon cou …

[I know your voice … Yes, your voice is turning mean. … I have the wire around my neck. I have your voice around my neck …]

Jean Cocteau, La Voix humaine[3]

The dynamic range that the human voice is capable of producing does not necessarily guarantee a vocal resonance. Bringing a poem to voice by specifically reading it out loud does not mean that it will create the desired effect. In his prose poem 'Pauvre enfant pâle' (M.*OC*.I, p.418), Mallarmé questions the effect of the child street-singer's attempts at singing:

> Pauvre enfant pâle, pourquoi crier à tue-tête dans la rue ta chanson aiguë et insolente, qui se perd parmi les chats, seigneurs des toits?
>
> [Poor pale child, why cry out in the street your harsh and insolent song at the top of your voice, which gets lost among the cats, the lords of the roofs?]

The acoustical padding of the bourgeois cityscape reinforces the extent to which the child's singing voice gets lost:

---

[1] F. Scott Fitzgerald, *Tender is the Night* (London: Penguin, 1934–1986), p.152.

[2] Pierre Louÿs, *Les Chansons de Bilitis* (Paris: Fayard, 1930), p.42.

[3] Jean Cocteau, *La Voix humaine* (Paris: Librairie Stock, Delamain & Boutelleau, 1930), p.66.

car elle ne traversera pas les volets des premiers étages, derrière lesquels tu
ignores de lourds rideaux de soie incarnadine.

[because it will not get through the blinds of the first floor, behind which you do
not know that there are heavy curtains of flesh-coloured silk.]

Read allegorically, the 'rideaux de soie incarnadine' could be interpreted as a
determined, or thick-skinned, refusal on the part of others to listen to the child's
singing which, in turn, aggravates the child to the extent that he redoubles his
efforts:

Et ta complainte est si haute, si haute, que ta tête nue qui se lève en l'air à mesure
que ta voix monte, semble vouloir partir de tes petites épaules.

[And your complaint is so high-pitched, so high-pitched, that your bare head
which rises up in the air as your voice rises, seems to want to break away from
your small shoulders.]

The intensification of the dynamic volume of the child's singing, reinforced here
by Mallarmé's repetition of 'si haute', is further heightened by the way Mallarmé
makes a parallel between the raising of the head and the raising of the voice.
Quite apart from the political, or at least socioeconomic, comment that Mallarmé
might be making in this poem, it offers an explanation as to why Mallarmé often
shies away from stronger dynamics in his poetry: in Mallarmé's poetic aesthetic,
there is no direct correlation between a loud volume and being heard or attaining
a response. In fact, for Mallarmé, it is frequently quite the contrary. As we have
seen, louder dynamics are often stifled and preference is granted to a quiet murmur.
The music that the child-beggar is trying to create is far from resonant because he
is straining too hard and does not take into account the real effect that his voice
creates. The louder he strains, the less likely he is to extract a penny or two from
any passers-by:

Pas un sou ne descend dans le panier d'osier que tient ta longue main pendue
sans espoir sur ton pantalon: on te rendra mauvais et un jour tu commettras un
crime.
    Ta tête se dresse toujours et veut te quitter, comme si d'avance elle savait,
pendant que tu chantes d'un air qui devient menaçant.

[Not a single penny drops into the wicker basket which is held in your long hand
hanging down hopelessly against your trouser leg: you will be turned bad and
one day you will commit a crime.
    Your head still stands tall and wants to leave you, as if it knew in advance,
whilst you sing in a way that becomes menacing.]

The inability to elicit the desired response and the inability to earn any money, transforms the child's singing into a menacing omen of a future crime. The warning is also a warning to Mallarmé's own poetic career. Published in 1864, during the years leading up to the 'crise' period of his poetic production, the poem's allegory portrays an aesthetics of voice which shies away from a vain striving. Mallarmé, at this time, is beginning to discover that in order to create a desired effect through poetry, there is much more involved than simply singing or shouting loudly enough to be heard. It is not simply a question of volume; it is more importantly a question of effective voice production.

Sounding out poetry is not simply about the action of creating noise, like the 'pauvre enfant pâle', it is also about creating meanings and feelings which go right to the heart of human experience. For Baudelaire and Mallarmé – as with so many other poets – unless their poetry is able spark some resonance with their reader, it will go just as unheard as the plangent singing of the 'pauvre enfant pâle'. Their aesthetic concerns suggest that it is important to be attentive to how a voice is able to resonate through poetry, and to what might happen if it does not. In this respect, an interaction between sound, sense and sensation comes into play. Although it is difficult to fully separate out each of these attributes of voice within the context of poetry, at times certain attributes are privileged over others.[4] Mallarmé is of particular relevance here, since he begins to privilege the notion of 'sensation' above both sound and meaning around the time of his 'crise' period. In this chapter, I shall focus on the inter-relationships between a number of poems composed during the mid 1860s, with particular attention to this notion of 'sensation' and the rhythmic effects that this will imply. I suggest that Mallarmé's increasing preoccupation with 'sensation' draws him to privilege particular interstices and gaps between different sounds, words and even between poems because it is within these spaces that the reader is able to listen out for all the different possible resonances that poetic language is capable of creating. Moving beyond Baudelaire's aesthetic of 'correspondances' where fragrances, colours and

---

[4]   The poetic theorist Becq de Fouquières, writing in 1879, discerns a particularly important relationship between the human voice and the ear in the composition of verse: 'En composant cet ouvrage, nous n'avons jamais oublié que l'art de la poésie exige le concours des deux organes de la parole et de l'ouïe. C'est la voix humaine qui forme les sons, les assemble et leur imprime un mouvement; mais c'est l'oreille qui juge de leur harmonie, de leur ordonnance et qui seule possède la mesure du temps' ['In composing this work, we have never forgotten that the art of poetry requires the competition between the two organs of the spoken word and hearing. It is the human voice which forms the sounds, assembles them, and gives them movement; but it is the ear which judges their harmony, their order and which alone possesses the measure of time']. Louis Becq de Fouquières, *Traité général de versification française* (Paris: Charpentier, 1879), p.xii. Becq de Fouquières's 'scientific' approach to poetry is, of course, quite distinct from that of Baudelaire and Mallarmé who were poetic practitioners rather than theorists. Both poets' sensitivity towards – and acceptance of – the necessary intervention of other human senses in conjunction with the voice and the ear forms an important part of their respective aesthetics of voice.

sounds respond to each other, it seems that Mallarmé's attention to the role of the body offers a more refined understanding of what it means to use 'voice' to create resonance. The implication is that unless the poet and his reader allow themselves to be attentive to what happens in the interstices between sounds, words and poems – in which potential meanings might flutter past evocatively – poetry will fail to create any effect at all.

Mallarmé's Resonant Intent

For a consummate wordsmith to declare that 'toutes les paroles [doivent] s'effacer devant la sensation' reveals what seems to be astonishingly poor business acumen, since it poses as a declaration that fundamentally imperils the future of his trade. This paradoxical doing-away with the very tools of his trade is formulated in an oft-cited letter from Mallarmé to his poet friend Henri Cazalis dated 30 October 1864: 'Le vers ne doit donc pas, là, se composer de mots, mais d'intentions, et toutes les paroles s'effacer devant la sensation' ['poetry should not be made up of words, but of intentions, and all [spoken] words should erase themselves before sensation'] (M.*OC*.I, p.663). This desire for the erasure of words from the poetic line is concomitant with Mallarmé's desire for an indirect, symbolic, use of language. This forms the very basis of Mallarmé's poetic design which searches for poetic 'intentions' (M.*OC*.I, p.663) rather than striving to 'présent[er] les objets directement' ['present objects directly'] (M.*OC*.II, p.699). The well-rehearsed distinction between direct and indirect language, and Mallarmé's predilection for the latter, elaborates Mallarmé's use of the word 'sensation'.[5]

The letter to Cazalis, however, remains laden with paradox. In expressing his desire to shift the emphasis away from words, Mallarmé rhetorically problematises the force of the words he is writing both within his poetic compositions and within the letter itself. The culmination of the sentence aims to wipe the page clean of words and replace them instead with a 'sensation'. Mallarmé's use of the word 'sensation' in this context still retains the potential to uncover a more profound meaning beyond the meaning of the words themselves, and this is to be found

---

[5]   In fact, Mallarmé's desire for poetic 'intentions' in order to create a particular effect is not an original one. Baudelaire had already identified this aptitude in Poe's language, in his 'Notes Nouvelles sur Edgar Poe' published in 1857 alongside Baudelaire's own translation of Poe in the *Nouvelles histoires extraordinaires*. However, Baudelaire talks specifically of the genre of the 'Tale' (or 'Nouvelle') that Poe exploits (where Mallarmé refers specifically to poetry): 'Dans la composition tout entière, il ne doit pas se glisser un seul mot qui ne soit une intention, qui ne tende, directement ou indirectement, à parfaire le dessein prémédité' ['Throughout the whole composition, not a single word should slip in which is not intended, which does not serve directly or indirectly to complete the premedidated design'] (B.*OC*.II, p.329). Of course the distinction between Baudelaire's Poe and Mallarmé is that Mallarmé sought more and more to avoid using language 'directement'.

within the 'intentions' of language. The paradoxical power struggle between words within the poetic line and their effacement from it dissolves into an aesthetic quandary for Mallarmé, which he begins to answer in his poetic compositions through an exploration of rhythmic patternings and relationships structured by the problematics of meaning(s). In order to explore what Mallarmé expresses through his use of the term 'sensation', I shall elaborate the relationship, first of all, between 'sensation' and meaning(s), before moving onto the relationship between 'sensation' and rhythm (which also raises the problematic of the meaning of rhythm itself). A notion of 'rhythmic sensation' begins to emerge from Mallarmé's use of language through the way he privileges the palpable patternings within human language which are felt in particular through the physical act of murmuring poetic language. It is this rhythmic sensation which Mallarmé is at pains to 'déchiffrer' ['decipher'] (M.*OC*.II, p.294).

'Sensation' and Meaning(s)

Understanding what Mallarmé means by the term 'sensation' is bound up with the relationship that he perceives between how words feel (perhaps their 'sensation') and what they mean (perhaps their 'sens'). Both terminologies ('sensation' and 'sens') are employed with some ambiguity at least in the initial stages of Mallarmé's exploration of poetic composition (particularly in the 1860s 'crise' period). The way Mallarmé links the term 'sensation' to the notion of an 'effet produit' ['effect produced'] (M.*OC*.I, p.654) is evident from the October 1864 letter to Cazalis cited above since the sentence which precedes the phrase I initially cited is the renowned phrase: 'Peindre non la chose mais l'effet qu'elle produit' ['To paint not the thing but the effect it produces']. Yet terminologies such as 'sensation' or 'effet produit' are fundamentally and necessarily vague for Mallarmé, because any effects or sensations produced by poetic language are not only difficult to verbalise, but perhaps should not be verbalised at all. Any language which tries to describe effects or sensations in words does a disservice not only to the words themselves but also to the effect or sensation produced (and this problematic indeed poses a potential methodological issue for critical analysis of such terms[6]). Mallarmé frequently uses the terms 'sensation' or 'effet produit' specifically in the singular, which suggests paradoxically that he is less concerned about uncovering a range of (perhaps even contradictory) sensations or effects, and is more concerned instead with discovering something more fundamental to poetic language per se. But the erasure of the words into some kind of overarching poetic 'sensation' which takes over from words can only happen after the words themselves have been explored: the diachrony of the poetic experience thereby starts with the words (which are

---

[6] This does not mean, however, that it is impossible to explore verbally what these 'sensations' or 'effets produits' might be: rather like a musicologist who endeavours to verbalise the effects of music, the task is a precarious but not impossible one.

laden with meanings), and leads thereafter towards a 'sensation' (which goes beyond meanings in the plural towards a more profound, singular, meaning which Mallarmé terms as the 'effet produit' or 'sensation').

This supposedly diachronic process – from words and their meanings towards the more profound 'meaning' of 'sensation' or 'effet produit' – requires careful attention. Five years after the letter to Cazalis cited above, Mallarmé re-introduces the notion of the 'effet produit' in relation to meaning within his fragmentary notes on language:

> Enfin les mots ont plusieurs sens, sinon on s'entendrait toujours – nous en profiterons – et pour leur sens principal, nous chercherons quel effet ils nous produiraient prononcés par la voix intérieure de notre esprit, déposée par la fréquentation des livres du passé. (M.*OC*.I, pp.508–509)

> [Fundamentally words have several meanings, otherwise we would always understand each other – we shall profit from this – and for their primary meaning, we shall search for the effect that they would elicit in us when spoken by the interior voice of our minds, collected from the habitual readings of old books.]

Mallarmé starts with the exploration of potential meanings of words before allowing these to dissolve and be governed instead by the 'effet produit' which will validate their 'sens principal', their fundamental, singular, meaning. In this respect, the 'effacement' of words that Mallarmé had longed for in the October 1864 letter to Cazalis is part of a process which is still beholden to words, but the words must be explored in their most transitory, ephemeral state, because they must be able to offer the potential for differing meanings if the more profound 'effet produit' is to be achieved. In order to elicit the longed-for poetic sensation, Mallarmé looks towards a use of language which persistently tries out words in their varying guises, that is to say, 'prononcés par la voix intérieure de notre esprit'. But although the effect produced by words which are 'prononcés par la voix intérieure de notre esprit' reveals a (singular) 'sens principal', Mallarmé is aware that the interior voice is not one which has primacy over that meaning. Mallarmé specifically allies the 'voix intérieure' with the 'livres du passé', creating an ambivalence between the various guises of language which slip between being written or spoken, since this is bound up with ways of remembering previous encounters with words. The 'voix intérieure' is what remains after reading the 'livres du passé', and Mallarmé exploits the possibility for meaning(s) through the process of reading which specifically involves the reader's voice which interacts, necessarily, with the ambiguities of meaning(s) ('sinon on s'entendrait toujours').

The constant battle for supremacy within Mallarmé's work between 'sensation', 'sens' and 'son' is evidenced in another letter to Cazalis dated 18 July 1868 where he considers the effect of the spoken word on the 'Sonnet en *yx*':

J'extrais ce sonnet, auquel j'avais une fois songé cet été, d'une étude projetée sur *la Parole*: il est inverse et je veux dire que le sens, s'il en a un, (mais je me consolerais du contraire grâce à la dose de poësie qu'il renferme, ce me semble) est évoqué par un mirage interne des mots mêmes. En se laissant aller à le murmurer plusieurs fois on éprouve une sensation assez cabalistique. (M.*OC*. I, p.731)

[I extract this sonnet, which I first dreamt of this summer, from a planned study on the *Spoken word*: it is inverse and by that I mean that the meaning, if there is one, (but I would console myself of the contrary thanks to the dose of poetry it contains, it seems to me) is evoked by an internal mirage of the words themselves. By letting yourself murmur them several times, you feel a rather cabalistic sensation.]

Mallarmé radically privileges 'sensation' over 'sens' in this sonnet, not simply by introducing neologisms forced by the difficult rhyme scheme (the infamous 'ptyx') but also by exploring the notion of trying out how the poem sounds and feels, murmuring it *'sotto voce'*, like an incantatory prayer.[7] The relationship between the 'sensation' and the 'sens, s'il en a un' of this sonnet calls upon the words themselves ('évoqué par un mirage interne des mots mêmes'), exploiting the etymological sense of evocation as *ex* + *vocare*. This latent ability within language to 'speak for itself' becomes an increasingly recurrent theme in Mallarmé's poetic aesthetic. In the prose poem 'Le Démon de l'analogie' (M.*OC*.I, pp.416–418) he allows the words in the phrase 'La Pénultième est morte' to speak for themselves: 'elle [la phrase] s'articula seule' ['it [the phrase] articulated itself of its own accord']. But in order for words to take on this evocative potency of being able to speak for themselves, they must first be brought to voice (that is to say vocalised, or in Mallarmé's terms, 'prononcés' or 'murmurés') by the voice of the poet and of his reader. Moreover, Mallarmé does not expect to attain this 'sensation' on a first reading, but rather he allows himself to murmur the poem to himself 'plusieurs fois', as in 'Le Démon de l'analogie':

je résolus de laisser les mots de triste nature errer eux-mêmes sur ma bouche, et j'allai murmurant avec l'intonation susceptible de condoléance: 'La Pénultième est morte, elle est morte, bien morte, la désespérée Pénultième'.

[I resolved to let the words wander sadly of their own accord on my lips, and I went along murmuring with an intonation susceptible to condolence: 'The

---

[7]   That Mallarmé has frequently likened his poetry to a religious act has been explored extensively in Bertrand Marchal's *La Religion de Mallarmé: poésie, mythologie, religion* (Paris: José Corti, 1988). For more on the idea of 'sotto voce' language, see Roger Pearson's chapter in *Mallarmé and Circumstance: the Translation of Silence* (Oxford: OUP, 2004).

Penultimate one is dead, it is dead, really dead, the despairing Penultimate
one'.]

That Mallarmé expects then to elicit a 'sensation' from this repetitive *sotto voce*
murmuring of poetic language remains predicated on the premise that the words
themselves have an agency ('un mirage interne des mots mêmes', 'les mots de triste
nature errer eux-mêmes sur ma bouche'). The 'sensation assez cabalistique' that he
elicits from his 'Sonnet en *yx*' implies that there is an enigma to be unravelled from
poetic language, and that in repeating the words to himself a process of decryption
is set in motion by the very words themselves. Poetry, for Mallarmé, is designed
to enshrine a linguistic enigma, as he expressed in the 1891 interview with Huret:
'Il doit y avoir toujours énigme en poésie' ['There always needs to be an enigma
in poetry'] (M.*OC*.II, p.700). The 'sensation assez cabalistique' of the 'Sonnet
en *yx*' is a sensation which delights in the process of exploring the ambiguous or
obscure elements of meaning (the art of 'évocation', 'allusion' or 'suggestion').
Mallarmé's uncertainty in the letter to Cazalis about the 'Sonnet en *yx*' concerning
whether the poem has any meaning at all ('le sens, s'il en a un') is part of the
process of unravelling the poetic enigma. The supposedly diachronic process of
exploring the meanings of words before experiencing the sensation elicited from
them thus turns in on itself in the 'Sonnet en *yx*': the sensation of poetic language
takes precedence over meanings as the search for the 'effet produit' becomes the
idealised site of the poetic 'mystère' with its singular, profound 'meaning'. The
relationship between meanings and poetic sensation in the Mallarméan aesthetic
thereby becomes a quasi-ritualistic rite-of-passage as the reader travels through
a range of different ways of experiencing the words of poetic language, and as
the words themselves begin to take over in the battle between meanings and the
meaning of sensation.

Although the poetic 'sensation' that Mallarmé privileges is a non-verbal one
(as referred to in the October 1864 letter to Cazalis where the words themselves
are replaced by 'sensation'), he recognises that this cannot be attained without
a verbal experience. Poetic language is to be constantly tried out in a range of
different guises. Through experiences of language which may be, for example,
semantic, physical, psychological, figurative, verbal or musical, Mallarmé
negotiates a relationship between meaning and sensation which pivots around the
precarious verbal/non-verbal divide. In 'Le Démon de l'analogie', he explores the
notion of 'sensation' by slipping in and out of different verbal experiences. He
takes as his starting point a verbalised description of a sensation which is replaced
by a different verbal experience, this time the form of a speaking voice:

Je sortis de mon appartement avec la sensation propre d'une aile glissant sur les
cordes d'un instrument, traînante et légère, que remplaça une voix prononçant
les mots sur un ton descendant: 'La Pénultième est morte'. (M.*OC*.I, p.416)

[I left my apartment with the sensation of a wing stroking the strings of an instrument, lingering and light, which was replaced by a voice speaking the words in a descending tone: 'The Penultimate one is dead'.]

That Mallarmé transposes the lingering sensation of the softly strummed stringed instrument into a verbalised description is evidence of his endeavour to explore the meaning of the sensation. The fact that the sensation is quickly superseded by the 'voix prononçant les mots' of a haunting four-word phrase indicates that the verbalisation of the sensation is precarious, perhaps even impossible. However, since the actual words of the description of the sensation remain on the page ('traînante et légère'), the very drawing attention to the notion of a 'voix prononçant les mots' requires the reader to explore the sensation of the wing gliding over the instrument in a different way. It is no longer merely a figurative, verbalised description of a sensation, but a sensation waiting to be re-explored through the process of pronouncing the words themselves. The strategy of persistently trying out poetic language forms part of the Mallarméan poetic aesthetic, and here in 'Le Démon de l'analogie' he begins to interweave the notion of poetic sensation with strategies of verbalisation and vocalisation which are no longer dependent solely on meanings, but on the more profound resonances of poetic language. As Pearson has outlined in *Unfolding Mallarmé*:

> this (and any other Mallarméan) sentence makes no sense if it is not vocalized and its etymological origins left unearthed. As readers we are not merely being asked an anodyne question about our psychological experience of language, we are being given a hint as to how to understand what is coming. We must, like the poet, let the words of the text play upon our own lips, murmur them, adapt them, 'remember' their past, try placing unexpected silences between them.[8]

The 'sense' that is to be made of Mallarmé's poetic language, then, is one which fundamentally relies on the sensation of the words themselves. Mallarmé's idealised strategy for attaining a profound poetic 'sensation' is to murmur the words so persistently that the words are no longer a hindrance in themselves; words are 'effaced' by the trying-out of language in its differing guises, in order to (in Pearson's terms) 'remember' their past so that meanings dissolve into a meaning ('sens principal') which is the profound, mysterious, singular 'sensation' of language.

A Most Irregular Meaning: Rhythmic Sensation

The sensation elicited in 'Le Démon de l'analogie', which Mallarmé verbalises in the description of a wing gliding over a stringed instrument, is one that lingers

---

[8]   Roger Pearson, *Unfolding Mallarmé* (Oxford: Clarendon, 1996), pp.78–79.

not simply throughout the prose poem itself, but also throughout Mallarmé's poetic œuvre. For example, about a decade after 'Le Démon de l'analogie' was published, Mallarmé published four poems in the November 1883 volume of the journal *Lutèce* at Verlaine's behest.[9] The poems 'Apparition', 'Sainte', 'Don du poème', and 'Cette nuit' (more usually known as the untitled sonnet 'Quand l'ombre menace ...') are all permeated by the same sensory-semantic world: the wing (perhaps of an angel), the stringed instrument, and the act of stroking or gliding all recur in various guises. The relationship between the prose poem and these four-verse poems suggests that the meaning behind Mallarmé's notion of 'sensation' can be uncovered beyond the supposed confines of a closed poetic unit, and that for Mallarmé, 'sensation' is of more profound import than simply being about meaning.

In the prose poem, the verbalisation of the sensation of the wing becomes dominated by the four-word phrase 'La Pénultième est morte'. The phrase is specifically governed by metrical constraints, not only because it comprises six syllables like those of a traditional hemistich within an alexandrine line,[10] but also because, as Mallarmé makes explicit, the words are expressed (M.*OC*.I, pp.416–417):

> de façon que
> > *La Pénultième*
> finit le vers et
> > *Est morte*
> se détacha de la suspension fatidique plus inutilement en le vide de signification.

> [in such a way that
> > *The Penultimate one*
> ended the verse line and
> > *Is dead*
> detached itself from the fatal suspension rather needlessly in the emptiness of meaning.]

---

[9]   Paul Verlaine, 'Les Poètes maudits', in *Lutèce*, 95 (24–30 November 1883).

[10]   Mallarmé does of course exploit the ambiguity of the syllable count of the phrase, but I would not go so far as to concur with Heath Lees who identifies the phrase as being made up of eight syllables, qualifying the phrase as a specifically musical sensation linked to an eight-note scale: 'As he leaves his apartment (his own domain?) Mallarmé is struck by a musical sensation from his phrase – the suggestion of a wing being passed lightly down the strings of an instrument, patterning the descending, scale-like analogy of sound in ordered steps, and giving birth to the phrase "La Penultième est morte" whose eight syllables fit the *ton descendant* of a typical eight-note descending scale.' Heath Lees, '"... depuis Wagner, la poésie": Mallarmé and the All-Embracing Word Work', in *Situating Mallarmé*, ed. by David Kinloch and Gordon Millan (Bern: Peter Lang, 2000), p.22.

The four words are tried out incessantly in varying guises and contexts throughout the prose poem, as the poetic narrator navigates through differing meanings and sounds. The relationship between the initial 'sensation' experienced by the poetic voice, and the dominating presence of the 'voix prononçant les mots' plays out the problematic that what Mallarmé perceives lies within the notion of 'sensation': in Mallarmé's vocabulary, sensation is necessarily verbal, and almost always linked to the notion of the spoken (murmured) word, and yet it must go beyond words themselves. By allowing the words themselves to take on an agency of their own, Mallarmé exploits the force of the suspension created by poetic language. The use of the term 'suspension' here is, in typical Mallarméan fashion, ambiguous. It implies the interruption (and breathing space) created by the verse line break of the line-end; the interruption furthermore, in rhetorical terms, is also an interruption of sense or direction; it has musical connotations created by the context of musical vocabulary (a musical suspension is a delayed resolution where a dissonant note is tied over from the previous chord before resolving); and this specific connotation also implies the broader sense of delay or uncertainty. But the 'suspension' is 'fatidique', and is itself left behind by the words 'Est morte' which are granted the agency of the verb 'se détacha'. That Mallarmé places the verb in the past historic, as an irrevocably completed past action, itself leaves the suspension hanging in mid-air, and complicates the implications of the relationship between the terms 'morte' and 'fatidique'. What has died remains suspended or hanging in the air in the 'vide de signification'. The relationship between sensation and sense here, therefore, is explored by Mallarmé through the notion of the suspension.

Mallarmé expresses this in 'Le Mystère dans les Lettres' published in the *Revue blanche* two years before his death:

> Les mots, d'eux-mêmes, s'exaltent à mainte facette reconnue la plus rare ou valant pour l'esprit, centre de suspens vibratoire. (M.*OC*.II, p.233)

> [The words, of their own accord, excite through many facets recognised as the most rare or valuable for the mind, the centre of vibrating suspension.]

Words, of their own accord, raise themselves up towards a suspended position within the mind, which is the epicentre of a 'suspens vibratoire'. The vibrating nature of this suspension is derived from the exploration of meaning, implied here by terms such as 'mainte facette' or 'valant'. For Mallarmé, words themselves are 'à facettes', that is to say that they are 'difficile[s] à déchiffrer' ['difficult to decipher'].[11] The vibrating suspension created by words themselves posits itself as a trembling of meaning behind which something more profound might reside. I term this vibrating suspension Mallarmé's 'rhythmic sensation', and it is a sensation that is best appreciated through the quiet murmuring of poetic language to oneself. That is to say, Mallarmé's rhythmic sensation is attained through strategies of

---

[11] See *Le Nouveau Petit Robert*.

verbal repetition (of a phoneme, of a rhyme ending, of the same word in a different poetic context, of speaking the same word or words to oneself, for example). It is within the interstices between the moments of repetition that the suspended vibration of rhythmic sensation is patterned. The recurrent patternings (which are not, however, necessarily regular)[12] incorporate (perhaps quite literally) a 'rhythmic sensation' that is dynamic (because it exploits the duration over time of the effect of a word, phoneme, or collection of words), palpable (because it has a corporeal potency) and immanent (because it is self-sufficient, created by the words themselves). The more oblique or hypothetical the meanings of a word ('la plus rare ou valant ...'), the more profound the rhythmic sensation, because the interstitial relationships between *possibilities* of meanings of each word – played out over time, tangibly moving between meanings and enacted by the words themselves – begin to set in motion a more profound possibility: by exploiting the strategy of quietly murmuring poetic language to oneself, the words themselves set off a rhythmic sensation which allows the reader to perhaps uncover, or to 'déchiffrer', the fundamental patternings of existence, which Mallarmé terms 'les purs motifs rythmiques de l'être' ['the pure rhythmic motifs of being'] (M.*OC*.II, p.294).

The process of 'déchiffrage' set in motion by Mallarmé's rhythmic sensation is all the while founded on the uncertainty of meaning. Mallarmé thwarts any possibility for regular, unproblematised meaning, just as much as he thwarts the possibility of regular, unproblematised rhythm, of both poetry and the human body. He stretches the distances between possible meanings by emphasising the overriding importance of rhythmic sensation which suspends meanings indefinitely in a more profound exploration of human language. As the October 1864 letter to Cazalis cited above insists, an individual 'mot' gives itself over to 'intentions', which in turn give themselves over to 'les paroles' which give themselves over to 'sensation'. The distance between the written word and the spoken word (the distinction between 'mots' and 'paroles') offers the possibility for eliciting a rhythmic sensation of language. However, it is the patterning of the interstices between the elements of the written poetic text that Mallarmé relies upon in order to attain the overriding 'sensation' or 'effet produit'[13] which is perhaps able to

---

[12] Commenting on Bertrand Marchal's interpretation of Mallarméan rhythm as a regular, natural 'pulsation originelle' (See *La Réligion de Mallarmé*, p.188), David Evans writes: 'Despite his lucid account of Mallarmé's poetic fictions, Marchal often seems to imply that the poet believes in a rhythmic constant in man which corresponds to regular rhythms in nature. ... Yet Mallarmé remains carefully unclear on the fundamental question of the origins of this apparent regularity.' Evans, *Rhythm, Illusion and the Poetic Idea* (Amsterdam and New York: Rodopi, 2004), p.251.

[13] Mallarmé says of 'L'Azur' in another letter to Cazalis dated 7 January 1864: 'Je te jure qu'il n'y a pas un mot qui ne m'ait coûté plusieurs heures de recherche, et que le premier mot, qui revêt la première idée, outre qu'il tend lui-même à l'*effet* général du poème, sert encore à préparer le dernier. L'*effet produit*, sans une dissonance, sans une fioriture, même

uncover not only what is at the heart of poetry itself, but also what is at the heart of human existence. By now it will have become clear that for Mallarmé the 'sens' that can be derived from a rhythmic sensation of language is both complicated and elusive, and the typically Mallarméan adjective 'mystérieux' captures this, as is clear from a letter to Leo d'Orfer dated 27 June 1884:

> La Poésie est l'expression, par le langage humain ramené à son rythme essentiel, du sens mystérieux des aspects de l'existence. (M.*OC*.I, p.782)

> [Poetry is the expression, through human language brought back to its essential rhythm, of the mysterious meaning of the aspects of existence.]

Any notion of rhythm for Mallarmé does not correlate with the hypothesis, such as that put forward by Henri Meschonnic's in *Critique du rythme* that 'le rythme est une organisation du sens' ['rhythm is the organisation of meaning'].[14] Any organisation of meaning goes against Mallarmé's poetics because it implies a regular order; the patternings of meaning in the suspended vibrations of a rhythmic sensation of poetic language take the form of irregular interstitial pulls that may be re-awakened or re-discovered on each re-reading of the texts of Mallarmé's poems.

The interstices set up through the inter-related repetitions of terms across the textual tissue of the *Lutèce* poems not only hark back to the verbalised description of the sensation in 'Le Démon de l'analogie' (a wing gliding over a stringed instrument), but also elaborate how the rhythmic sensation of poetic language retains meaning through a persistently suspended and irregular vibration which is established across junctures within and around poetic texts. The meaning of the relationships between words is based on a rhythmic sensation, because, as Mallarmé expresses in a letter to Edmund Gosse dated 10 January 1893, he is concerned with exploring 'le rythme entre des rapports' ['the rhythm between relationships'] (M.*OC*.I, p.807). So whilst the terms of the verbalised description of the sensation in 'Le Démon de l'analogie' do not always recur exactly or directly in the four poems published in *Lutèce*, the relationships and the interstices between the relationships are clear, as the two tables (Table 3.1 and Table 3.2) below demonstrate.

---

adorable, qui distrait, – voilà ce que je cherche' ['I swear to you that there is not a single word which did not cost me hours of research, and that the first word, which takes on the first idea, as well as itself leading towards the general *effect* of the poem, also serves to prepare the last word. The *effect produced*, without dissonance, without embellishment, even charming, which distracts, – that is what I am looking for'] (M.*OC*.I, p.654).

[14] Henri Meschonnic, *Critique du rythme: anthropologie historique du langage* (Lagrasse: Verdier, 1982), p.71.

Table 3.1   Description of sensation

Poem title	Diction of 'sensation'
'Le Démon de l'analogie' (M.*OC*.I, pp.416–418)	la sensation propre d'une aile glissant sur les cordes d'un instrument
'Apparition' (M.*OC*.I, pp.113–114)	Des séraphins en pleurs Rêvant, l'archet aux doigts, dans le calme des fleurs Vaporeuses, tiraient de mourantes violes De blancs sanglots glissant sur l'azur des corolles. (v.1–4)
'Sainte' (M.*OC*.I, p.114)	sa viole (v.3) Que frôle une harpe par l'Ange Formée (v.10–11) le plumage instrumental (v.15)
'Don du poème' (M.*OC*.I, pp.115–116)	l'aile saignante et pâle, déplumée (v.2) la lampe angélique (v.5) rappelant viole et clavecin (v.11)
'Cette nuit' (M.*OC*.I, p.115)	Il a ployé son aile indubitable en moi (v.4)

Table 3.2   Sensation keywords

'Le Démon de l'analogie'	*Lutèce* poems
aile [wing]	aile, plumage, déplumée, ange, angélique, séraphins
glissant [gliding]	frôle, tiraient
instrument [instrument]	harpe, viole, clavecin, archet, instrumental

These recurrences of diction pertaining to the same verbalised description of a sensation from 'Le Démon de l'analogie' found within the *Lutèce* poems are by no means regular recurrences, precisely because of the distance established between the individual poems themselves. The irregular patternings of meaning that Mallarmé establishes in his poetic œuvre are spread out across differing kinds of interstitial distances. The interstices between words at times come in the form of a verse-line break, at others in the spaces established within a poem, or in the spaces set up between individual poems. And it is the complicated, irregular interplay between these different interstitial relationships that firmly places the notion of a rhythmic sensation at the heart of poetic experience for Mallarmé.

The initial sensation of the wing gliding down the stringed instrument in 'Le Démon de l'analogie' is quickly replaced by the poetic phrase 'La Pénultième est morte' in which he very swiftly creates a gulf by inserting a verse-line break (which is, moreover, interspersed with commentary describing the verse strategy, thus widening the gulf). The relationship between each of the four words of the phrase 'La Pénultième est morte' themselves, as well as the relationship between the four-word phrase and the sensation of the wing gliding down the stringed instrument, incessantly weaves in and out of the prose poem, first of all with:

'La Pénultième' puis la corde de l'instrument, si tendue en l'oubli sur le son *nul*
... (M.*OC*.I, p.417)

['The Penultimate one' then the string of the instrument, strained into oblivion
on the sound *nul* ...]

and then later:

j'allai murmurant avec l'intonation susceptible de condoléance: 'La Pénultième
est morte, elle est morte, bien morte, la déseperée Pénultième' ... quand, effroi!
... je sentis que j'avais, ma main réfléchie par un vitrage de boutique y faisant
le geste d'une caresse qui descend sur quelque chose, la voix même. (M.*OC*.I,
p.417)

[I went along murmuring with an intonation susceptible to condolence: 'The
Penultimate one is dead, it is dead, really dead, the despairing Penultimate one'
... when, a fright! ... I felt that I possessed, with my hand reflected by the shop
window doing the descending caressing gesture on something, the voice itself.]

and furthermore at the conclusion of the prose poem:

je vis ... que j'étais devant la boutique d'un luthier vendeur de vieux instruments
pendus au mur, et, à terre, des palmes jaunes et les ailes enfouies en l'ombre,
d'oiseaux anciens. Je m'enfuis, bizarre, personne condamnée à porter
probablement le deuil de l'inexplicable Pénultième. (M.*OC*.I, p.418)

[I saw ... that I was in front of a stringed instrument maker's shop selling old
instruments hung up on the walls, and, on the ground, the yellow palms and the
wings buried in the shadows of ancient birds. I flew away, an oddity, a person
condemned no doubt to carry the mourning of the inexplicable Penultimate
one.]

The sensation of the gesture ('le geste d'une caresse qui descend sur quelque
chose') and the sensation of the four-word phrase are inextricably linked by the
rhythmic patterning of the poem which is enacted through the interstices that
Mallarmé inserts first of all between 'La Pénultième' and 'Est morte' with the
supposed verse-line structure, and between the gesture of the wing on the stringed
instrument and the four-word phrase, as well as between the different recurrences
of the elements of the phrase throughout the prose poem.

The strongest recurrence of the verbalised sensation of 'Le Démon de l'analogie'
is found in 'Apparition' (M.*OC*.I, pp.13–14) where the angels are playing stringed
instruments. The 'sanglots' extracted from the angels' viols figuratively thematise
the anguished irregular suspense inherent in the notion of rhythmic sensation.
Mallarmé establishes a sense of irregular interstitial relationships through the

enjambement of the first four lines of the poem. After the initial sentence unit of the first hemistich of the first line, the remainder of the quatrain takes the form of one long sentence whose syntax flows over the verse line-ends:

> La lune s'attristait. Des séraphins en pleurs,[15]
> Rêvant, l'archet aux doigts, dans le calme des fleurs
> Vaporeuses, tiraient de mourantes violes
> De blancs sanglots glissant sur l'azur des corolles. (v.1–4)

> [The moon grew sad. Crying seraphims,
> Dreaming, with a bow in their fingers, in the calm of flowers
> Vaporous, drew out from dying viols
> White tears gliding down the blue of the corollas.]

The disruptive interstices established by the 'rejets' of 'Rêvant' and 'Vaporeuses' linger throughout the rest of the poem, even where the alexandrine line is employed regularly, because the interstice of the verse line-end is problematised from the very outset of the poem. The disruptive metrical patternings, coupled with small-scale repetitive devices within this poem (in particular the extensive use of the [ã] sound throughout), show Mallarmé's poetic language in a state which endeavours to capture the rhythmic sensation of the interstices established between irregular recurrent patternings. The anguish of the irregularity of the rhythmic sensation established in the 'sanglots' extracted by the angels' string-playing persists throughout. The poem is one of romantic torment, as is signalled not only by diction such as 'martyriser' or 'tristesse' which come at the ends of lines six and seven respectively, but also by the metrical angst of further sense units that continue to run on beyond the line end:

> Ma songerie aimant à me martyriser
> S'enivrait savamment du parfum de tristesse
> Que même sans regret et sans déboire laisse
> La cueillaison d'un Rêve au coeur qui l'a cueilli. (v.6–9)

> [My dream delighting in causing me pain
> Became knowledgeably intoxicated with the perfume of sadness
> Which even without regrets or residue leaves
> The gathering of a Dream to the heart which has gathered it.]

The piling-up of alliterative patterns, particularly on 'm' and 's' sounds in lines six, seven and eight, and on the accentual 'c' sounds in line nine, intensifies the irregularity of the patternings inherent to this poem. The insertion of traces of

---

[15]   In the Deman edition of 1899, there is no comma at the end of the first line. The version referred to here is the *Lutèce* version of 1883.

anaphora (the repeated 'sans' in line eight) and of hints at a mirrored structure in line nine (with the 'cueillaison' at the beginning reflecting the 'cueilli' at the end of the line) create the impression of a rhythmic coherence which is yet undermined by the actual appearance of anaphora on the 'Et' at the beginning of lines 12 and 13, coupled with the culmination of the narrative drama with the arrival of the apparition, 'tu m'es en riant apparue' (v.12), which has been prepared by the pivotal 'Quand' at the beginning of line 11:

> J'errai donc, l'œil rivé sur le pavé vieilli,
> Quand, avec du soleil aux cheveux, dans la rue
> Et dans le soir, tu m'es en riant apparue
> Et j'ai cru voir la fée au chapeau de clarté
> Qui jadis sur mes beaux sommeils d'enfant gâté
> Passait, laissant toujours de ses mains mal fermées
> Neiger de blancs bouquets d'étoiles parfumées. (v.10–16)

> [And so I wandered, eyes riveted on the aged cobblestones,
> When, with sun in your hair, in the street
> And in the evening, you appeared to me laughing
> And I thought I saw the fairy with a halo of light
> Which of old in my beautiful slumbers as a spoilt child
> Passed by, always letting from half-closed hands
> Snow down white bouquets of perfumed stars.]

The evocation of the poetic voice's childhood in line 14 establishes an even wider gap between the words of the poem and a suspended vibration of meaning which recalls what Pearson describes as being able to 'remember' the past of words. The relationship between what passes and what remains is played out significantly at the beginning of the penultimate line of the poem through the juxtaposition of the verbs 'Passait, laissant'. That between 'Passait' and 'laissant' there is nothing more than a comma (and that the two words not only look but also sound similar in the reflected patterns of the [a] vowel and the double 's') establishes a tight rapport which is at once challenged by the syntactic pull of each of the words. The interstice between what is past and what remains is one of both proximity and distance:[16] the proximity is textual, the distance is semantic. The interstice between the memory of a word which has been murmured out loud and its presence on the page exploits both textual proximity and semantic distance, and this interstitial

---

[16] In her analysis of the 'plis' of the Mallarméan 'éventail', Elizabeth McCombie explores Mallarmé's predilection for the oxymoronic coupling of proximity and distance: 'The air of the intervening space pulsates in rhythms of mobile stasis, resistant affinity, and open closure.' Elizabeth McCombie, *Mallarmé and Debussy: Unheard Music, Unseen Text* (Oxford: Clarendon, 2003), p.197.

relationship is fundamental to Mallarmé's rhythmic sensation which suspends meaning and effaces words.

Mallarmé's rhythmic sensation, then, goes beyond the meanings of the individual words of a poem towards a vibrating suspension of meaning which is patterned by irregular recurrences of past meanings. For words to be 'self-effacing' according to the Mallarméan model does not mean that words must be done away with altogether, and does not imply that Mallarmé denigrates semantics. By striving to attain an overriding rhythmic sensation of poetic language, which is best explored through the murmuring of poetic language in order to allow the words to speak for themselves, Mallarmé seeks to move beyond the individual meanings of words into a more profoundly meaningful poetic space. By exploring the sensation elicited by poetic interstices – whether on a small scale (such as the gaps between alliterative patterns or anaphora, for example) or on a larger scale (such as the gaps between syntactical, semantic or metrical patterns within a poem or across poems) – Mallarmé also explores the possibility of a poetic memory which lingers within the mysteries of existence, and which validates the poetic urge. It is on this basis that the monumental 'Coup de dés' is founded, where not only the typography but also the oblique diction and tense moods – in particular the imperfect subjunctives of 'EXISTÂT-IL; COMMENÇÂT-IL ET CESSÂT-IL, SE CHIFFRÂT-IL; ILLUMINÂT-IL' ['WERE IT TO EXIST; WERE IT TO COMMENCE AND WERE IT TO CEASE, WERE IT TO ADD UP; WERE IT TO ILLUMINATE'] (M.*OC*.I, p.383) – establish the lingering pull of memories of poetic regularity (perhaps 'LE NOMBRE' ['THE NUMBER'] of the alexandrine which is governed by the list of imperfect subjunctives above, and which perhaps, ultimately, is what Mallarmé wishes to 'déchiffrer'). Poetic regularity is no longer able to validate human existence in Mallarmé's aesthetic world. Being able to 'déchiffrer' what Mallarmé calls 'les purs motifs rythmiques de l'être' ['the pure rhythmic motifs of being'] (M.*OC*.II, p.294) offers a way of exploring the uncertainties, or suspensions, set in motion by the dissolution of regularity. A new sensation of language is elicited which provides a more profound validation for existence, which is no longer governed by a spurious model of direct, regular language, but which instead thrives on the interstitial rhythmic pulls between the possibilities set in motion by a most irregular meaning.

Remembering Baudelaire

My lengthy focus on Mallarmé and the notion of (rhythmic) sensation seems to have altogether sidelined Baudelaire. Whilst it is true that Baudelaire did not develop the same notion of 'sensation' as Mallarmé was later to do (Baudelaire talks of 'sensation' more in terms of an aesthetically pleasing by-product of poetry rather than its essential quality), Mallarmé's indebtedness to Baudelaire's poetic aesthetic cannot be ignored. The Baudelairean take on 'sensation' is much more beholden to his aesthetics of 'correspondances' as in the sonnet of the same title

(B.*OC*.I, p.11) where an intermingling of the senses – of perfumes, colours, sounds – is explored in order to create a resonant echo:

> Comme de longs échos qui de loin se confondent
> Dans une ténébreuse et profonde unité,
> Vaste comme la nuit et comme la clarté,
> Les parfums, les couleurs et les sons se répondent. (v.5–8)

> [Like long echoes which mingle from afar
> Into a shadowy and profound unity
> Vast like the night and like the daylight
> Perfumes, colours and sounds respond to each other.]

Where the perfumes, colours and sounds reply or speak to each other in this sonnet, Baudelaire elsewhere employs a range of different verbs to describe how this intermingling of the senses is able to work. When talking of the differing senses in the verse and prose poems which portray 'la chevelure' ['hair'], Baudelaire employs the verbs 'boire', 'humer', 's'enivrer' ['to drink', 'to inhale', 'to become intoxicated'] ('La Chevelure') and 'voir', 'sentir', 'entendre', 'respirer', 's'enivrer' ['to see', 'to feel', 'to hear', 'to breathe', 'to become intoxicated'] ('Un hémisphère dans une chevelure'). What this kind of diction confirms is that, for Baudelaire, the sensation of poetic language is a very physical or corporeal experience which is dependent on the senses: the interaction between sense, sensation, sound and meaning becomes an intricate and convoluted physical endeavour which is somehow able to spark resonances. It is not by accident that Baudelaire rhymes 'se confondent' with 'se répondent', for the echoes and resonances set in motion by poetry are mysteriously able to intermingle in 'La Chevelure' in such a way that he finds himself drinking perfumes, sounds and colours ('où mon âme peut boire / A grands flots le parfum, le son et la couleur' ['where my soul can drink / In great torrents the perfume, the sound and the colour'] v.16–17) where normally each of the senses described would require a separate verb, that is to say, to smell, to listen, to see. For Baudelaire, it is the 'culte de la sensation multipliée' ['cult of multiplied sensation'] which counts and which, moreover, must be glorified. This comment, from 'Mon cœur mis à nu', refers to the dual notions of vagabondage and music:

> Glorifier le vagabondage et ce qu'on peut appeler le Bohémianisme, culte de la sensation multipliée, s'exprimant par la musique. (B.*OC*.I, p.701)

> [To glorify vagabondage and what we could call Bohemianism, cult of multiplied sensation, expressing itself through music.]

The figurative nature of 'vagabondage' for Baudelaire draws it close to music, and reinforces what he expresses through the 'culte de la sensation multipliée'. The mind which is able to wander freely, unhindered by meaning (hence the reference to music which, unlike poetry, is more free of direct meaning), is thereby able to experience a multiplicity of sensations – of sounds, perfumes and colours together as one. The step that Baudelaire makes between these multiplied sensations and poetic language is something on which Mallarmé was later to draw: by glorifying the cult of multiplied sensations, Baudelaire is able to experience profound memories which validate poetic experience.

It is by exploring Baudelaire's memories together with Mallarmé's memories of Baudelaire that the complex notion of vocal resonance begins to take shape. The complexity is established by the persistent concern on the part of both poets that their poetry may fail to resonate at all, that it may fail to create any effect. Where Baudelaire was content to 'embrasser la gloire' ['embrace the glory'] ('La Chevelure' v.19) and to glorify the wanderings and intermingling of sounds, senses and sensations through his aesthetic of 'correspondances', Mallarmé is more wary, and seeks to stifle the cry of poetic glory ('Le cri des Gloires qu'il étouffe' ['The cry of the Glories which he stifles'] in 'Quelle soie aux baumes de temps' v.14) through his insistence, expressed in subtle, murmured undertones, on the illusory nature of poetry which in a letter to Cazalis dated 28 April 1866 he famously declared as '*La Gloire du Mensonge*, ou *Le Glorieux Mensonge*' ['*The Glory of Lying*, or *The Glorious Lie*'] (M.*OC*.I, p.696). On this issue of vocal resonance, the relationship between Baudelaire and Mallarmé stems from resonances established between their poems. I take as my primary example the relationship between three poems already cited: the two Baudelaire poems (verse and prose) about 'la chevelure' and Mallarmé's sonnet 'Quelle soie aux baumes de temps'. I seek to demonstrate that not only do the relationships between the poems elaborate upon the possibility of vocal resonance in poetry, but that this vocal resonance is also indebted to the models of 'actio' and 'memoria' that I outlined above. That is to say, making poetry resonate necessitates putting the voice into 'action' (or 'pre-action', or 'reaction') and establishing memories of a how a word, a phoneme, a rhyme, or a rhythmical pattern may feel in other contexts. The key here is to recall that, just as Quintilian reminds us that the voice is at once unique and infinite, so too are vocal resonances unique and potentially infinite – provided that they are actually able to resonate.

Resonance and Movement

In relation to the important motif derived from Poe, that of the 'mouvement dans l'air', we remember that Mallarmé favoured the 'agitation solennelle par l'air / De paroles' over 'l'irascible vent des mots' in 'Toast funèbre' (M.*OC*.I, p.28). The implication of Mallarmé's preference is that he is preoccupied with moderating the movement of air, or resonance, created by words in order that the ultimate effect may be more marked. Baudelaire, on the other hand, allows 'impulses on the air' to be less tautly controlled. In 'La Chevelure' (B.*OC*.I, p.26), he writes of the hair: 'Je la veux agiter dans l'air comme un mouchoir!' ['I want to shake it in the air like a handkerchief!'] (v.5). The exclamation mark at the end reinforces the uncontrolled dynamic of the vocal enactment within the line, and this has been prepared by the direct address of the apostrophe of the opening two lines of the poem:

> Ô toison, moutonnant jusque sur l'encolure!
> Ô boucles! Ô parfum chargé de nonchaloir!
> Extase! Pour peupler ce soir l'alcôve obscure
> Des souvenirs dormant dans cette chevelure,
> Je la veux agiter dans l'air comme un mouchoir! (v.1–5)

> [O mane, curling down to the neckline!
> O curls! O perfume laden with nonchalance!
> Ecstasy! In order to populate this evening the dark alcove
> With memories sleeping within this hair,
> I want to shake it in the air like a handkerchief!]

These apostrophes, as Elissa Marder has demonstrated, 'perform like poetic speech acts that actually seem to propel the poet into a state of intoxicated bliss', revealing the relationship between speaking and movement.[17] Already within this first stanza of the poem the dynamics of the vocal enactment ('actio') of the apostrophe serve to evoke a set of memories ('memoria') in the form of the 'alcôve obscure / Des souvenirs' (v.3–4). The direct relationship between movement and resonance, between action and memory, is established through the motif of the hair. In the prose poem version of this same motif, Baudelaire expands this relationship by reinforcing the role of the senses. The 'parfum' of the second line of the verse poem is reiterated twice in the opening sentence of the prose poem 'Un hémisphère dans une chevelure' with the noun 'odeur' and the adjective 'odorant':

> Laisse-moi respirer longtemps, longtemps, l'odeur de tes cheveux, y plonger tout mon visage, comme un homme altéré dans l'eau d'une source, et les agiter avec ma main comme un mouchoir odorant, pour secouer des souvenirs dans l'air. (B.*OC*.I, p.300)

> [Let me breathe in at length, at length, the sweet smell of your hair, plunge my whole face into it, like a parched man in the water from a spring, and shake it with my hand like a sweet-smelling handkerchief, in order to shake out memories in the air.]

---

[17]   Elissa Marder, *Dead Time: Temporal Disorders in the Wake of Modernity (Baudelaire and Flaubert)* (Stanford: Stanford University Press, 2001), p.52.

The strategies of redoubling in this sentence – not simply of the twice-iterated odour, but also of the repeated 'longtemps, longtemps' and of the two similes signalled by the word 'comme' – further reinforce the relationship between movement/action and resonance/memory. The movement is untamed (the verb 'agiter' of the verse form (v.5) is also transposed into 'secouer' in the prose form), and the memories are multiple (or at the very least double).

While in the verse poem the memories were purely inhaled by the poetic voice ('je hume à long traits le vin du souvenir' ['I inhale deeply the wine of memory'] v.35), in the prose poem this inhalation is reiterated in the opening sentence cited above, only to then morph into an even more palpable action of taking the hair into his mouth, biting at it in order to taste it. This typically Baudelairean intermingling of the senses means that smell and taste take on an equal role through the repetition of the 'Laisse-moi' of the opening paragraph. These words then also open the final paragraph of the prose poem. The alteration of the infinitive which follows each instance of the anaphora-at-a-distance (which has also been interspersed by three anaphoric repetitions of 'dans' in the central paragraphs) is rendered all the more subtle by the inclusion of the word 'longtemps' in the second repetition. Thus 'Laisse-moi respirer longtemps' of the opening sentence and 'Laisse-moi mordre longtemps' of the final sentence are equated notwithstanding the spatial distance which separates them on the page.

An even greater transformation has taken place in the prose version.[18] The untamed 'agitation dans l'air' of the verb 'secouer' in the opening paragraph – a movement which provides a source for re-evoking memories – is transformed in the final paragraph into the act of ingesting memories, a movement which takes these memories right into the mouth of the poetic voice:

> Laisse-moi mordre longtemps tes tresses lourdes et noires. Quand je mordille tes cheveux élastiques et rebelles, il me semble que je mange des souvenirs. (B.*OC*.I, p.301)

> [Let me bite at length your heavy and black tresses. When I nibble your elastic and rebellious hair, it is as if I am eating memories.]

Reading the poem allegorically, as the words 'il me semble' invite the reader to do, the hair – which is elastic and rebellious – designates poetic form. The prose poem form itself is elastic and rebellious, and by taking it into the mouth, the poetic voice ingests memories of a verse form, in a process that Barbara Johnson calls 'manger

---

[18]   The dates of publication of the two poems, 'La Chevelure' in 1859 and 'Un hémisphère dans une chevelure' in 1857 (under the original title 'La Chevelure'), have created a critical quandary concerning the order of composition. Whilst it is generally accepted that Baudelaire composed his prose poems later than his verse poems, I do not wish to impose my own chronology where critical enquiry has hitherto proven inconclusive.

la poésie' ['to eat poetry'].[19] This is precisely what the strategies of doubling and repetition throughout the poem invite the reader to do – to sense on his or her lips, in his or her mouth, in his or her voice, the remnants and memories of poetic form. The profound corporality of the experience of the hair in both the verse and prose poem translates into a physical sensation for the reader (in imagining the smell and taste, the reader is engaged in a 'pre-action'). Furthermore, the reader is invited to bury his whole face or head within the poetry in order to sense its different possibilities on his or her lips ('Je plongerai ma tête amoureuse d'ivresse / Dans ce noir océan' ['I will plunge my head enamoured with intoxication / Into this dark ocean'] v.21–22; 'y plonger tout mon visage' ['to plunge my whole face into it']).

Reading Baudelaire's 'chevelure' poems in this way – without negating the more obvious reading of these two poems as love poems which rhapsodise the mistress' hair – opens up a rather intriguing contrast with Mallarmé's untitled sonnet 'Quelle soie aux baumes de temps' (M.*OC*.I, p.43). The same key themes of 'agitation', 'souvenirs', 'gloire', 'respiration' and 'morsure' ['agitation/shaking', 'memories', 'glory', 'breathing' and 'biting'] are to be found in Mallarmé's octosyllabic sonnet, albeit treated in a very different way. 'Quelle soie ...', like Baudelaire's 'chevelure' poems can also be read simply as a poem addressed to his beloved (he does, after all, describe himself as 'ton princier amant' ['your princely lover'] v.11), but by focusing on the notion of the possibility of vocal resonance (through 'actio' and 'memoria'), a rather different reading offers itself:

> Quelle soie aux baumes de temps
> Où la Chimère s'exténue
> Vaut la torse et native nue
> Que, hors de ton miroir, tu tends!
>
> Les trous de drapeaux méditants
> S'exaltent dans une avenue:
> Moi, j'ai ta chevelure nue
> Pour enfouir des yeux contents.
>
> Non la bouche ne sera sûre
> De rien goûter à sa morsure,
> S'il ne fait, ton princier amant,
>
> Dans la considérable touffe
> Expirer, comme un diamant,
> Le cri des Gloires qu'il étouffe.

---

[19] Barbara Johnson, *Défigurations du langage poétique: la seconde révolution baudelairienne* (Paris: Flammarion, 1979), p.52.

[What silk in the solace of time
Where the Chimera wears itself out
Is worth the twisted and natural cloud
Which, beyond your mirror, you hold out!

The emptiness of meditating flags
Exalt themselves in a wide street:
Me, I have your bare hair
In which to bury my contented eyes.

No, the mouth can never be sure
Of tasting anything in its bite,
If your princely lover does not,

In the enormous tufts
Breathe out, like a diamond,
The cry of the Glories which he stifles.]

The fading chimera is not simply the fading away of a love story, but also the fading away of poetry, which needs to be veiled in silk in order to shut out the cries of old-fashioned poetic glory. Rather like the raucous singing of the child in 'Pauvre enfant pâle' which is shut out by the 'soie incarnadine' of the curtains (M.*OC*.I, p.418), the narrative progression in 'Quelle soie …' uses the veil of silken hair to stifle the cry of (poetic) glory and prevent it from being heard. The Baudelairean act of taking the hair into the poetic voice's mouth in order to bite and taste it is explicit in Mallarmé's first tercet, but where Baudelaire was more certain of getting something out of this physical act (in the form of 'souvenirs'), the Mallarméan poetic voice is much less convinced. Mallarmé must kill off, or at least breathe out, through the verbs 'expirer' and 'étouffer', any notion of glory if any poetic resonances are to be attained. The close rapport between 'gloire' and 'souvenir' in Mallarmé's poetic language is attained not simply through the Baudelairean resonance with the 'chevelure' poems, but also in 'Le Démon de l'analogie', where he specifically writes of 'le glorieux Souvenir' ['the glorious Memory'], granting the 'Souvenir' the status of a proper noun through the capitalisation of its initial letter, whereas in 'Quelle soie …', it is 'Gloires' which are granted this status. However, a paradox remains: the hair is also the very symbol of that glorious memory, or memory of the glory, of poetry that he wishes to stifle or extinguish.

The analogy which draws together 'chevelure' and 'drapeaux' in the second quatrain implies that 'la chevelure' is also governed by the verb of glory 's'exaltent' (v.6). Yet the resonances that this analogy has with the Baudelairean image of the hair being waved like a handkerchief ('Je la veux agiter dans l'air comme un mouchoir!', 'La Chevelure', v.5), suggest that here we are to bid farewell to the glory of poetry. In order to do so, the poet needs to envelop himself completely in the veil of poetry (the silk, the flag, the handkerchief, the hair). Just as Baudelaire writes of the hair that 'Je plongerai ma tête amoureuse d'ivresse / Dans ce noir océan' ('La Chevelure' v.21–22) or 'Laisse-moi ... y plonger tout mon visage' ('Un Hémisphère dans une chevelure'), Mallarmé in the second quatrain writes 'Moi, j'ai ta chevelure nue / Pour enfouir des yeux contents' (v.7–8). The transposition from Baudelaire's diction of 'plonger' into the Mallarméan verb 'enfouir' intensifies the notion of extinguishing poetic glory. Just as in 'Toast funèbre', the cry of poetic doubt needs to be tamed ('L'espace a pour jouet le cri: "Je ne sais pas!"' v.31), here in 'Quelle soie ...', the poetic voice is determined to stifle the cry of poetic glory in order to allow the poem to emerge. For Mallarmé, the uncontrolled dynamic volume of the 'cri' is abhorrent to his poetic endeavour. In a sonnet which scholars believe to have been written in 1886, the year after 'Quelle soie ...', the preference for a softer dynamic is made explicit through the same motif of the hair, which serves as an acoustic damper. The untitled sonnet 'Ô si chère de loin et proche et blanche ...' (M.*OC*.I, p.67), composed for Méry Laurent (who is explicitly referred to in the second line), contrasts the poet's own endeavours with his voice to the words which emanate from Méry's hair. The two tercets read:

> Mon cœur qui dans les nuits parfois cherche à s'entendre
> Ou de quel dernier mot t'appeler le plus tendre
> S'exalte en celui rien que chuchoté de sœur
>
> N'était, très grand trésor et tête si petite,
> Que tu m'enseignes bien toute une autre douceur
> Tout bas par le baiser seul dans tes cheveux dite. (v.9–14)
>
> [My heart which at night sometimes yearns to be heard
> Or to call to you with some final most tender word
> So that in it nothing might be exalted than that which had been whispered by you,
>
> Dear sister, very great treasure and head so small,
> That you might teach me some completely different pleasure
> Spoken very quietly, simply by the kiss within your hair.]

In contrast to the 'cri' of 'Quelle soie ...', then, here in 'Ô si chère', the dynamics are tamed to a whispered level, 'tout bas'. It is only by taming the dynamics, by exploiting the acoustic damper of the motif of the woman's hair, that poetry is able to resonate and create the all-important effect or sensation that Mallarmé yearns for.

Using the Body

For Mallarmé, then, in order for poetry to resonate, that is, to create an effect or a sensation through a suspended vibration of meaning, a certain set of conditions is required. Mallarmé privileges a soft dynamic range, favouring the 'chuchotement' ['whisper'] over the 'cri' ['cry / shout']. This then averts the possibility that unpleasant sounds might tarnish his poetic endeavour, which would result in a failure to resonate with the reader. The implications of this preference not only cause the reader to take care over his or her own reading (whether out loud or internally), but also to assume the kind of mindset that will listen out for potential resonances. This is why, as Mallarmé expresses in a letter to Eugène Lefébure, dated 27 May 1867, 'il faut penser de tout son corps' ['one should think with one's whole body'], in order not to limit the potential for resonance. Using the voice in poetry is not simply about the physical action of moving ones lips or vocal chords, but also about allowing the mental mimicry (or 'pre-action') of using one's voice in order, precisely, to attain that yearned-for 'sensation' (or 'reaction'). It is only through allowing the whole body of sound to resonate within the mind that poetry will achieve its effect. Mallarmé exploits a musical analogy to express why, on his emergence from his poetic 'crise' ['crisis'], the involvement of the whole body in creating poetic ideas is so important:

> il faut penser de tout son corps – ce qui donne une pensée pleine et à l'unisson comme ces cordes du violon vibrant immédiatement avec sa boîte de bois creux. Les pensées partant du seul cerveau (dont j'ai tant abusé l'été dernier et une partie de cet hiver) me font maintenant l'effet d'airs joués sur la partie aiguë de la chanterelle dont le son ne réconforte pas la boîte – qui passent et s'en vont sans se *créer*, sans laisser de trace d'elles. (M.*OC*.I, p.720)[20]

> [one should think with one's whole body – which leads to a thought which is complete and in unison, like the strings of a violin vibrating immediately with its body of hollow wood. Thoughts which emanate from the mind alone (the kind of thoughts which I overused last summer and for a part of this winter) now give me the effect of airs played on the most taut part of the E-string, the sound of which does not fortify the body – which pass and go by without *creating* themselves, without leaving any trace of themselves.]

Mallarmé's realisation here that mental machinations are not sufficient to create effect, reinforces the status of the human voice within his poetic aesthetic. Even though, in contrast to Baudelaire's more assertive use of vocal designations and stronger dynamics, Mallarmé softens or dampens the vocal dynamic, he nevertheless does this in order that they might resonate to the fullest. The distaste

---

[20]   The straining of the violin here is like the straining of the pauper's voice in 'Pauvre enfant pâle' (M.*OC*.I, p.418) discussed above.

that Mallarmé feels for non-resonant language is expressed through the image of the violin straining to resonate when it is played at the most taut point of the highest string – 'la partie aiguë de la chanterelle' is like the 'chanson aiguë' of the 'Pauvre enfant pâle' (M.*OC*.I, p.418). It is through the action of using the whole body in relation to the human voice, in unison with the inner thoughts of the mind, that memories are created by the poetic text.

Mallarmé confirms this in his advice to would-be poets in 'Quant au livre', composed 20 or so years after the letter to Lefébure. He writes in the opening 'L'Action restreinte' section:

> Ton acte toujours s'applique à du papier; car méditer, sans traces, devient évanescent, ni que s'exalte l'instinct en quelque geste véhément et perdu que tu cherchas. (M.*OC*.II, p.215)

> [Your action always applies to paper; because to medidate, without traces, becomes fleeting, nor does the instinct glorify itself in some vehement and lost gesture that you searched for.]

The creative action of writing rejects a glorified 'geste véhément' (which recalls uncontrolled 'cri des Gloires' of 'Quelle soie ...') in favour of a focused attention on the written page. This attention, in turn, is described in an earlier paragraph as an action which will generate a particular response:

> Agir, ... signifia, ... produire sur beaucoup un mouvement qui te donne en retour l'émoi que tu en fus le principe (M.*OC*.II, p.214)

> [To act, ... meant, ... to produce upon many a movement which gives you in return the emotion of which you were the origin]

So where Poe, in Baudelaire's translation, declared that all words are a 'mouvement créé dans l'air', here we find the result of that movement: it generates, in return, an emotive response, an effect, or 'sensation'. Although Genette, in the 1960s, had lamented how a 'rhétorique restreinte' seemed to sideline the 'actio' and 'memoria' elements of rhetorical production in favour of the 'elocutio', here in fact we find Mallarmé talking of an 'action restreinte' which incorporates not simply the action of writing, but also the action of reading, where these actions are both externally and internally experienced through the intervention of the written page. The trace of voice on the page animates, and will re-animate upon each re-reading, the involvement of the whole body, of the mutually interior and exterior qualities of the human voice, so that sound, sense and sensation interact to give, in return, a productive, creative, resonant effect as language begins to speak for, and converse with, itself.

PART III
Exchange

Chapter 4

Exchanging Voices

La parole est moitié à celuy qui parle, moitié à celuy qui l'escoute.
[Speech belongs half to the person who speaks, half to the person who listens.]
Michel de Montaigne, 'De l'expérience'[1]

La conversation est le lien de la société de tous les hommes.
[Conversation is what links all men together in society.]
Madeleine de Scudéry, 'De la conversation'[2]

From merely a cursory reading of Baudelaire's poetry, it is clear that he employs a vast array of different voices. By contrast, voices in Mallarmé's poetry seem more oblique because the designation of who or what is speaking is frequently rendered ambiguous or unclear. That is not to say that Baudelaire's voices are entirely self-evident or unproblematic; rather it is that Baudelaire typically signals different voices on the page by clearer typographic indications. This distinction in typographic decisions appears, at an initial glance, to be quite a superficial difference between the two poets; in fact, it offers an insight into their differing attitudes towards what 'voice' implies. Each poet's preoccupation with resonance (which, as explored above, is often expressed in terms of an echo, a vibration, or an 'impulse on the air') suggests that theirs is a poetry which aspires to some form of vocal exchange – between poet, reader and language itself, in the form of differing 'voices' inscribed within their poetic texts. Baudelaire's attitudes towards speaking and listening through and within poetry set the scene for Mallarmé's later developments. Mallarmé idealised the notion that language should be able to speak for itself, even though, like Baudelaire, he remains aware that it needs, somehow, to be animated by the human voice.

Just as the array of different voices in the works of each poet is so wide-ranging, so too are the conditions of vocal exchange. Rather like the varied parameters of a dynamic range explored in earlier chapters, the number of vocal protagonists involved in an exchange of voices can vary from an intimate conversation with a mistress, for example, through to a very public interaction such as raising one's voice amongst a crowd. An awareness of the different effects created by the diverse conditions of a vocal exchange is highlighted by the ways in which each poet designates voice through particular textual strategies. Even though we

---

[1]   Michel de Montaigne, *Essais*, 3 vols (Paris: Garnier-Flammarion, 1979), III, p.299.

[2]   Madeleine de Scudéry, *Conversations sur divers sujets* (1680), in *L'Art de la conversation* ed. by Jacqueline Hellegouarc'h (Paris: Garnier, 1997), p.104.

might find direct speech signalled by quotation marks, or verbs in the imperative form, or particular names or personal pronouns which designate an addressee or vocal protagonist, the poets' texts do not, however, respond readily to the question 'who (or what) is speaking?', because each of the designated voices interact, intermingle and intervene in a complex process of exchange. By exploring how each poet employs different strategies for designating voice, and how, therefore, different voices are brought into contact with one another through a poetic text, I shall analyse whether conversation is, in Baudelaire's or Mallarmé's eyes, what both constitutes and safeguards poetry.

My analysis will touch briefly on literary conventions surrounding conversation and conversational techniques, exploring vocal designations such as direct or indirect speech, imperatives, personal pronouns and apostrophe. Since each poet employs a range of different techniques within each poem, I shall not address each element in turn, but rather explore how various strategies are combined in order to create a particular effect. These ways of designating voice through text not only raise questions about the register of a vocal exchange, but also about the potential artificiality of the vocal exchanges set up by Baudelaire and Mallarmé. If the poet seeks to capture conversations within a poetic text, is this because he seeks to exploit the transience that a conversation implies (as the Baudelairean stance on modernity would suggest)?[3] Is the urge to enact a conversation through poetry (with or without the theatrical connotations that this may imply) driven by a desire both to record and replay the ephemerality of a vocal exchange? The fleeting nature of conversational exchanges (even those which seem to endure through their presence on the printed page) would imply that achieving either a lasting impression or a profoundly productive interaction is nigh on impossible.

Nonetheless, problems that are inherent to conversational scenarios, such as miscomprehension or an inability to make one's voice heard, are embraced rather than eschewed by both poets. As I shall explore, Baudelaire revels in thwarting conversational exchange by employing rhetorical questions, by opening up his voice amongst a crowd even though this entails the potential risk of his voice being lost or unheard, and by exploiting foreign voices which pose potential communication problems. In turn, Mallarmé delights in rendering a voice ambiguous, by dislocating any direct relationship between voice and subject in order to avert any preconceptions that a nuanced subjective voice might bring to the text. Yet in so doing, he renders his poetic voices more oblique, foreign and strange, which threatens the communicative, resonant potential of the model of conversation. Does the conversational model break down in these instances, especially in poems where conversations are thwarted, or are not textually represented, or does the model of an exchange of voices thrive on these potential risks? I shall explore, first of all, Mallarmé's reflections on conversation between 1869–1870 before moving

---

[3]   As Baudelaire writes in his section on 'La Modernité' in 'Le Peintre de la vie moderne': 'Il s'agit … de tirer l'éternel du transitoire' ['It is a question … of extracting the eternal from the transitory'] (B.*OC*.II, p.694).

on to consider how these relate to poetic language in particula
I shall relate these more theoretical reflections to particul
questioning the extent to which voices are clearly designate
the implications of this for a system of conversational excha
consider ways in which the problems arising from conversat
either feed or hamper the ability to create and enjoy a lasting

Mallarmé on Conversation 1869–1870

Mallarmé's interest in the burgeoning notion of a science of language or linguistics in 1869–1870 led him to write several notes on conversation (spread across five different 'feuillets') which I take as a basis for my analysis of the model of conversation. The value of this contribution to a science of language based on conversation could be considered somewhat dubious, however. These notes are somewhat fragmentary and indeed were subsequently crossed out by Mallarmé. Nowhere in the notes does he specifically refer to poetic language, but in citing his five notes on conversation in full, I seek to evaluate whether in fact they contributed to Mallarmé's stance on the use of voice in his poetic language. For convenience of reference, I have outlined them in a numerical list below (M.*OC.* I, pp.508–509):[4]

1. la Conversation; non dans une conversation, ce qu'elle est au moment (c'est fini) ni dans la partie de son Abstraction que nous voulons connaître, mais dans sa Fiction, ici telle qu'elle est exprimée par rapport à ces deux phases qu'elle réfléchit. Arriver de la *phrase* à la *lettre*, par le mot; en nous servant du *signe* ou de l'écriture, qui relie le mot à son Sens.

   La Science n'est donc pas autre que la Grammaire, historique et comparée, afin de devenir générale, et la Rhétorique.

   [Conversation; not in a conversation, that which it is at that moment (it is finished) nor in that part of its Abstraction that we would like to get to know, but in its Fiction, here in the way that it is expressed in relation to these two phases that it reflects. To get from the *phrase* to the *letter*, via the word; by making use of the *sign* or of writing, which joins the word to its Meaning.

   Science, then, is nothing other than Grammar, historical and comparative, so as to become general, and Rhetoric.]

---

[4]   I have not conserved the typographic layout used in the Bertrand Marchal edition of the *Œuvres complètes* cited since this does not specifically influence my argument.

2. Méthode

Conversation – Sens des mots, diffère, d'abord, puis le *ton*; on trouve du nouveau dans le ton dont une personne dit telle et telle chose

– Nous prendrons le ton de la conversation, comme limite suprême, et où nous devons nous arrêter pour ne pas toucher à la science – comme arrêt des cercles vibratoires de notre pensée.

Enfin les mots ont plusieurs sens, sinon on s'entendrait toujours – nous en profiterons – et pour leur sens principal, nous chercherons quel effet ils nous produiraient prononcés par la voix intérieure de notre esprit, déposée par la fréquentation des livres du passé (Science, Pascal), si cet effet s'éloigne de celui qu'il nous fait de nos jours.

[Method

Conversation – Meaning of words, differs, first, then the *tone*; we find something new in the tone in which a person says such and such a thing

– We will take the tone of the conversation, as the ultimate limit, and where we should stop so as not to infringe upon science – as the limit of the vibrating circles of our thought.

In short, words have several meanings, otherwise we would always understand each other – we shall profit from this – and for their primary meaning, we shall search for the effect that they would elicit within us when spoken by the interior voice of our mind, collected from the habitual readings of old books (Science, Pascal), if this effect is removed from the one which it creates in us these days.]

3. C'est donc puisque nous retrouvons dans la conversation le procédé essentiel du Langage, qui est d'abstraire; dans la conversation que nous étudierons le Langage, et

C'est donc, puisque la conversation nous permet une abstraction de notre objet, le Langage, en même temps que, site du Langage, elle nous permet d'offrir son moment à la Science.

Ainsi nos deux termes ne se tiennent dans l'adhésion momentanée de notre esprit que grâce au procédé de la conversation.

[It is therefore because we find in conversation the essential process of Language, which is to abstract; therefore we will study Language in conversation, and

It is therefore, because conversation allows us to abstract our object, Language, at the same time as being the site of Language, it allows us to offer its moment to Science.

Thus our two terms only hold together in the fleeting union within our mind thanks to the process of conversation.]

4. Toutefois puisque nous en avons retiré déjà le procédé d'Abstraction qui l'a réfléchie, étudions-la, telle qu'elle demeure, non plus en tant qu'abstraction elle-même, mais telle qu'elle nous apparaît dans sa manifestation habituelle et telle que nous la possédons dans le cas présent, et si ce dernier concorde avec le premier comme il le fait déjà avec l'abstraction de la conversation, nous en conclurons que nous pouvons continuer à nous en servir, et que ses différences devenant des équivalences, seront évaluées, et nous serviront de mesure commune.

[Nonetheless since we have already removed the process of Abstraction which has reflected it, let us study it, as it remains, no longer as an abstraction itself, but as it appears to us in its usual manifestation and as we grasp it in the present situation, and if this latter accords with the former as it does already with the abstraction of conversation, we shall conclude that we can continue to make use of it, and with its differences becoming equivalences, these will be evaluated, and will be useful to us as a common measure.]

5. Le moment de la Notion d'un objet est donc le moment de la réflexion de son présent pur en lui-même ou sa pureté présente.
   En tirer une époque de réflexion du langage.
   la pensée vient de sortir de la conversation: nous nous servirons de cela pour y rentrer.

[The moment of the Notion of an object is therefore the moment of the reflection of its pure presence within itself or its present purity.
   To take from this an era of reflection of language.
   Thought has just emerged from conversation: we shall make use of this in order to go back into it.]

Note 1 draws attention to the written manifestation of a conversation and its relevant conventions (grammar and rhetoric). Note 2 highlights the role of different individuals within a conversation, and the effects that this creates, which thrive on the differences not only in meanings and interpretations but also on sound qualities: the onus on each individual, then, is to explore these differences in order to understand the effect of meaning. Note 3 evidences the notion that conversation is a process or action rather than a static use of language, and this process allows for the possibility of isolating language in its most essential state. Note 4 suggests that within the process of abstraction or isolation of language-in-conversation it is possible to explore moments of divergence and moments of convergence in interpretations, meanings and effects (which relates to the points made in note 2). Note 5 points out that the moment that is of most interest is the moment of re-reading or re-hearing a conversation in the present moment, and the reciprocal rapport (of potential divergences and convergences) that is established between the originary conversation and its mental manifestation in the 'voix intérieure' of note 2.

The ideas put forward by Mallarmé are complex, but I would suggest that a schematic representation of what he implies about conversation could read as follows: conversation is a method for using language which implicates the imagination or an interior voice. It is a process that allows us to isolate (or abstract) language at its most transient moment. Because of its transience, however, the scope for differences in interpretations and effects is broad. The transient moment of a conversation is precisely the moment which is both the most elusive and the most mentally rewarding because of its differing resonant possibilities. Such a reduction obviously fails to do justice to the fuller complexity of Mallarmé's notes on language and conversation, but it allows us to draw out some key elements which affect Mallarmé's position on conversation.

The context of Mallarmé's notes from this period highlights that he is indebted not only to contemporary linguistic theories such as those propounded by Renan, Bopp or Müller, but also to seventeenth-century figures such as Descartes, La Bruyère and Fénelon:

> Aux autres, la grande et longue période de Descartes
> Puis, en général: du La Bruyère et du Fénelon, avec un parfum de Baudelaire
> (M.*OC*.I, p.505)

> [To the others, the great and long period of Descartes
> Then, in general, some La Bruyère or some Fénelon, with a whiff of Baudelaire]

This is also elaborated in note 2 above where, through the mention of another seventeenth-century figure, Pascal, Mallarmé brings attention to the different meanings of words as they have been used in the past. His clear indebtedness to two particular eras – the seventeenth century and his own century, the nineteenth – suggests that Mallarmé's attitude towards conversation within the context of seeking to understand how language works is not simply a question of the here and now, even though in note 5 he talks of the 'pureté présente' of language. The temporal element that Mallarmé introduces into his schematic argument, then, is twofold: on the one hand, he demonstrates an indebtedness to a bygone era of using and studying language in a particular way (which was predominantly rule-bound and governed by conventions), whilst on the other hand, he seeks to grasp the very contemporary moment of using and studying language.

That a 'parfum de Baudelaire' is introduced into Mallarmé's musings on language and conversation during the 1869–1870 period reveals that Baudelaire's position is an important one for Mallarmé at that time. Where, in note 2, Mallarmé talks of profiting from the fact that the many different meanings of words can lead to misunderstanding, Baudelaire too had formulated a similar thought perhaps 10 or so years previously in 'Mon cœur mis à nu':

> Dans l'amour comme dans presque toutes les affaires humaines, l'entente cordiale est le résultat d'un malentendu. Ce malentendu, c'est le plaisir. L'homme crie: 'Oh! mon ange!' La femme roucoule: 'Maman! maman!' Et ces deux imbéciles sont persuadés qu'ils pensent de concert. – Le gouffre infranchissable, qui fait l'incommunicabilité reste infranchi. (B.*OC*.I, pp.695–696)[5]

> [In the case of love as with almost all humain affairs, the entente cordiale is the result of a misunderstanding. This misunderstanding is pleasure. The man cries out: 'Oh! my angel!' The woman coos: 'Mummy! mummy!' And these two imbeciles are convinced that they are thinking in harmony. – The impassable gulf, which creates the incommunicable, is never bridged.]

The typical Baudelairean irony that pervades this fragment leaves a latent ambiguity over his attitude towards the relationship between misunderstanding and the incommunicable: the pleasure resides, it seems, in the vast gulf that separates two different opinions.[6] Baudelaire's decision to portray the divergence of opinion through an imagined conversation between lovers captures the moment of transience that Mallarmé yearns for in his 'Notes sur le langage' above. This capturing of a conversation by recording it through text elaborates what Mallarmé described in note 1 above of exploring conversation in its state as a fictitious use of language (rather than the moment of conversation itself). The recording of a conversation through text grants it its 'pureté présente' as it resides on the written

---

[5]   Baudelaire reinforces this perspective in the prose poem 'Les Yeux des pauvres' where the narratorial voice of the poem finds himself utterly at odds with his mistress; she voices her horror at seeing a poor man and his children staring in wonder at the café in which she and her lover are sitting. The poem concludes with the narratorial voice lamenting 'Tant il est difficile de s'entendre, mon cher ange, et tant la pensée est incommunicable, même entre gens qui s'aiment' ['It is so difficult to understand each other, my dear angel, and thought is so incommunicable, even between people who love each other'] (B.*OC*.I, p.319).

[6]   Baudelaire also goes on to say that: 'Le monde ne marche que par le Malentendu. – C'est par le Malentendu universel que tout le monde s'accorde. – Car si, par malheur, on se comprenait, on ne pourrait jamais s'accorder. / L'homme d'esprit, celui qui ne s'accordera jamais avec personne, doit s'appliquer à aimer la conversation des imbéciles et la lecture des mauvais livres. Il en tirera des jouissances amères qui compenseront largement sa fatigue' ['The world only works through Misunderstanding. – It's through the universal Misunderstanding that everyone is able to get on with each other. – For if, by misfortune, we understood each other, we could never agree with each other. / A great wit, someone who will never get on with anyone, should apply himself to getting to like the conversation of imbeciles and reading bad books. He will get bitter pleasures from this which will largely compensate for his fatigue'] (B.*OC*.I, p.704).

page. And it is this recorded conversation that allows for a more mentally rewarding conversation to take place, as the closing words of note 5 suggest: 'la pensée vient de sortir de la conversation: nous nous servirons de cela pour y rentrer'. From the original conversation comes a new conversational exchange sparked by the written text: one created between word and the interior voice of the imagination which explores different possible meanings.

This relationship between text and interior voice has already been elucidated by Mallarmé in another note in which he gives a chronological hierarchy for linguistic terminologies, from 'le Verbe', to 'le Langage', to its two divisions 'la Parole' and 'l'Écriture', which, in turn, are united by 'l'Idée du Verbe':

> Le Verbe ... devient le *Langage*.
> Le Langage est le développement du Verbe, son idée, dans l'Être, le temps, devenu son mode: cela à travers les phases de l'Idée et du Temps en l'Être ...
> D'où les deux manifestations du Langage, la Parole et l'Écriture, destinées ...
> à se réunir toutes deux en l'Idée du Verbe: la Parole, en créant les analogies des choses par les analogies des sons, l'Écriture en marquant les gestes de l'Idée se manifestant par la parole, et leur offrant leur réflexion, de façon à les parfaire, dans le présent (par la lecture), et à les conserver à l'avenir comme annales de l'effort successif de la parole et de sa filiation: et à en donner la parenté. (M.*OC*. I, p.506)

> [The Word ... becomes *Language*.
> Language is the development of the Word, its idea, within each Being, time, becomes its mode: this through the phases of the Idea and of Time within each Being ...
> From which come the two manifestations of Language, the Spoken and the Written, destined ... to both unite themselves in the Idea of the Word: the Spoken, by creating analogies of things by the analogies of sounds, the Written by marking the gestures of the Idea which manifest themselves by the spoken, offering them their reflection, in order to complete them, in the present (through reading), and to conserve them for the future, like annals of the successive effort of the spoken and its filiation: and to grant them parentage.]

For Mallarmé, the ideal manifestation of a direct relationship between 'parole' and 'écriture' is found in conversation, more specifically in conversation which is recorded in order to give birth to further conversations. Once again, Mallarmé establishes a relationship between previous encounters with words and a present encounter. In this particular fragment, the notion of a previous encounter with a word is represented in a hypothetical future anterior, through the suggestion that words will have a future past if they are conserved through writing.[7] The present

---

7   Although Kristeva does not use this excerpt when analysing Mallarmé's revolutionary use of language, she nonetheless recognises that, for this generation of poets, 'le texte est

moment that Mallarmé refers to in this fragment recalls the 'pureté présente' discussed in note 5 above; that Mallarmé qualifies what he means by the present as being the moment of 'lecture' is significant to the understanding of Mallarmé's perspective on the model of conversation.

An idealised form of conversation takes place on two levels: first of all, between the written word and the spoken word as they become a reflection of each other at the moment of writing, and then between the written word and the spoken word at the moment of reading. What is important to both these moments of conversation is that they should be productive: analogies and gestures are created through sounds and signs, which, for Mallarmé, emphasise the importance of the mobility of language. The model of conversation allows for words to retain their sense of an originary movement (of sound, of gesture), since Mallarmé seeks to 'rendre au mot ... sa mobilité' ['give back to the word ... its mobility'] (M.*OC*.I, p.510).[8] That mobility is due, in part, to the nature of conversation as both a written and a spoken model, and also to the nature of a communicative exchange system that seeks to bring different voices into play in order to arrive at misunderstandings and divergences of opinions, which, in turn are able to become 'les équivalences' (see note 4 above) – the very model, perhaps, already instigated by Baudelaire's 'correspondances' which, in the second quatrain of the sonnet of the same title, allows such diverse elements as 'les parfums, les couleurs et les sons' ['perfumes, colours and sounds'] to answer one another 'Dans une ténebreuse et profonde unité' ['In a dark and deep unity'] (B.*OC*.I, p.11).

The complex model of conversation expounded in Mallarmé's critical writings from the 1869–1870 period highlights the significance of establishing a resonant or productive exchange. However, it also raises the question about poetry's place within this idealised conversational exchange of voices. How does Mallarmé incorporate or establish conversations within or through his poetic texts? Is there a greater or lesser prevalence of conversational exchange in poetry than in everyday, or non-poetic, language? Is there a greater or lesser prevalence of conversational exchange in his verse poetry than his prose poetry? What is the role of theatrical dialogue within this context? Is Mallarmé's advocacy of the model of conversation in the 'Notes' merely a momentary diversion or does it have greater relevance for his poetic output? As a preliminary answer to these questions, I would suggest that even though Mallarmé did not put his fragmentary notes on conversation and language to use in any of his critical articles, the way in which he incorporates conversations in his poetry, increasingly dissociating

---

toujours un "futur antérieur": écho et précurseur ... Mais par sa disposition et seulement par elle, le texte est un contemporain: il est présent' ['the text is always a "future anterior": echo and precursor ... But through its layout and only through this, the text is contemporary: it is present']. Julia Kristeva, *La Révolution du langage poétique* (Paris: Seuil, 1974), p.364.

[8]   Of course, we have already encountered this concept of words being movements or impulses on the air in the preceding section, with the notion put forward by Poe in 'The Power of Words'.

voice from a specific speaking subject is precisely the means through which Mallarmé isolates (or abstracts) that transient moment of conversation explored in his reflections on linguistics. Mallarmé's poetic conversations reveal, it seems, a more profound interpretation as to what it means to bring a poem to voice than is the case with Baudelaire. In drawing together Mallarmé's emphasis on 'différences devenant des équivalences' (see note 4 above) and Baudelaire's notion of 'correspondances', I glossed over this issue of the subjectivity of voices in a conversation. Yet as his delight in 'le malentendu' ['misunderstanding'] highlights, Baudelaire retains the notion that subjective voices are necessary parties to a conversation. In the conversation from 'Mon cœur mis à nu' referred to above (B.*OC*.I, pp.695–696), the protagonists were an 'homme' and a 'femme', but elsewhere, as will be demonstrated, he grants a subjective voice to colours, demons and other inanimate or fictitious objects. Mallarmé, by contrast, seeks increasingly to dislocate 'voice' from 'subject' within his poetry in order, it seems, to allow for the 'procédé essentiel du langage' (see note 3 above) to take place, which abstracts and isolates voices from subjects in a model of conversation that allows poetic language to speak to and for itself.

Baudelaire's Conversations

Although in Baudelaire's poetic conversations there is typically a fairly clear alliance between 'voice' and 'subject', this does not mean that his conversations are banal or ordinary; in fact, Baudelaire's conversations tend towards the more extraordinary by beginning to break down accepted conventions of conversational exchange. In the prose poem 'Portraits de maîtresses' (B.*OC*.I, pp.345–349), hints of conventionality are persistently undermined. Baudelaire chooses a very conventional topic of conversation between the four male protagonists of the poem: they discuss the various merits (or otherwise) of taking on a mistress. The conventional topic seems to be set against a conventional backdrop:

> Dans un boudoir d'hommes, c'est-à-dire dans un fumoir attenant à un élégant tripot, quatre hommes fumaient et buvaient.

> [In a men's boudoir, that is to say in a smoking room resembling an elegant gaming house, four men were smoking and drinking.]

With typical Baudelairean irony, the 'boudoir d'hommes' is set within an oxymoronically 'élégant tripot', where 'tripot' bears the negative connotations not only of a gaming house, but also of a sordid love intrigue. The style of the prose poem also harks back to the tradition of literary conversations from the late sixteenth or seventeenth centuries (such as those composed by Marguerite de Navarre in her *Heptaméron* or Madeleine de Scudéry's *Conversations*) where, once the scene has been set, each protagonist is allowed to speak in turn. However, as the prose poem reaches its culmination, the stylistics of the exchange are undermined by a dissolution into disbelief and speechlessness. Furthermore, Baudelaire is quick to point out – through the voice of a third-party narrator – that this conversation is not of a particularly elegant register; the banality of the subject matter renders the parties involved in the conversation somewhat indifferent:

> L'un d'eux jeta la causerie sur le sujet des femmes. Il eût été plus philosophique de n'en pas parler du tout; mais il y a des gens d'esprit qui, après boire, ne méprisent pas les conversations banales. On écoute alors celui qui parle, comme on écouterait de la musique de danse.

> [One of them turned the chat to the topic of women. It would have been more philosophical to not talk about such a matter at all; but there are certain high-minded people who, after drinking, do not disdain banal conversations. So you listen to the person who is speaking like you would listen to dance music.]

The alliance of a low register ('causerie', 'conversations banales') with dance music serves to ironise the verb 'écouter': in fact the protagonists are not really listening to each other at all (at least in the initial phase of the conversation). The string of banalities and conventional assumptions about women that the first male protagonist reels off also reinforces the reason behind the apathy. That this first protagonist does not even bother to list all the conventional elements that typically assist female beauty once the flower of youth has passed ('le parfum, la parure, et cætera' ['perfume, attire, et cætera']) requires the other conversational protagonists (including the reader) to use their own imagination, and prepares the reader for the incomplete conclusion to the tale which closes the prose poem.

As the conversation unfolds, other protagonists intervene, and other conversations exterior to that taking place in the 'boudoir d'hommes' are recounted. The different levels of exchange are distanced by different temporal moments: past conversations are signalled within the context of a textual present, which in turn is distinct from the actual present moment of reading. Negotiating these different levels of exchange is relatively unproblematic, since the text mimics conventional strategies for representing conversations in written form, with each speaking voice clearly signalled by quotation marks. Although the subject–voice alliance is clear, the interaction between voices is not. The development in the level of interest in the conversation (as the other protagonists slowly shift away from indifference towards the purported banality of the subject matter) comes from the narrative drive which exploits instances where the conversational exchange is thwarted by differing perspectives or misunderstandings. In the case of the first protagonist who talks of his most recent mistress, the divergence of opinion between himself and his mistress is expressed through reported speech:

C'était une femme qui voulait toujours faire l'homme. 'Vous n'êtes pas un homme! Ah! si j'étais un homme! De nous deux, c'est moi qui suis l'homme!' Tels étaient les insupportables refrains qui sortaient de cette bouche d'où je n'aurais voulu voir s'envoler que des chansons.

[She was a woman who always wanted to play the role of a man. 'You're not a man! Ah! if I were a man! Of the two of us, it is I who is the man!' Such were the unbearable refrains which came out of her mouth, a mouth from which I would rather only have seen songs pour out.]

A new musical analogy recalls the narrator's musical analogy cited above: the implication is that certain ways of speaking, as with certain types of music, fail to appeal. The imperfection of this mistress is her desire to be something that her lover wishes her not to be; by contrast, the second male protagonist's mistress is imperfect because she only desires to do whatever he wishes:

'Je le veux bien, puisque cela vous est agréable.' C'était sa réponse ordinaire.

['I'd like that, because it pleases you.' That was her usual response.]

The monotony of the woman's habitual reply contrasts to the unpredictability of the mistress recounted by the previous protagonist. The two different styles of mistress are represented by two different styles of conversation with their lovers.
     The negative monotony of repetition seen in the way the second mistress speaks becomes a positive trait in the case of the mistress of the third male protagonist.

Elle avait une manière douce, rêveuse, anglaise et romanesque de dire: 'J'ai faim!' Et elle répétait ces mots jour et nuit en vous montrant les plus jolies dents du monde, qui vous eussent attendris et égayés à la fois.

[She had a sweet, dreamy, English and romantic way of saying: 'I'm hungry!' And she repeated these words day and night, showing you the most beautiful teeth in the world, which would have made you feel both tender and excited at the same time.]

The different repetitive refrains of each of these three mistresses are ridiculed by the fourth male protagonist. He tells his three listeners that the way they complain about their mistresses is inappropriate:

Je vous trouve mal venus, trop fortunés mortels, à vous plaindre des imperfections de vos maîtresses.

[I find it bad timing of you, all too fortunate mortals, to complain about the imperfections of your mistresses.]

This recourse to a 'bienséant' ['seemly'] language reminiscent of the seventeenth-century literary conventions surrounding the appropriateness of certain topics of conversational exchange is, however, rapidly ironised. In contrast to the descriptions of the three mistresses which rely on reported speech, the fourth male protagonist does not give voice to his mistress. The reasons for this become clear as his tale unfolds: her control over him came in the form of a persistent 'reproche muet' ['silent reproach'].

The persistent silence of the fourth mistress, however, drives the fourth male protagonist to the point of fury, to the extent that he wants to shout at her, but never does:

> Combien de fois ne me suis-je pas retenu de lui sauter à la gorge, en lui criant: 'Sois donc imparfaite, misérable! afin que je puisse t'aimer sans malaise et sans colère!'

> [How many times did I stop myself from wanting to grab her by the throat and cry out: 'Be imperfect, you wretch! so that I can love you without uneasiness and anger!']

Under the control of his silent mistress, he remains silent. That his desire to shout at her has now been voiced poses as an ominous indication of the conclusion of their affair. In recounting this silence to the other three male protagonists, the fourth protagonist instigates a new level of silence, refusing to speak fully of what became of her. Silence is built up by ellipsis:

> Un soir, dans un bois ... au bord d'une mare ..., après une mélancolique promenade où ses yeux, à elle, réfléchissaient la douceur du ciel, et où mon cœur, à moi, était crispé comme l'enfer ...

> [One evening, in a wood ... on the banks of a pond ..., after a melancholy walk during which her eyes reflected the sweetness of the sky back to her, and during which my heart was tensed up like hell ...]

This strategy of denying fullness of explanation leads the other three protagonists to cry out:

> – Quoi!
> – Comment!
> – Que voulez-vous dire?

> [– What!
> – Howso?
> – What do you mean?]

But these questions remain unanswered, reinforced by a concluding rhetorical question on the part of the fourth protagonist:

> 'C'était inévitable. ... Que vouliez-vous que je fisse d'elle, *puisqu'elle était parfaite?*'

> ['It was inevitable ... What would you have wanted me to do with her, *since she was perfect?*']

The piling up of elliptical silence, followed by the piling up of unanswered questions leaves the conversation to dissolve into speechlessness:

> Les trois autres compagnons regardèrent celui-ci avec un regard vague et lentement hébété, comme feignant de ne pas comprendre.

> [The three other companions looked at him with a vague and slightly stunned look, as if they were pretending that they did not understand.]

The speechlessness, however, is not unresonant: implicitly, internally, using their own imagination, the other protagonists sense only too profoundly the implications of what the fourth man has left unsaid. The initial banality of the conversation has dissolved into an extraordinary internal conversation which is far more meaningfully resonant.

The apparently light-hearted 'causerie' of 'Portraits de maîtresses' and its dissolution into a more serious internal conversation shows the Baudelairean perspective on conversation to be a process of exchange that is not an equally-matched exchange. As with his comment from 'Mon cœur mis à nu' cited above in which he privileges 'le malentendu', Baudelaire revels in scenarios where a conversational exchange is thwarted or problematised by the inability to reply. In another rather extraordinary 'causerie sur le sujet des femmes', this time in verse form from the 'Spleen et Idéal' section of *Les Fleurs du Mal*, the one-sidedness of the conversation belies its supposedly frivolous register implied by the title. 'Causerie' (B.*OC*.I, p.56) is a sonnet where not only are no replies given, but no outward exchange seems to be established at all. Baudelaire does not include typographic markers of direct speech, but signals an addressee through imperatives and personal pronouns. What renders this supposed conversation extraordinary is that Baudelaire's designation of his female addressee slips between two different personal pronouns, either a 'tu' or a 'vous':

> Vous êtes un beau ciel d'automne, clair et rose!
> Mais la tristesse en moi monte comme la mer,
> Et laisse, en refluant, sur ma lèvre morose
> Le souvenir cuisant de son limon amer.

Ta main glisse en vain sur mon sein qui se pâme;
Ce qu'elle cherche, amie, est un lieu saccagé
Par la griffe et la dent féroce de la femme.
Ne cherchez plus mon cœur; les bêtes l'on mangé.

Mon cœur est un palais flétri par la cohue;
On s'y soûle, on s'y tue, on s'y prend aux cheveux!
– Un parfum nage autour de votre gorge nue! …

O Beauté, dur fléau des âmes, tu le veux!
Avec tes yeux de feux, brillants comme des fêtes,
Calcine ces lambeaux qu'ont épargnés les bêtes!

[You are a beautiful autumn sky, clear and pink!
But the sadness within me rises up like the sea,
And leaves behind, as it ebbs, on my morose lips
The stinging memory of its bitter lemon.

Your hand slides in vain over my swooning breast;
What it is looking for, dear woman, is a place which has been plundered
By the claws and ferocious teeth of woman.
Do not look for my heart any more; the beasts have eaten it.

My heart is a palace blackened by the crowd;
People get drunk there, kill each other, tug each other's hair!
– A perfume swims around your bare neck! …

Oh Beauty, harsh scourge of souls, you desire it!
With your eyes of fire, shining as if in festival,
Burn these remnants which the beasts have left behind!]

The 'vous' opens the poem, and is reiterated implicitly in line eight with the imperative 'Ne cherchez plus' and in line 11 with the possessive adjective 'votre gorge nue'. The 'tu' first appears in line five with the possessive adjective 'Ta main', and in line 13 with the personal pronoun 'tu le veux', and again in line 14 with the possessive adjective 'tes yeux', and finally implicitly in line 15 with the imperative 'Calcine'. The interweaving of the two personal pronouns throughout the poem reveals the complexity of Baudelaire's rapport with the poem's addressee (who, according to biographical data, is Marie Daubrun). There is no scope for reply in this supposed 'causerie' because the other party to the conversation is denied a clear subjective position, and instead is doubled confusingly through the two personal pronouns 'tu' and 'vous'.

The 'tu'/'vous' persona is not granted a concerted presence within the conversation although she does have a linguistic potency; the poetic 'moi' seemingly overwhelms the 'tu'/'vous' persona, and yet presents itself as being overwhelmed by the suggestion of a female presence. On the one hand, the excess of alliteration in the second line on the letter 'm' ('Mais la tristesse en moi monte comme la mer') reinforces the 'moi' at the end of the first hemistich, whose presence is reiterated in line three with 'ma lèvre morose', in line five with 'mon sein', in line eight with 'mon cœur', and finally in line nine again with 'Mon cœur'. Yet on the other hand, the 'moi' remains empty, it is a 'lieu saccagé' (v.6) by a woman, and it calls out to be totally destroyed by the persona designated as 'tu' in the final line of the sonnet: 'Calcine ces lambeaux qu'ont épargnés les bêtes!'. The protagonists of the 'causerie' dissolve as the poem closes; the textual voices are weakened by the subjective designations of 'moi', 'tu' or 'vous' because the act of conversing does not seem to actually take place. The imagined nature of the conversation suggests that where protagonists are designated only by the fluctuating status of personal pronouns, the inability to actually speak is intensified. This raises questions about the status of conversation in this poem: does an unstable subject result in an inability to speak? A focus on other poems where conversation is more clearly designated by direct speech, even though the subject is unstable, would suggest otherwise.

Three successive poems in *Les Fleurs du Mal* all contain questions and answers clearly signalled by quotation marks; these are the conversations of two poems I have already addressed in earlier chapters, 'Semper eadem' and 'Tout entière', followed by the untitled sonnet 'Que diras-tu ce soir?' (B.*OC*.I, pp.41–43). This is a sonnet where the use of voice is a central thematic of the whole poem: the verbs 'dire', 'chanter' and 'parler' ['to say', 'to sing' and 'to speak'] are used in the quatrains and the second tercet. As is the case in 'Causerie', the Baudelairean 'je' persona imagines a conversation with a female protagonist, and in doing so, both his own poetic 'je', and the female persona become multiple and unstable. By weakening the clarity of a subjective position and its relationship with a particular vocal enactment, Baudelaire reinforces the internal, imaginative and fictitious nature of the conversational exchanges established in his poetry. The main poetic voices of 'Que diras-tu' (B.*OC*.I, p.43) seem to revolve around a male and a female protagonist. From biographic data, in the form of a letter dated 16 February 1854 in which the sonnet was enclosed, it is clear that the sonnet was composed for Mme Sabatier:

> Que diras-tu ce soir, pauvre âme solitaire,
> Que diras-tu, mon cœur, cœur autrefois flétri,
> À la très belle, à la très bonne, à la très chère,
> Dont le regard divin t'a soudain refleuri?

> – Nous mettrons notre orgueil à chanter ses louanges:
> Rien ne vaut la douceur de son autorité;
> Sa chair spirituelle a le parfum des Anges,
> Et son œil nous revêt d'un habit de clarté.

Que ce soit dans la nuit et dans la solitude,
Que ce soit dans la rue et dans la multitude,
Son fantôme dans l'air danse comme un flambeau.

Parfois il parle et dit : 'Je suis belle, et j'ordonne
Que pour l'amour de moi vous n'aimiez que le Beau;
Je suis l'Ange gardien, la Muse et la Madone.'

[What will you say this evening, poor lonely soul,
What will you say, my heart, heart which had faded long ago,
To the very beautiful, to the very good, to the very dear woman,
Whose divine look has suddenly revived you?

– We will turn our pride to singing her prasies:
Nothing is as sweet as her authority;
Her spiritual flesh has the perfume of Angels,
And her eye covers us in a cloak of light.

Whether it be in the night, in solitude,
Whether it be in the street, among the multitude,
Her ghost dances in the air like a flame.

Sometimes it speaks and says: 'I am beautiful, and I decree
That out of love for me you love only Beauty;
I am your guardian Angel, your Muse and Madonna.']

Although upon publication of this sonnet within *Les Fleurs du Mal*, Mme Sabatier no longer features specifically as the main female addressee, she is represented by the more oblique turns of phrase such as 'belle' / 'bonne' / 'chère' (v.3) or 'Ange gardien' / 'Muse' / 'Madone' (v.14). These triplicate designations have the same function as the duple 'tu'/'vous' pronouns of 'Causerie': they dissolve her subjective position into a more abstract position. This is further emphasised by the third-person designations that the female addressee is allocated ('ses louanges' v.5, 'son autorité' v.6, 'Sa chair' v.7, 'son œil' v.8, 'Son fantôme' v.11). Just as the female protagonist becomes triplicate in this poem, so too is the male protagonist of the poem presented in triplicate in the first two lines of the poem: as 'âme' v.1, 'cœur' v.2 and the 'je' who asks the question that opens the poem. The anaphora of the first two lines 'Que diras-tu' sets up a hypothetical question contained within the first quatrain. The reply comes in the first person plural 'Nous mettrons' (v.5). By uniting together the 'âme' and 'cœur' into a plural 'nous', who together imagine singing the woman's praises, Baudelaire answers the hypothetical question with a hypothetical answer. The speculative nature of the dialogue between the male protagonist's 'je' and 'nous' is further emphasised by the use of future tense verbs ('que diras-tu', 'nous mettrons').

Where in the second quatrain Baudelaire's 'âme' and 'cœur' speak in unison in response to the question posed in the first quatrain, it is the singular voice of the woman's 'fantôme' who purportedly speaks in the tercets ('parfois il parle et dit'). The hypothetical voice of the woman's 'fantôme' denies any conversational exchange by the use of the verb 'j'ordonne'. The woman's vocalised demand stifles any possibility of exchange or reply on the part of the male protagonist. Although the woman's speaking voice is presented at the closure of the poem, it is not presented as a culmination of the initial question and answer of the first two quatrains. The adverbial 'parfois' reminds the reader that the woman's demands are hypothetical, temporally ungrounded, and take place against varied backdrops. From the solitude of the night, to the multitude of the street (v.9–10), the fluctuating presence of the woman's phantom raises questions as to the status of the reported speech of the final tercet.[9] The anaphora of 'Que ce soit' mirrors the anaphora of the opening question 'Que diras-tu', and expresses an ambivalence towards the different settings in which the woman's phantom is presented and occasionally speaks. Whereas in 'Portraits de maîtresses', the protagonists involved in the conversational exchange were presented within the same environment of a 'boudoir d'hommes', here in 'Que diras-tu', the instability of the backdrop against which voices are raised renders the possibility for conversational exchange more problematic.

Conflicts with the Crowd

For Walter Benjamin, the most unstable backdrop against which Baudelaire can raise his voice is the noisy hubbub of the Parisian cityscape. Benjamin suggests, in his 'Zentralpark' reflections, that the presence of background noise entails certain risks for Baudelaire as he attempts to use his voice. In the conversational scenarios that I have analysed above – 'Portraits de maîtresses', 'Causerie' and 'Que diras-tu' – no other extraneous noises are brought into play in the scene. However, Benjamin's comment suggests that in using his voice within the context of the Parisian cityscape (which is the city in which, after all, he published his poetry), Baudelaire runs the gauntlet, first of all, of not being heard, and in the second instance, of his voice being hijacked by extraneous noises:

> Baudelaire élève la voix au milieu du mugissement de Paris comme quelqu'un qui parlerait sur le bruit de fond des vagues. Sa parole est claire dans la mesure où elle est perceptible. Mais quelque chose vient se mêler à elle, qui lui porte

---

[9]   The distinction between multitude and solitude is, of course, famously broken down by Baudelaire in the prose poem 'Les Foules': 'Multitude, solitude: termes égaux et convertibles pour le poète actif et fécond' ['Multitude, solitude: equal and convertible terms for the active and fertile poet'] (B.*OC*.I, p.291).

préjudice. Et elle demeure mêlée à ce mugissement qui l'emporte plus loin et qui lui donne une obscure signification.[10]

[Baudelaire raises his voice in the midst of the roar of Paris like someone who is speaking against the backdrop of waves. His word is clear insofar as it is perceptible. But something comes to mix itself in with his voice, which prejudices it. And it remains intermingled with this roar which carries it further away and gives it an obscure meaning.]

Benjamin's description of Baudelaire raising his voice 'au milieu du mugissement de Paris' is a metaphorical description. He does not refer to Baudelaire going out and proclaiming his poetry on the streets of Paris; he refers to a different level of vocal exchange beyond the interiority of conversations portrayed in Baudelaire's poems. This vocal exchange is one that takes place between poet and his readership, this latter group being represented by Benjamin as a babbling hubbub. Although Benjamin recognises that Baudelaire is willing to take on the challenge of raising his voice against this backdrop, he does not take into account the fuller implications of Baudelaire's varying degrees of involvement with the city's inhabitants.

In the 'Tableaux parisiens' section of *Les Fleurs du Mal*, for example, the sonnet 'A une passante' (B.*OC*.I, pp.92–93) portrays the poet as he thrives on the context of 'La rue assourdissante' ['The deafening street'] (v.1), whereas just two poems later in 'Le Crépuscule du soir' (B.*OC*.I, pp.94–95), the poet figure seeks to distance himself from the 'rugissement' ['roar'] (v.30) of the city:

> Recueille-toi, mon âme, en ce grave moment,
> Et ferme ton oreille à ce rugissement. (v.29–30)

> [Step back, my soul, in this serious moment,
> And shut your ears to this roar.]

So for Baudelaire to raise his voice against the background noise of the Parisian cityscape is nuanced by the poetic context. Benjamin's comment recognises the potential negativity of raising one's voice against a background noise – perhaps that of other voices – but this is counterbalanced (in typically Baudelairean fashion) by the potential positive outcome of gaining in return 'une obscure signification'. The point that Benjamin makes here is that Baudelaire, as a poet, had no choice other than to try to raise his voice in the city of Paris. In deciding to publish his poetry, Baudelaire accepted the double-edged sword of the potential risks and rewards of trying to make his voice heard by the Parisian public.

---

[10] Walter Benjamin, *Charles Baudelaire: un poète lyrique à l'apogée du capitalisme*, trans. by Jean Lacoste (Paris: Payot, 2002), p.233.

In this respect, Baudelaire aspired to a form of conversational exchange between his own voice and the indistinct, unknown voices of his reading public. For Mallarmé, too, poetry necessarily needed to be opened up to the public in order to establish an exchange. An unpublished draft article, which probably dates from the latter years of Mallarmé's career explains the following (M.*OC*.II, p.474):[11]

> Le Vers et tout écrit au fond par cela qu'issu de la parole doit se montrer à même de subir l'épreuve orale ou d'affronter la diction comme un mode de présentation extérieur et pour trouver haut et dans la foule son écho plausible, au lieu qu'effectivement il a lieu au-delà du silence que traversent se raréfiant en musiques mentales ses éléments, et affecte notre sens subtil ou de rêve.

> [The Poem and all writing fundamentally by that which, coming from the spoken word, should present itself as if in order to undergo an oral test or to confront diction as an exterior mode of presentation and in order to discover its plausible echo out loud and in the crowd, whereas effectively it takes place beyond the silence in which its elements cross and become rarefied into mental music, and it affects our subtle or ideal sense.]

Three main points can be derived from this comment: first of all, that Mallarmé perceived poetry to be founded on the spoken word ('la parole'), second, that the ideal for poetry would be to be spoken out loud ('l'épreuve orale', 'la diction', 'présentation extérieur') and finally, that poetry is very rarely actually spoken out loud ('il a lieu au-delà du silence', 'musiques mentales'). These points bring us back to the dilemma between internal or external uses the human voice discussed above:[12] where I borrowed from recent studies in neuroscience to suggest that the distinction between an internal and an external reading is not a clear-cut division, Mallarmé himself goes on to comment that 'Ce n'est pas à dire … qu'il [le vers] soit fait exclusivement pour les yeux' ['This does not mean to say … that it [poetry] is designed exclusively for the eyes']. Mallarmé acknowledges, then, that the subtle nuances in the relationship between using one's eyes and using one's voice and ears in reading poetry, render the ideal of speaking poetry out loud one that remains beholden to reading a written text. Mallarmé makes the point that only upon reading the text will the reader be able to notice 'l'*s* du pluriel' ['the *s* of a plural ending'], for example, from which can be derived the pleasure which would allow a contrast with 'une rime nette sur un son le même au singulier' ['a clear rhyme on a sound which is the same in the singular']. This is how poetry, for Mallarmé, goes beyond silence.[13] Poetry is able to spark resonances that go beyond the written page.

---

[11]   Bertrand Marchal follows Bonniot's suggestion that this text dates from 1895.

[12]   See Chapter 2.

[13]   As Leo Bersani also outlines, 'Mallarmé's references to the silences of poetry may be thought of as a way of emphasizing the non-adherence of sense to the words which

Rather like the way Baudelaire, in his poetry, writes at times of thriving on being in amongst the crowd, and at others seeking to distance himself from it, Mallarmé's relationship with 'la foule' in this instance is nuanced by context. The 'épreuve orale' that he demands for poetry seems to require, on the one hand, an intimate one-on-one rapport with the text, whilst on the other hand providing a means of contact with a wider public. That Mallarmé recognises that poetry rarely enjoys a 'présentation extérieur' does not damage a rapport with 'la foule'; it merely interiorises it. For Mallarmé 'la foule' is not simply a body of individuals but also a body of text, words and language. The action of reading poetry, then, takes place ('il a lieu') both through the voice of the individual person reading, and through the voice of the body of language represented by 'la foule'.

The way in which Mallarmé breaks down the distinction between internal and external readings of poetry is reinforced by his careful choice of words. In claiming that poetry 'doit se montrer à même de subir l'épreuve orale', the verb 'devoir' takes on its dual significance of being both a requirement and a suggestion. By selecting the words 'épreuve' and 'un mode', Mallarmé chooses to nuance the notion that the process of reading out loud is only one of the ways of reading poetry. The notion of an 'épreuve', furthermore, is reinforced by the verbs 'subir' and 'affronter' which qualify the status of the action of reading poetry out loud: a 'présentation extérieur' of poetry is a challenging test for poetry. From this challenging or risk-filled scenario, however, a potential reward is to be gained in the form of a resonant 'écho'. The adjectival qualifier of 'plausible' reminds us that experiencing a resonant echo from reading poetry out loud is subject to the laws of possibility or probability, rather than to the law of certainty. The 'écho plausible' comes from a process of evaluation (the 'épreuve') carried out by 'la foule': the 'foule' is able either to accept or to reject the possibilities thrown open by reading poetry. If 'la foule' designates the corpus of language itself, then it is not surprising that the process of reading out loud does not always actually take place. The exchange that is established by poetry is one that goes beyond both reading out loud and the silence of an internal reading, because it enters a fictitious world of exchange of opinions and meanings within the imagination. By imagining and exploiting previous encounters with poetic language, through a process of evaluation, the reader is able to establish the yearned-for resonant echo latent within poetic language.

In suggesting that 'la foule' in this context is a symbolic designation for the body of language, I have circumvented the complexity of Mallarmé's relationship with his reading public, which has been discerned by critics to be on the one hand negative and elitist, whilst remaining on the other hand positive and inclusive. Louis Marvick, for example, claims that:

---

produce sense'. Leo Bersani, *The Death of Stéphane Mallarmé* (Cambridge: CUP, 1982), p.76.

> In Mallarmé ... a certain ambivalence toward the crowd can be felt. Even
> allowing for the evolution of his thought over thirty years, the horror of the
> masses which he expressed in 'Hérésies artistiques – L'Art pour tous' (1862)
> is echoed in the pessimism of his mature reflections on the competence of the
> audience.[14]

It is true that Mallarmé struggled with the question of the competence of his
reader. The Huret interview of the late 1890s makes this explicit, since he talks
of the instability of readers' intelligence and therefore of their ability to grasp the
kind of poetry that he writes (M.*OC*.II, p.700). Damian Catani, following Jacques
Rancière, nuances this deficiency on the part of the reading public in grasping
Mallarmé's poetry, by suggesting that it is a product of the very instability of
poetry itself during the time in which Mallarmé was writing:

> Mallarmé did not seek to derive a universally pertinent source of solace
> exclusively from language, but from those more concrete, tangible
> manifestations of modern life that were invariably shaped and motivated by
> economic or political factors, were instantly reognisable by 'la Foule', and
> which, unlike language, demanded no degree of concentrated intellectual
> engagement. Mallarmé's reason for embarking on non-linguistic avenues of
> enquiry ... is related to his awareness (as Rancière has aptly pointed out) of
> living in an interrègne, a period of historical transition in which 'la Foule' is not
> yet ready to grasp his aesthetic in its abstract theoretical form.[15]

By separating out the relationship between the crowd and language, however,
calling instead upon 'economic or political factors' as more 'tangible manifestations
of modern life', Catani circumvents the fact that the comprehension of such factors
is itself carried out through language. Thus the distinction between what 'la foule'
can grasp and what it fails to grasp is to be found in the way language manifests
itself: language is not distinct or separate from 'la foule', but an inherent part of
it. The poetic 'interrègne' does not dislocate poetic language from 'la foule', but
rather brings the process of evaluation (the process of the 'épreuve orale') into
sharper focus. In Peter Dayan's words:

> 'La foule' becomes, then, to Mallarmé, by the 1880s, the repository of as well as
> the universal metaphor for the artistically accessible ideal.[16]

---

[14]   Louis Marvick, *Waking the Face That No One Is* (Amsterdam and New York:
Rodopi, 2004), p.2.

[15]   Damian Catani, *The Poet in Society: Art, Consumerism and Politics in Mallarmé*
(Bern: Peter Lang, 2003), p.13.

[16]   Peter Dayan, *Mallarmé's 'Divine Transposition': Real and Apparent Sources of
Literary Value* (Oxford: Clarendon, 1986), p.76.

This does not mean that the 'foule' must necessarily understand everything, however; the instability and incompatibility of differing opinions, meanings, sounds and effects offers the precise moment of linguistic difficulty that Mallarmé seeks to exploit through an 'épreuve orale', testing out language under the most strenuous or challenging conditions, the condition of a conversational exchange.

In 'Conflit', for example, written in the same year as the comment from his draft article cited above (1895), Mallarmé expresses the difficult challenge posed by conversational exchange by imagining starkly divergent uses of language on the part of each of the parties involved. Catani suggests that the conversation in 'Conflit' is based on a conflict of ideologies:

> What is notable about this (imaginary) dialogue is the incompatibility of two views of society.[17]

But as other critics such as Bertrand Marchal have pointed out, 'Conflit' is not simply about a class struggle.[18] This conflict of ideologies is also based on a conflict in language and what it means to converse. The 'je' protagonist of the prose poem, who finds his rented country retreat disturbed each Sunday afternoon by the drunken carousing of a group of railway construction workers, contemplates – with much trepidation – the prospect of entering into conversation with these workers in order to regain his peace and quiet. He explores the various ways in which he might use language to address his complaint towards the workers:

> Quelque langage, la chance que je le tienne, comporte du dédain, bien sûr, puisque la promiscuité, couramment, me déplaît: ou, serai-je, d'une note juste, conduit à discourir ainsi? – Camarades, par exemple, vous ne supposez pas l'état de quelqu'un épars dans un paysage celui-ci, où toute foule s'arrête, en tant qu'épaisseur de forêt à l'isolement que j'ai voulu tutélaire de l'eau (M.*OC*.I, p.436)

> [Such language, the chance that I might possess it, carries some disdain, of course, because promiscuity, being common, displeases me: or, will I, on such a note, be led to speak like that? – Friends, for example, you do not imagine the state of someone dispersed in a landscape such as this, where all crowds stop, in

---

[17] Catani, *The Poet in Society*, p.190.

[18] 'S'il y a donc un conflit, comme l'indique le titre, le poète refuse expressément que ce conflit soit interprété comme une illustration trop évidente de la lutte des classes, n'hésitant pas à en appeler à la compréhension des envahisseurs pour sa réaction de rejet' ['If there is a conflict, then, as the title indicates, the poet expressly refuses the possibility that this conflict be interpreted as an all too self-evident illustration of class struggle, not hesitating to call this to the attention of the invaders for their reaction of rejection']. Bertrand Marchal, *La Religion de Mallarmé: poésie, mythologie et religion* (Paris: José Corti, 1988), p.353.

the sense of the density of the forest to the isolation which I wanted protecting the water]

Although his imagined choice of address, 'Camarades', seeks to place the workers and himself on the same level, the gulf that separates them remains considerable. It is not simply a gulf of class, but a gulf of language.

The way in which Mallarmé uses language here – which, after all, is his fundamental métier – is elliptical and far from self-assured. The Mallarméan 'je' is trying to find a way of using language that the workers will comprehend, but he struggles in his aim: the 'conflit' of the title, then, becomes not a class struggle but a struggle of linguistic register. He qualifies, for example, the word 'promiscuité' with 'couramment' (which in its original version was the more extended 'pour parler couramment'). Mallarmé seeks to find a popular register which would, theoretically, be totally at odds with his own poetic language. Of course, the status of 'Conflit' itself as a poem is uncertain. It was published, first of all as the seventh article of 'Variations sur un sujet' in *La Revue blanche*, which would grant it the status of literary criticism; later it was included in *Divagations* as one of the 'Anecdotes ou poèmes', which would grant it the status of prose poem. This ambiguity seems to be presented also in the confusion of the imagined conversational register which seeks to be 'fréquent' ['common'] (M.*OC*.I, p.438), yet which is enclosed within a much higher register verging on the poetic.

In the imagined exchange with these supposed 'camarades', the poetic 'je' fears a rebuttal of his initial address:

> à moins qu'un ne répondit, tout de suite, avec égalité. – Nous, le travail cessé pour un peu, éprouvons le besoin de se confondre, entre soi: qui a hurlé, moi, lui? son coup de voix m'a grandi, et tiré de la fatigue, aussi est-ce, déjà, boire, gratuitement, d'entendre crier un autre. (M.*OC*.I, p.436)

> [unless one of them replies, straight away, with equality. – We feel, with work having stopped for a bit, the need to lose ourselves in each other: who shouted, me, him? the rap of his voice fortified me, and brought out of my fatigue, so it is, already, to drink, for free, to hear another one shout.]

The imagined rebuttal is rhetorically persuasive, although far from what the Mallarméan 'je' had hoped for. The workers seem simply to claim that they deserve a break from their work over a drink with friends: in fact, the drink serves merely as a premise for a more profound form of exchange. Their voices are able to 'se confondre', and this merging of their voices is presented as a profound necessity in the break from work, because in the uncertainty as to whose voice was shouting, each of the workers is revived from his fatigue. For the Mallarméan 'je' whose very métier is to bring language to voice (where for the workers, using their voice specifically signals a break from work), the sense of failure on his part to spark a resonance with the workers is exacerbated by the realisation that they are able to converse with each other so readily. The cavernous gap between the poet and the workers is expressed by a sense of 'animosité' ['animosity'] (M.*OC*. I, p.437). Dayan suggests in relation to 'Conflit' that 'the artist ... cannot hope to communicate with "la foule" in its present form'.[19] In order for the conversation between the poet and the workers to be successful, some form of rapprochement – both physical, ideological and linguistic – needs to take place.

The physical gap that separates the poet from the workers is expressed in the context of another imagined conversation that the poet conducts from inside the country house, through an open window. However, the desire to go and join them in person is never realised:

> M'abstraire ni quitter, exclus, la fenêtre, regard, moi-là, de l'ancienne bâtisse sur l'endroit qu'elle sait; pour faire au groupe des avances, sans effet. Toujours le cas: pas lieu de se trouver ensemble; un contact peut, je le crains, n'intervenir entre des hommes. (M.*OC*.I, p.438)

> [To cut myself off nor leave, outcast, the window, look, me there, from the old building in the place that it knows; to advance upon the group, without effect. Always the case: no reason to end up together; contact cannot, I fear, take place between men.]

Just as no physical contact is established between the poet and the workers, so too do their respective ideologies remain separate, because no conversation between them is actually able to take place. The Mallarméan 'je' nevertheless imagines the dialogue:

> 'Je dis' une voix 'que nous trimons, chacun ici, au profit des autres.' – 'Mieux,' interromprais-je bas, 'vous le faîtes, afin qu'on vous paie et d'être légalement, quant à vous seuls.' – 'Oui, les bourgeois,' j'entends, peu concerné 'veulent un chemin de fer'. – 'Pas moi, du moins' pour sourire 'je ne vous ai pas appelés dans cette contrée de luxe et sonore, bouleversée autant que je suis gêné'. (M.*OC*.I, p.438)

> ['I say' a voice 'that we are slaving away, each one of us here, for the benefit of others.' – 'Better still,' I interrupted in a low voice, 'you are doing it so that you can be paid and in order to be alone, legally, for yourselves.' – 'Yes, the middle class,' I hear, somewhat concerned, 'want the railway'. – 'Not me, at least' to smile 'I did not call you to this luxurious and sonorous countryside, which has been disrupted just as much as I have been put out'.]

The alliance between the conflict in ideology and the impossibility of the conversational exchange is further nuanced by the fact that, even in this imagined

---

[19]   Dayan, *Mallarmé's 'Divine Transposition'*, p.78.

dialogue, numerous assumptions on the part of each protagonist are challenged by the each of the responses. The poetic 'je' becomes increasingly agitated by the failure of this conversation, partly because it remains on the lowly level of popular exchange, failing to reach the profound conclusion that the poet hopes to share. The yearned-for conversation becomes nothing more than a vain attempt at speaking, dissolving instead into silence:

> Ce colloque, fréquent, en muettes restrictions de mon côté, manque, par enchantement; quelle pierrerie, le ciel fluide! Toutes les bouches ordinaires tues au ras du sol comme y dégorgeant leur vanité de parole. J'allais conclure: 'Peut-être moi, aussi, je travaille.' – À quoi? n'eût objecté aucun, admettant, à cause de comptables, l'occupation transférée des bras à la tête. À quoi – tait, dans la conscience seule, un écho – du moins, qui puisse servir, parmi l'échange général. Tristesse que ma production reste, à ceux-ci, par essence, comme les nuages au crépuscule ou des étoiles, vaine. (M.*OC*.I, p.438)

> [This chat, common, holding back in silence from my side, lacks, by way of enchantment; some gems, fluid sky! All the common mouths silent at ground level as if discharging there the vanity of the words they spoke. I was going to conclude: 'Perhaps I, too, work.' – Doing what? no doubt someone would have objected, admitting, because of accountants, the occupation transferred from the arms to the head. Doing what – staying silent, only in the mind, an echo – at least, which could be useful in the general exchange. Sadness that my production remains, to them, in essence, like clouds at evening time or stars, in vain.]

The 'tristesse' on the part of the poetic 'je' resides in the fact that his own métier, which uses language as its tool, has proven vain in this instance: no resonant echo has been established because the workers' assumptions and beliefs lie so far from the poet's own stance. Between themselves, the workers can successfully exchange voices, but between poet and worker, no exchange can be established because the workers do not perceive any value in the contribution that the poet makes. Mallarmé implicitly places a greater value in the exchange established through poetic language than that established through an informal conversation or 'colloque fréquent'. The ideal of a conversational exchange through the medium of poetry is put at risk because the proletarian worker cannot accept that language itself has a value. This is why, for Mallarmé, conversing with the 'foule' must be a metaphorical, rather than a practical or physical, endeavour. By the later stages of his career, he understands that poetic language must function amongst the 'échange général' but that such an exchange, between all parties and all social classes, is impossible at that particular time of writing.

The risks posed by opening up one's voice to the crowd through poetry are approached in different ways by Baudelaire and Mallarmé. Baudelaire never tires of raising his voice against the backdrop of the city and its crowds, granting both intimate conversations (within the realm of 'solitude') and public conversations (within the realm of the 'multitude') the same status; Mallarmé, on the other hand, cannot allow public conversations to bear the same status as intimate ones. Increasingly, Mallarmé renders the voices of his poetic protagonists more and more abstract, no longer allowing voices a clear subjective persona. Where Baudelaire thrived on the conflicts that arise out of misunderstandings (or 'le malentendu'), by the latter stages of his career, Mallarmé's preoccupation with the potential misunderstandings that arise from conflicting perspectives sees him retreat into a more abstract realm where poetic conversations can only take place in the abstract, symbolic realm where 'voice' and 'subject' become more and more dissociated from each other.

Transparency, Opacity and the Role of Punctuation

Over the course of Mallarmé's career, a marked change takes place in the way he uses punctuation. Where Baudelaire, throughout both his verse and prose poetry, clearly signals (hypothetical, imagined or reported) conversational exchanges through the traditional system of speech marks (using either 'guillemets' or the 'trait' where relevant), Mallarmé, by contrast, has much fewer instances of direct speech signalled by speech marks. Only five verse poems use speech marks, and all of these date from the pre-1880s period.[20] Of course, by 1886 Mallarmé had begun to compose poems which included no punctuation at all, with 'M'introduire dans ton histoire' being the first unpunctuated verse poem. In the prose 'Anecdotes ou poèmes', the percentage is somewhat higher: of the 13 prose poems, six contain instances of direct speech signalled by speech marks, but all of these instances are relatively minor interventions within the broader scope of each prose poem.[21] This tendency of Mallarmé not to signal direct speech clearly by speech marks carries an aesthetic agenda. Rather like the way he develops a symbolic nature for 'la foule', Mallarmé develops a symbolic way of designating poetic conversation without using the traditional punctuation.

Jean-Claude Milner, in his analysis of the sonnet 'Le vierge, le vivace et le bel aujourd'hui', proposes that Mallarmé reserves speech marks solely for those elements of a poem which represent speaking out loud:

> Il est vrai que les guillemets ne lui sont pas habituels dans les poésies, parce que peut-être ils relèvent à ses yeux du roman. ... Ajoutons que l'apparente clarté

---

[20]   I have excluded the two 'theatrical' poems ('Hérodiade' and 'L'Après-midi d'un faune') from this analysis, since they are specifically designed as theatrical dialogue. The poems which include speech marks are 'Le Guignon', 'Tristesse d'éte', 'Toast funèbre', 'Dans le jardin' and 'Sonnet' ('Sur les bois oubliés').

[21]   These are 'Le Phénomène futur', 'Un Spectacle interrompu', 'Réminiscence', 'La Déclaration foraine', 'Le Nénuphar blanc' and 'Conflit'.

typographique des guillemets n'eût pas laissé de tromper. Ceux-ci accompagnent d'ordinaire une profération à voix haute.[22]

[It is true that speech marks are not usual in his poems, because perhaps they remind him too much of the novel. ... I should add that the apparent typographic clarity of speech marks would not allow for any misunderstanding. These usually accompany something which has been said out loud.]

Milner's suggestion that Mallarmé's distaste for speech marks is due to his desire to distinguish poetic language from that of the novel might offer some explanation as to why Mallarmé employs them more frequently in that more ambiguous poetic genre, the prose poem. But Milner's suggestion that speech marks are only reserved for 'une profération à voix haute' requires careful attention, particularly since the critical distinction that is often made between reading poetry out loud and reading internally cannot be unproblematically upheld.[23] Milner seeks to qualify his statement by making a distinction between different types of speaking voice:

Or, s'il y a bien, dans le [premier] quatrain, parole du point de vue structurale, il n'y a pas de parole prononcée. La pensée du cygne demeure silencieuse et intérieure à la conscience.[24]

[Now, if there really is, in the [first] quatrain, the spoken word from the structural point of view, there is no actual spoken word. The thought of the swan remains silent and interior within the mind.]

The distinction that Milner makes between the 'parole prononcée' and 'parole structurale' suggests that a speaking voice represented by speech marks in Mallarmé's poetry from the 1860s and 1870s is granted the status either of having been spoken out loud on a past occasion, or of speaking in a poetic present. In the second quatrain of 'Tristesse d'été', the poetic 'je' recounts a woman's voice as having once spoken:

De ce blanc flamboiement l'immuable accalmie
T'a fait dire, attristée, ô mes baisers peureux
'Nous ne serons jamais une seule momie
Sous l'antique désert et les palmiers heureux!' (M.*OC*.I, p.13)

---

22   Jean-Claude Milner, *Mallarmé au tombeau* (Lagrasse: Verdier, 1999), pp.18–19.
23   See Chapter 2.
24   Milner, *Mallarmé au tombeau*, p.19.

[From this white blaze the immutable lull
Made you say, saddened, oh my fearful tears
'We will never be one sole mummy
Under the ancient desert and the happy palm trees!']

In 'Sonnet' ('Sur les bois oubliés', M.*OC*.I, p.66), the entire poem is enclosed in speech marks, as if the male protagonist were speaking the whole poem. Numerous other moments within Mallarmé's poetry (and particularly his later poetry), which Milner designates as a 'parole structurale', also present instances of speaking voices, even though these are not enclosed within speech marks (as would be the case in Baudelaire). It is difficult, however, to maintain Milner's distinction between speaking out loud and speaking internally, because even in instances where Mallarmé does use speech marks, such as in 'Tristesse d'été' cited above, the status of the speaking voice remains bound to the poetic text. The poem neither specifically represents a voice speaking out loud, nor requires that the voice be spoken out loud. These more oblique uses of voice in poetry now form part of a poetic texture whose symbolic language seeks to render the possibility of a speaking persona more and more abstract.

The increasing disappearance of punctuation in Mallarmé's poetry occurs through a range of strategies. Not only does he cease to use speech marks (whether or not these are supposed to represent, in some way, a 'proféation à voix haute' or otherwise), but he also begins to use exclamation marks in place of question marks when designating a (rhetorical) question, moving ultimately towards relying more and more on verb constructions, together with (ambiguous) personal pronouns, to designate voice(s) within his poetic texts.[25] In earlier poems (typically from the 1860s and 1870s), such as those published in the 1866 *Parnasse contemporain*, Mallarmé employs the question mark in its accepted role as serving to designate a question.[26] Similarly, in this earlier period, the exclamation mark is used, as is the case in Baudelaire's poetry, as

---

[25]   Indeed, as Malcolm Bowie has pointed out, 'For the speculative poet ... questions are an indispensable natural resource, a way of safeguarding the plurality and mobility of his mental world. It is curious, therefore, to find that Mallarmé, in his later poems, should make very little use of this resource. For these poems, as is well known, are the products of an inveterately questioning mind and are plural in their meanings to a degree unprecedented in French verse. What is even curioser than the paucity of questions, however, is the distrust shown by Mallarmé towards the interrogative mode at those points where questions do occur'. See 'The Question of *Un Coup de dés*', in *Baudelaire, Mallarmé, Valéry: New essays in honour of Lloyd Austin*, ed. by Malcolm Bowie, Alison Fairlie and Alison Finch (Cambridge: CUP, 1982), p.142.

[26]   See 'Les Fenêtres' v.37–40: 'Est-il moyen, mon Dieu qui voyez l'amertume, / D'enfoncer le cristal par le monstre insulté / Et de m'enfuir, avec mes deux ailes de plume / – Au risque de tomber pendant l'éternité?'; 'L'Azur' v.36: 'Où fuir, dans la révolte inutile et perverse?'; 'A un pauvre' (later entitled 'Aumône'), v.11–12: 'Robes et peau, veux-tu lacérer le satin, / Et boire en la salive heureuse l'inertie?'; 'Épilogue' (later untitled 'Las de

a way of reinforcing the dynamic volume or by way of emphasis.[27] But in the latter two decades of his career, Mallarmé began to replace the question mark with an exclamation mark (and the exclamation mark ceases to designate what it had designated previously).[28] This seemingly minor detail in fact signals an important development in Mallarmé's aesthetics of voice: the exclamation mark is no longer used for emphasis but for questioning, questions aren't signalled as questions by punctuation, and speech marks are no longer used to signal speaking. All of these traits serve to render his voices more and more oblique and abstract, a symbolic process instead of a direct representation.

So Milner is right to recognise that the first quatrain of 'Le vierge, le vivace et le bel' (M.*OC*.I, p.36) implies a speaking voice because it comes in the form of a (rhetorical) question, signalled by a verbal inversion ('Va-t-il'), but with an exclamation mark at the end of the stanza, rather than the expected question mark. Mallarmé has also picked up on the Baudelairean trait of dividing the speaking voice into multiple subjective designations (here the triplicate 'vierge' / 'vivace' / 'bel' recalls the 'belle' / 'bonne' / 'chère' of Baudelaire's 'Que diras-tu' analysed above). This combination of strategies – using more subtle punctuation, and granting a third-person singular verb to a triplicate subject which is contrasted to the first-person plural pronoun 'nous' (v.2) – calls the status of 'voice' into question. This is, after all, a poem about the fear of poetic impotence, with its images of a swan who is neither able to sing nor to fly (with flight and song both being heavily-laden metaphors in Mallarmé's aesthetic):

> Le vierge, le vivace et le bel aujourd'hui
> Va-t-il nous déchirer avec un coup d'aile ivre
> Ce lac dur oublié que hante sous le givre
> Le transparent glacier des vols qui n'ont pas fui!

---

l'amer repos') v.8–10: 'Que dire à cette Aurore, ô Rêves, visité / Par les roses, quand, peur de ses roses livides, / Le vaste cimetière unira les trous vides?'.

[27]   See, for example, Baudelaire's 'L'Ennemi' v.12–14: 'O douleur! ô douleur! Le Temps mange la vie, / Et l'obscur Ennemi qui nous ronge le cœur / Du sang que nous perdons croît et se fortifie!'; or 'Obsession' v.9–11: 'Comme tu me plairais, ô nuit! sans ses étoiles / Dont la lumière parle un langage connu! / Car je cherche le vide, et le noir, et le nu!'; or 'Alchimie de la Douleur', v.1–4: 'L'un t'éclaire avec son ardeur, / L'autre en toi met son deuil, Nature! / Ce qui dit à l'un: Sépulture! / Dit à l'autre: Vie et Splendeur!'. Mallarmé's earlier poems such as 'Brise marine' makes use of exclamation marks in this same way, such as v.1–3: 'La chair est triste, hélas! et j'ai lu tous les livres. / Fuir! là-bas fuir! Je sens que des oiseaux sont ivres / D'être parmi l'écume inconnue et les cieux!'.

[28]   See, for example, Mallarmé's use of the exclamation mark to designate a question, coupled with a verbal inversion, in 'Petit air II' v.13–14: 'Déchiré va-t-il entier / Rester sur quelque sentier!' (the similarity between the diction employed here and that used in the first stanza of 'Le vierge, le vivace et le bel' will be discussed later); or 'Tout Orgueil' v.1–4: 'Tout Orgueil fume-t-il du soir, / Torche dans un branle étouffée / Sans que l'immortelle bouffée / Ne puisse à l'abandon surseoir!'.

Un cygne d'autrefois se souvient que c'est lui
Magnifique mais qui sans espoir se délivre
Pour n'avoir pas chanté la région où vivre
Quand du stérile hiver a resplendi l'ennui.

Tout son col secouera cette blanche agonie
Par l'espace infligée à l'oiseau qui le nie,
Mais non l'horreur du sol où le plumage est pris.

Fantôme qu'à ce lieu son pur éclat assigne,
Il s'immobilise au songe froid de mépris
Que vêt parmi l'exil inutile le Cygne.

[The virginal, the vivacious and the beautiful today
Will it break for us with some drunken flapping of the wing
This hard forgotten lake within which, beneath the ice, haunts
The transparent glacier of the flights which have not flown!

A swan from times past remembers that it is he
Magnificent but who without hope liberates himself
For not having sung of the place to be lived in
When during the sterile winter boredom was shining.

His whole neck will shake off this white agony
Inflicted by the space on this bird who denies it
But not the horror of the ground in which his feathers are trapped.

Ghost which assigns to this place his pure brilliance,
He immobilises himself in the cold dream of contempt
Which within this useless exile clothes the Swan.]

The poetic heritage of the swan ('un cygne d'autrefois' v.5) stretches back not only towards the swan poems of Baudelaire or Hugo but also right back towards classical antiquity: the weight of the past weighs heavily on Mallarmé as he contemplates the future for poetry. Even though the second quatrain of the sonnet portrays the swan of the past who was unable to sing ('n'avoir pas chanté' v.7), the question of what will happen next has already been formulated in the first quatrain by the rhetorical question. By moving from questioning the future in the first quatrain to evaluating the past in the second, Mallarmé not only distorts the chronological flow, but also disrupts any possibility for an answer to the question posed in the first quatrain. The poem seems to recount the impossibility of a response or exchange in answer to the fearful question of the first quatrain: is today the day that poetry will finally be able to resonate (that is to say, to sing and to fly)?

In the first tercet, an image of movement offering the potential for poetic resonance is evoked through the verb 'secouera', whose future tense expresses the hope of release from the 'stérile hiver' (v.8) of the preceding quatrain. The movement remains an idealisation of the future: if the symbolic implication of the 'blanche agonie' (v.9) is the unwritten page that lies before the poet, then 'le plumage' (v.11) trapped on the ground is that of the poet's pen. The prevailing negativity of the swan's fate trapped by the frozen lake ('sans espoir' v.6, 'stérile' v.8, 'l'ennui' v.8, 'agonie' v.9, 'infligée' v.10, 'nie' v.10, 'horreur' v.11, 'mépris' v.13, 'inutile' v.14) mirrors the poem's own fate trapped by the white page. The aspiration for a movement which might release the swan-poem from its impotent state comes in the form of an uncontrolled 'secouement', as if waving the page around in the air might create some effect. Yet the uncontrollability of the movement leads to nothing, instead 'Il s'immobilise' (v.13). Paralleled to this aspiration for movement, however, is also an aspiration for the sound of the poem to emerge: but both movement and sound are trapped within the poetic text, by the icy sheet of its texture. Notwithstanding the supposed speaking voice in the first quatrain (which has already been shown to be of ambiguous status), the poem struggles to allow sound to emerge, and if sound does emerge, is it anything more than an uncontrolled noise, like the uncontrolled movement of the 'secouement'?

The presence of sound in the poem is muted by symbolic, periphrastic and ambiguous diction. In particular, the first line of the final tercet offers a range of different possible interpretations and meanings because of the ambivalence of its diction and the possibilities that it opens up:

Fantôme qu'à ce lieu son pur éclat assigne (v.12)

Mallarmé is undoubtedly aware of the homonymic status of 'son', both as a possessive pronoun and as a noun to designate sound. If a 'son pur' is allowed to emerge, it is only very briefly as it is taken over by the 'éclat', which may be the brightness of the 'blanche agonie' of the page, but may just as equally be a sharp, violent noise or shout. If the 'éclat' carries this latter meaning of an uncontrolled noise, then this resonates (perhaps paradoxically in the context of a poem about impotence) with the verb 'déchirer' in the opening quatrain (v.2), which not only means to shatter, but also implies the kind of violent sound that might pierce the air (to such an extent that it might be the driving force behind 'cette blanche agonie / Par l'espace infligée à l'oiseau' v.9–10). Of course the further figurative implication of 'nous déchirer' is that physical or emotional pain might be inflicted on the 'nous' persona (which, by implication, contains both the swan and the poet).[29]

---

[29]   In 'Le Crépuscule du matin' (B.*OC*.I, pp.103–104), Baudelaire allies the figure of a bird with the noise it creates through its song, using the same verb 'déchirer': 'Comme un sanglot coupé par un sang écumeux / Le chant du coq au lointain déchirait l'air brumeux' ['Like a sob cut by a foaming blood / The far-off song of the cock would tear through the misty air'] (v.19–20).

This, too, is mirrored in line 12 if the sound element of the verse line is privileged over its visual impact on the page: 'éclat' could take on the initial 'a' of 'assigne' to become a past historic verb 'éclata', and 'signe' of course is homophonous with its rhyming word in the final line of the sonnet, 'cygne'. If both the swan and its written sign on the page have been split open into their component parts, then what emerges are these more subtle readings that break down the poetic texture into its various components. In this way, homonymic, homophonic and semantic resonances are able to emerge. The supposed negative impotence of poetry that this poem represents is transformed into a positive resonant potency through the subtle manipulations of the poetic texture – by nuancing punctuation, by rendering the relationship between voice and subject ambiguous, by drawing attention to the poem's constituent elements, Mallarmé is able to overcome the terror of the 'vols qui n'ont pas fui!' (v.4). Mallarmé seeks to create new ways of establishing the fluttering of poetic resonance by denying his poetic voices any stridency that might lead to banality, and by seeking out the detachment of pure, naked sounds ('son pur' v.11 and 'sons nus', see below) through a process of a silent flight of abstraction ('envol tacite d'abstraction', see below).

The 'déchirure' and the 'éclat' become symbols of Mallarmé's fears for poetic language, and begin to take on a further significance in the burgeoning aesthetic dilemma about the potential precedence of music over poetry. This is elaborated in an article published in *La Revue blanche* in September 1896, 'Le Mystère dans les Lettres' (emphases mine):

> – Je sais, on veut à la Musique, limiter le Mystère; quand l'écrit y prétend.
>
> Les *déchirures* suprêmes instrumentales, conséquence d'enroulements transitoires, *éclatent* plus véridiques, à même, en argumentation de lumière, qu'aucun raisonnement tenu jamais; on s'interroge, par quels termes du vocabulaire sinon dans l'idée, écoutant, les traduire, à cause de cette vertu incomparable. Une directe adaptation avec je ne sais, dans le contact, le sentiment glissé qu'un mot détonnerait, par intrusion.
>
> L'écrit, *envol tacite d'abstraction*, reprend ses droits en face de la chute des *sons nus*: tous deux, Musique et lui, intimant une préalable disjonction, celle de la parole, certainement par effroi de fournir au bavardage. (M.*OC*.II, p.232)

> [– I know that people would like to limit the Mystery of Music; when writing aspires to it.
>
> The supreme instrumental *ruptures*, the consequence of a transitory rolling out, *ring out* more truthfully, just like, in the argumentation of light, which no reasoning ever held; we ask ourselves, according to certain terms of vocabulary if not within the idea, listening, to translate them, because of this incomparable virtue. A direct adaptation with, I don't know, in the contact, the slippery sentiment which a word sets off, by intrusion.
>
> Writing, *silent flight of abstraction*, takes back its rights in the face of the collapse of *naked sounds*: both, Music and itself, intimating a pre-existing

ion, that of the spoken word, certainly out of fear of adding to
g.]

...embering that 'le Livre' is itself an 'instrument spirituel' ['a spiritual instrument'] (the title of the final section of 'Quant au livre'), the slippage in Mallarmé's vocabulary as he talks about music and literature is significant. The sounds created by a 'déchirure' or an 'éclat' may also be a 'son nu' (or the 'son pur' of line 12 of 'Le vierge, le vivace et le bel') but these kind of sounds must take second place to the silent thought processes of the written poetic text ('L'écrit, envol tacite d'abstraction'). And, since for Mallarmé, the process of 'abstraction' takes place through the model of conversation as his 1869–1870 notes on language suggest, it is not surprising, then, that he perceives a necessary dislocation between the spoken word and the written word. 'La parole' in this context signifies not simply the difference between speaking and writing, but also the difference between 'bavardage' and poetic language. By restricting any overt indications of a speaking voice in his poetry, Mallarmé averts the kind of insignificant chattering conversation that the poetic voice seemingly overheard in 'Conflit', and instead opens up the possibility for a more abstract contact with language which is able not only to listen carefully to its component parts but to get them to speak to each other in a resonant exchange, the 'envol tacite d'abstraction'.

Mallarmé's aesthetic tendency to explore the resonant conversational exchange established within the 'musiques mentales' ['music within the mind'] (M.*OC*.II, p.474) of the 'envol tacite d'abstraction' places much more emphasis on abstract voices than textual voices. This also places more emphasis on the instability of hypotheses and on the uncertainty of grammatical postures, requiring an inquisitive attitude on the part of the reader of his poetry. This is why he reduces the amount of clear punctuation which would signal textual voices in his poetry, since this enables the reader to be unhindered by any supposed voices expressed on the page (since these would risk being too colloquial or banal) and to explore instead the vocal exchange and resonances established within and between the symbolic textures of the poem itself. The increasing opacity of Mallarmé's poetic voices is inherent in his aesthetic: 'voices' in Mallarmé's poetry dissociate themselves from being subject-specific (with individual or personal agendas), and in their place, ambiguous voices and subjects emerge, conflict, disappear and reappear in the universal exchange system (or 'échange général', M.*OC*.I, p.438) of the conversational model that abstracts language at its most transient and unstable moment.

Jacques Rancière's analysis of Mallarmé suggests that the literary endeavour becomes an internalised process for which no literary work is appropriate, and he perceives that Mallarmé therefore negates any notion of 'subject' or 'author':

> L'acte poétique nie la futilité sociale – le hasard – de l'objet, chevelure ou
> éventail, en retenant son aspect essentiel, la virtualité du geste de monde que
> décrit son mouvement. Il marque le déploiement de l'apparaître, la scansion de
> l'apparaître et du disparaître qui réduit la nature à sa 'symphonique équation',

soit à son idée. Réciproquement, la tresse ou l'éventail de mots, dans lequel l'acte poétique a nié le hasard du 'sujet', fait disparaître, dans ses plis et ses déplis, l'autre hasard, celui qui lie le poème à la 'personnalité' des sentiments, idées ou sensations de tel individu. Aussi le hasard de la langue, celui du sujet et de l'auteur sont-ils ensemble niés. Les principes contradictoires de la poétique semblent alors conciliés. Le principe de symbolicité, qui ramène tout spectacle empirique au principe d'indifférence qui trouve le ciel de l'idée poétique dans l'éclat d'un lustre, une pantomime de foire ou le frou-frou d'une robe ... la littérature ramenée à son propre est une littérature évanouie dans une vie de l'esprit, à laquelle aucune œuvre n'est adéquate.[30]

[The poetic act denies the social futility – chance – of the object, hair or fan, by retaining its essential aspect, the virtual nature of the gesture of the world which describes its movement. It marks the display of appearance, the scansion of appearance and disappearance which reduces nature to its 'symphonic equation', or rather, to its idea. Reciprocally, the hair or the fan of words, in which the poetic act has denied the chance of the 'subject', makes the other chance disappear in its folding and unfolding, that chance which links the poem to the 'personality' of sentiments, ideas or sensations of a particular individual. Therefore the chance of language, that of the subject and of the author are all denied. The contradictory principles of poetry therefore seem to be reconciled. The principle of symbolisation, which brings any empirical spectacle back to the principle of indifference which finds the pinnacle of the poetic idea in the brilliance of a chandelier, the pantomime of a fun fair or the swishing sound of a dress ... literature brought back to itself is a literature which has vanished within the life of the mind, for which no work is adequate.]

This process of negation, however, does not allow for the important, though complicated and ambiguous, role of the human (subjective) voice (at once an internal and an external voice) which necessarily remains at work in Mallarmé's poetic texts. What is in fact at stake in Mallarmé's poetry is the dislocation between, or the distancing of, 'voice' and 'subject' rather than the total negation of subject, poetry and language that Rancière implies.

Direct Address and Response

On the surface, then, Mallarmé's ideas in this regard could not be further removed from Baudelaire's aesthetics of voice, where supposed speaking voices in his poetry are granted a more-or-less stable subjective persona thanks to (primarily) the transparency of his punctuation (even if a 'voice' is pluralised into a 'nous'

---

[30] Jacques Rancière, *La Parole muette: essai sur les contradictions de la littérature* (Paris: Hachette, 1998), pp.127–130.

perspective of the poet's 'âme' and himself, for example). The poems (both in verse and prose) in which Baudelaire employs direct speech signalled by quotation marks are so numerous that they barely require specific consideration within the context of understanding the role of punctuation. By contrast, those poems which do not incorporate speech marks – and therefore do not clearly signal a conversational interlocutor – require closer attention. Whereas, in Mallarmé, the absence of speech marks or other punctuation does not necessarily imply an absence of (speaking) voice(s), and certainly does not imply an absence of conversational exchange (at least on a symbolic level), does the absence of speech marks in Baudelaire imply that no conversational voices are established within his poems?[31]

We have already seen in 'Causerie' (B.*OC*.I, p.56) that the conversational element seems to be thematic rather than structural: there is no direct speech signalled by quotation marks, but the poetic 'je' addresses his mistress through the ambiguous second-person pronouns. Elsewhere, Baudelaire uses imperatives or apostrophe as another strategy for direct address, along with instances where he uses descriptive passages to recount a voice or a conversation. In the first 'Spleen' poem ('Pluviôse, irrité contre la ville entière', B.*OC*.I, p.72), for example, there is also no direct speech, but he employs direct address by apostrophising a personified figure (the faux-classical goddess of rain, 'Pluviôse', v.1), combined with descriptions of the poet's voice ('L'âme d'un vieux poète erre dans la gouttière / Avec la triste voix d'un fantôme frileux' ['The soul of an old poet wanders in the gutter / With the sad voice of a shivering ghost'] v.7–8) and of a lovers' conversation ('Le beau valet de cœur et la dame de pique / Causent sinistrement de leurs amours défunts.' ['The handsome jack of hearts and the queen of spades / Chat ominously of their dead love affair.'] v.13–14).[32] Or in 'Mœsta et errabunda' (B.*OC*.I, pp.63–64), for example,

---

[31]   Even in Mallarmé's first poem without punctuation, 'M'introduire dans ton histoire', for example, he still includes the direct address of an imperative which requires a spoken response on the part of his addressee in the first line of the first tercet: 'Dis si je ne suis pas joyeux' ['Say if I am not joyous'] (M.*OC*.I, p.44).

[32]   The last line of this sonnet of course inspired Verlaine's 'Colloque sentimentale' which was published in *L'Artiste* in 1868. The precedent that Baudelaire set for the poetic representation of a conversation between former lovers is taken up by Verlaine through a mixture of narrative devices: first of all, a third-person narrator sets the scene in three sets of decasyllabic couplets before the two lovers begin to converse in turn, and then the third-person narrator closes the poem in a final couplet. The first lover talks in rapturous tones of the time of their affair, but each memory is denied by the second protagonist. The conversation thus represents once again the typical 'malentendu' that Baudelaire had theorised in 'Mon cœur mis à nu' cited above. The closing couplet of Verlaine's poem, however, subtly reminds the reader that it is impertinent to eavesdrop on such an intimate conversation by claiming that 'la nuit seule entendit leurs paroles' ['the night alone heard their words']. This raises questions as to the validity of presenting such an intimate conversation in poetic form: Baudelaire merely describes it, Verlaine boldly portrays it, but Mallarmé would eschew such a level of intimacy altogether (because it is too specific to the two lovers involved and therefore excludes the reader, as Verlaine's poem demonstrates).

Baudelaire combines imperatives – addressing first a female figure ('Dis-moi, ton cœur parfois s'envole-t-il, Agathe?' ['Tell me, does your heart sometimes fly away, Agatha?'] v.1 and 5) and then apostrophising two modes of transport ('Emporte-moi, wagon, enlève-moi, frégate?' ['Carry me away, carriage, take me away, frigate?'] v.11 and 15) – with descriptions of voices ('la mer, rauque chanteuse' ['the sea, raucous singer'] v.7, 'd'une voix argentine' ['with a silvery voice'] v.29), and with a hypothetical reported speech without traditional speech marks which also integrates the imperative mood apostrophising the modes of transport in a different context ('Est-il vrai que parfois le triste cœur d'Agathe / Dise: Loin des remords, des crimes, des douleurs, / Emporte-moi, wagon, enlève moi, frégate?' ['Is it true that sometimes the sad heart of Agatha / Says: Far away from remorse, crimes, sorrows / Carry me away, carriage, take me away, frigate?'] v.13–15). The intermingling of different narrative techniques for signalling voice without the clarity of speech marks reveals that Baudelaire's conversations, like Mallarmé's up to a point, do not require transparency of punctuation in order to function.

What 'Mœsta et errabunda' also reveals is Baudelaire's predilection for the interrogative mode, or the rhetorical question. As a means of direct address which expects a response that is sometimes thwarted because no response is voiced, Baudelaire demonstrates that the model of conversation is not simply a question of his own poetic persona conversing with himself within his own imagination. Baudelaire, following Asselineau, recognises himself to be a 'homo duplex' (B.*OC*.II, p.87), and dubs the imagination 'la reine des facultés' ['the queen of faculties'] ('Salon de 1859', B.*OC*.II, p.619), and there are a number of poems in which he presents himself as speaking to himself.[33] Yet the expectation in Baudelaire, through his use of the interrogative, is that a response must be elicited also within his reader.[34] In 'Mœsta et errabunda' there are six rhetorical questions, each punctuated (in contrast to Mallarmé) by a question mark. Each one remains unanswered, and seems – on the surface – not to require a response. However, as the final question which culminates the poem expresses, the piling up of rhetorical questions within the typically Baudelairean context of hankering after a foreign paradise draws attention to the role of the voice in this inquisitive longing:

---

[33] In 'L'Amour du mensonge' (B.*OC*.I, pp.98–99), Baudelaire writes: 'Je me dis: Qu'elle est belle! et bizarrement fraîche!' ['I say to myself: Oh how beautiful she is! and peculiarly fresh!' (v.9); or in 'La Fin de la journée' (B.*OC*.I, p.128), he writes: 'Le Poète se dit: "Enfin!"' ['The Poet says to himself: "Finally!"'] (v.8); or in 'Les Projets' (B.*OC*. I, p.314), he opens the prose poem with: 'Il se disait, en se promenant dans un grand parc solitaire: "Comme elle serait belle ..."' ['He said to himself, whilst walking alone in the large park: "How beautiful she would be ..."'].

[34] 'Dans la musique, comme dans la peinture et même dans la parole écrite, qui est cependant le plus positif des arts, il y a toujours une lacune complétée par l'imagination de l'auditeur' ['In music, as in painting and even in the written word, which is nonetheless the most positive of all the arts, there is always a gap which is filled by the imagination of the listener'] (B.*OC*.II, pp.781–782).

> Peut-on le rappeler avec des cris plaintifs,
> Et l'animer encor d'une voix argentine,
> L'innocent paradis plein de plaisirs furtifs? (v.28–30)[35]

> [Can one call it back through plaintive cries,
> And give it life again with a silvery voice,
> The innocent paradise full of furtive pleasures?]

Each question posits not just the possibility of an unknown response on the part of the reader, but also of a memory or recollection which is brought to the surface through the act of using one's voice.[36] It is not a certainty, but a possibility, and the responsibility for that possibility is placed not just on Baudelaire himself, but also on those who read his poem (who are included in the impersonal 'on' persona). Is it possible, by using one's voice through poetry, by putting one's voice into action, that a faraway poetic paradise of childhood innocence can be brought back to life?

That Baudelaire allies the 'cris plaintifs' with a 'voix argentine' is interesting, however, given that a 'cri' would typically imply an uncontrolled, disruptive element to a conversational exchange, whereas the adjective 'argentine' implies a clarity of sound. This intermingling of clarity and disruption is also, however, a feature of the rhetorical question in which it is phrased: a rhetorical question should theoretically be so clearly self-evident that no actual reply is required, but this then disrupts the possibility of establishing a productive conversational exchange. By asking the question in this way, specifically in the context of a strict poetic form, Baudelaire questions not simply whether a plaintive cry in a clear voice will be able to revive the memory, but also whether, specifically, a poetic voice will be able to do it. The 'strophes encadrées' form of this poem sets out a system of 'memoria' on a miniature scale through the repetition of the first line of each five-line stanza as the last line of that same stanza. The notion of the 'plainte' is a typical mournful topos which vocalises the strain of loss or death, but the effectiveness of the topos is called into question. Where Gautier in a 'Lamento' had been content to tell of a 'blanche tombe / Où flotte avec un son plaintif / L'ombre d'un if' ['white tomb / Where flutters with a

---

[35]   Lamartine had already used this expression of a 'voix argentine', also rhyming with 'enfantine' (which Baudelaire uses as a preceding rhyme word in v.21 and 25 of 'Mœsta et errabunda'). In 'Le premier regret' from the fourth book of *Harmonies poétiques et réligieuses* Lamartine writes: 'Son pas insouciant ... // ... courait pour courir; et sa voix argentine / Écho limpide et pur de son âme enfantine, / Musique de cet âme où tout semblait chanter / Egayait jusqu'à l'air qui l'entendait monter!' (v.62–67). ['His insouciant step ... // ... ran for the sake of running; and his silvery voice / Limpid and pure echo of his childish soul, / Music of this soul in which everything seemed to sing / Enlivened even the air which heard it rise!'] Alphonse de Lamartine, *Œuvres poétiques complètes* (Paris: Gallimard, 1963), p.469.

[36]   This evidently, once again, allies the 'actio' and 'memoria' elements of rhetorical practice outlined in my first chapter.

plaintive sound / The shadow of a yew tree'] (v.1–3) and of being able to 'Écouter la pâle colombe / Chanter, sur la branche de l'if, / Son chant plaintif!' ['Hear the sound of the pale dove / Singing, on the branch of the yew tree, / Its plaintive song!'] (v.34–36) hinting that 'On sent lentement revenir / Un souvenir' ['One hears slowly returning / A memory'] (v.20–21), Baudelaire calls into question the purpose of the 'plainte' suggesting that the topos has become clichéd and ineffectual.[37] This is, of course, exactly what Baudelaire had done with the rhetorical question of the second stanza which calls into question why the sea is typically personified as a 'berceuse' (v.9). So just as the 'amours enfantines' (v.21 and 25) of 'l'innocent paradis plein de plaisirs furtifs' (v.26 and 30) that Baudelaire considers reviving are in fact now outmoded, lost or dead, so too are the metaphorical topoi that he exploits in the poem.

The balancing act between outmoded topoi or conventional textual designations and effective poetic language is enacted through the relationship between voice, memory and poetic language. Poetic language will be ineffective if it over-uses traditional topoi or conventions because the reading voice can access the memory of such topoi or conventions too readily. By calling into question the rhetorical effect of outmoded language and ideals, Baudelaire places a greater responsibility on his reader to seek out new 'plaisirs furtifs' that are not beholden to tired clichés. The response to the rhetorical question posed in the final stanza of this poem – if there can be any at all – is that 'cris plaintifs' and a 'voix argentine' (v.28–29) will not revive tired, past 'plaisirs furtifs', but will create new pleasures (perhaps the pleasure elicited by poetic language itself). In this way, the manifold 'plaisirs furtifs' remain ephemeral and clandestine, just like the 'response' that is formulated by the reader to the rhetorical question itself. Using one's voice in order to revive memories becomes a perennial game of questions and answers which must not become stultified into traditional topoi, but which must be furtive in their rapidity and transience. This is, after all, a poem entitled 'Mœsta et errabunda' which translates as 'Triste et vagabonde' ['Sad and vagabond'], and Baudelaire sought to 'Glorifier le vagabondage' ['Glorify vagabondage'] (B.*OC*.I, p.701) and find a reviving force in the 'Fugitive beauté' ['Fugivite beauty'] (v.9) of 'A une passante' (B.*OC*.I, pp.92–93). The effects of using one's voice through poetry are themselves transient, but this does not mean that they are not lasting. The iterability of the poetic text means that on each encounter with a poem, new voices, new pleasures and new memories are brought to life through a process of exchange, each time reviving a past voice, yet each time in a new guise.

Remembering Conversations: Response and Responsibility

If Baudelaire, in 'Mœsta et errabunda', questions whether the voices of poetic language are able to re-evoke memories of a childhood past, Mallarmé answers that

---

[37] Théophile Gautier, 'Poésies diverses' in *Poésies complètes*, ed. by René Jasinski, 3 vols (Paris: Nizet, 1970), II, pp.179–180.

question in 'Apparition' (M.*OC*.I, p.7) with the image of the 'enfant gâté' (v.14) and again in the prose poem 'Réminiscence' (originally entitled 'L'Orphelin'). The two very different versions of this prose poem – the first, 'L'Orphelin' (M.*OC*.I, pp.445–446) was published initially in *La Revue des lettres et des arts* in November 1867, and the revised version, 'Réminiscence' (M.*OC*.I, p.423) was published in *Le Chat noir* in 1889 – not only portray what seems to be a childhood memory, but portray it in two very different forms, the earlier version being much less elliptical than the later 1880s version. Mallarmé revives voices of the past by recounting a conversation, but each time it appears in a different guise – not just because the words are different, but because the effect of those words is different on each recounting. Like Baudelaire, the appeal of transience is powerful, as Mallarmé recounts in 'Réminiscence': 'j'aimais le parfum des vagabonds' ['I liked the fragrance of vagabonds']. The 'je' of the poem is the 'orphelin' ['orphan'], who, according to the earlier version was an 'enfant avec tristesse pressentant le Poète' ['child with a sadness pre-empting that of the Poet']. The noise-scape of this poem is theatrical, but of the most transitory kind, being set within the context of a travelling band of players. Whereas in 'L'Orphelin' the theatrical setting is made explicit by a variety of vocabulary ('ces comédiens', 'planches', 'tréteaux' ['these actors', 'boards', 'stage']), 20 years later in 'Réminiscence' the description is somewhat more terse ('le drame' ['the drama']). Where in the earlier version the sound of what is going on on stage is transmitted both to the poetic 'je' and to the reader, in 'Réminiscence', these personæ are transposed into a negative 'aucun […], ni'. In remembering the voices of the theatre, Mallarmé misremembers, and re-transcribes the voices in a new iteration in the later version:

'L'Orphelin'	**'Réminiscence'**
Par les planches m'arrivaient, brise ancienne des chœurs, des voix d'enfants maudissant un tyran, avec de grêles tirades, car Thalie habitait la tente et attendait l'heure sainte des quinquets. Je rôdais devant ces tréteaux, orgueilleux, et plus tremblant de la pensée de parler à un enfant trop jeune pour jouer parmi ses frères […]. L'enfant, je le vois toujours, coiffé d'un bonnet de nuit taillé comme le chaperon du Dante.	Aucun cri de chœurs par la déchirure, ni tirade loin, le drame requérant l'heure sainte des quinquets, je souhaitais de parler avec un môme trop vacillant pour figurer parmi sa race, au bonnet de nuit taillé comme le chaperon de Dante.

[Across the boards came to me, ancient breeze of choirs, the voices of children cursing a tyrant, with reedy declamations, because Thalia was living in the tent and was waiting for the sacred hour of the oil lamps. I prowled around the stage, proud, and trembling more at the thought of speaking to a child who was too young to play amongst his brothers [...]. The child, I can still see him, wearing a night cap cut in the style of Dante's hood.]

[No cry of choirs by way of rupture, nor any far off declamation, the drama requiring the sacred hour of the oil lamps, I wanted to speak to a kid who was too unsteady to feature amongst his peers, wearing a night cap cut in the style of Dante's hood.]

The desire on the part of the young poetic 'je' to speak to one of the children remains in both versions: this child is, however, a precarious interlocutor because he is a misfit, an outsider within the context of other children. The transposition from the more direct description of 'un enfant trop jeune pour jouer parmi ses frères' to the more indirect and succinct 'un môme trop vacillant pour figurer parmi sa race' reinforces the instability of the child's position. Mallarmé is at pains to reduce the stability of his poetic subjects so that when the child speaks it is removed from any originary subject and granted instead the instable textual subjectivity of language.

Mallarmé's memory of language, like each of his readers' memory of language, is governed by this instability, so that in the reworked version of the late 1880s, the textual presentation of the conversation between the child and the young poetic 'je' is significantly less colloquial. The change in register between the versions, the first of which predates Mallarmé's notes on language composed in 1869–1870, reminds us of Mallarmé's struggle in 'Conflit' to find the appropriate register for his poetic conversations:

'L'Orphelin'

Il était tout nu dans un maillot lavé, et pirouettait avec une turbulence surprenante; ce fut lui qui m'adressa la parole: '– Où sont tes parents? – Je n'en ai pas, lui dis-je. – Ah! tu n'as pas de père? moi, j'en ai un. Si tu savais comme c'est amusant, un père, ça rit toujours ...'

'Réminiscence'

Nu, pirouetter dans sa prestesse de maillot à mon avis surprenante, lui, qui d'ailleurs commença: 'Tes parents? – Je n'en ai pas. – Allons, si tu savais comme c'est farce, un père ...'

[He was completely naked in a clean vest, and he pirouetted with a surprising turbulence; it was he who spoke to me: 'Where are your parents? – I don't have any, I said to him. – Ah ! you do not have a father ? as for me, I have one. If you knew how fun they are, fathers, it's always a laugh a minute ...']

[Naked, to pirouette in his borrowed vest to my mind surprising, he, who moreover started: 'Your parents? – I don't have any. – Come on, if you knew how entertaining it is to have a father ...']

This seems, on the surface, to be an exercise in developing elliptical language, but it also highlights the way in which Mallarmé's developments in language over the course of his career affect his poetic voices. Again, he seems to misremember the conversation, giving in the later version a much more succinct rendering. Even though, when the child moves on to asking the poetic 'je' about his mother, there are fewer alterations in the text, there are still some apparent memory slips, or at least Mallarmé is content to give a new iteration of the original version:

'L'Orphelin'

'– Et de ta maman, tu n'en as pas non plus, que tu es tout seul? La mienne mange de la filasse et tout le monde tape des mains. Tu ne connais pas cela, toi. Voilà, des parents sont des gens drôles qui nous font rire.'

['– And as for your mother, you don't have one either, so you are all alone? Mine eats cast-off threads and everyone claps their hands. You, you don't know what it's all about. So there you go, parents are fun people who make us laugh.']

'Réminiscence'

'Ta maman, tu n'en as pas, peut-être, que tu es seul? la mienne mange de la filasse et tout le monde bat des mains. Tu ne sais rien, des parents sont des gens drôles, qui font rire.'

['Your mother, you don't have one, perhaps, then, you are alone? mine eats cast-off threads and everyone claps their hands. You don't know anything, parents are fun people, who make you laugh.']

Notwithstanding these alterations in the later version, the effect of this conversation remains the same: the poetic 'je' feels 'triste' ['sad'] ('L'Orphelin') and 'déçu' ['disappointed'] ('Réminiscence') because he is still without parents.

In contrast to the prolixity of the other child, the 'orphelin' speaks only the words 'Je n'en ai pas' (which remains the same in both versions). The poetic 'je' himself has remembered his conversational reply only too well, where the other child's boast about his own parents have undergone transformations as the memory of his exact words in the mind of the 'orphelin' falters. It would be erroneous to suggest that Mallarmé's own memory has faltered in the retelling: one can only assume that in re-writing, he had the original version to hand. The supposed 'misremembering' of the (fictitious) children's conversation, then, is a conscious effort of alteration and refinement which exploits the ephemerality of language. The conversational exchange in 'L'Orphelin' and 'Réminiscence' creates, in both instances, a lasting impression, even though the actual words of the exchange have undergone a transformation. Is this, then, what Mallarmé means when he claims in his 1869–1870 notes on language that conversation is 'le procédé essentiel du Langage, qui est d'abstraire' ['the essential process of Language, which is to abstract'] (M.*OC*.I, p.509)? Being able to abstract the essential effect of language from a conversational exchange suggests that Mallarmé's aesthetics of voice relies on a poetic exchange which can be reiterated, modified and misremembered. The emotion – the 'effet produit' or 'sensation' perhaps – remains the same, but the language is altered.

If the response of the young poetic 'je' in 'L'Orphelin' / 'Réminiscence' indicates that a conversation's effect is inevitable (irrespective of the precise words spoken), then this suggests that the process of exchange established through poetry is one which moves beyond the meaning of the words on the page, towards the effect that they are able to create (with the implication that different words, or different ways of reading or pronouncing words, will still be able to elicit the same effect). This brings us back to the question of rhetoric: in constructing their poetic narrative, are Baudelaire and Mallarmé driven solely by the response or effect that they wish to create? The persuasive force of a conversational interlocutor can contain a certain inevitability of conversational response. Baudelaire in particular is all too aware of how to manipulate rhetorical rules to subvert or ironise the ultimate outcome. In 'L'Avertisseur' (B.*OC*.I, p.140), for example, Baudelaire not only demonstrates a petulant refusal to do his duty, but he also refuses to adhere to the rules of sonnet form, by opening and closing with quatrains, and placing the tercets in the centre of the poem.[38] The opening quatrain implies that the voice of good battles against the voice of evil, but the response will always be the same:

> Tout homme digne de ce nom
> A dans le cœur un Serpent jaune,
> Installé comme sur un trône,
> Qui, s'il dit: 'Je veux!' répond: 'Non!' (v.1–4)

> [Any man worthy of this name
> Has in his heart a yellow Serpent,
> Installed there as on a throne,
> Who, if he says: 'I want!' replies: 'No!']

In 'Le Rebelle' (B.*OC*.I, p.139), the Baudelairean 'je' eschews the demands of the 'bon Ange' ['good Angel'] (v.4) who reminds him '"Tu connaîtras la règle!"' ['"You knew the rule!"'] (v.3). Where the angel had stated at the end of the first quatrain '"Je le veux!"', the Baudelairean 'je' vehemently responds in the closing words of the poem '"Je ne veux pas!"'. This response is inevitable (due in part to the inevitable necessity of the rhyme which closes the poem). The persuasive force of the angel's argument in the second quatrain and first tercet which demands that the 'mécréant' ['heathen'] (v.2) should love 'Le pauvre, le méchant, le tortu, l'hébété' ['The poor man, the evil man, the cripple, the idiot'] (v.6) is not only ineffective, but will always be ineffective, since 'le damné répond toujours: "Je ne veux pas!"' ['the damned soul always replies "I don't want to!"'] (v.14). The adverb 'toujours' emphasises that, even knowing the rules of the persuasive conversational game, the Baudelairean 'je' will always refuse to play the game that is expected of him.

---

[38]   This is the only instance of this particular irregularity in Baudelaire's use of sonnet form.

The inevitability and unalterability of Baudelaire's conversational responses, like Mallarmé's 'orphelin', suggest that once a response has been given, the poet is beholden to it. In another poem published in the 1866 *Le Parnasse contemporain* alongside 'L'Avertisseur' and 'Le Rebelle', entitled 'La Voix' (B.*OC*.I, p.170), Baudelaire reinforces this notion, namely that when responding within a conversational exchange, the respondent must take responsibility for this action. In 'La Voix', Baudelaire answers with an affirmative 'Oui!' (v.14) to the temptations proffered by 'Deux voix' (v.5), and even though he later regrets this response, the act of saying yes carries with it an unavoidable responsibility:

> Deux voix me parlaient. L'une, insidieuse et ferme,
> Disait: 'La Terre est un gâteau plein de douceur;
> Je puis (et ton plaisir serait alors sans terme!)
> Te faire un appétit d'une égale grosseur.'
> Et l'autre: 'Viens! oh! viens voyager dans les rêves,
> Au-delà du possible, au-delà du connu!'
> Et celle-là chantait comme le vent des grèves,
> Fantôme vagissant, on ne sait d'où venu,
> Qui caresse l'oreille et cependant l'effraie.
> Je te répondis: 'Oui! douce voix!' C'est d'alors
> Que date ce qu'on peut, hélas! nommer ma plaie
> Et ma fatalité. (v.5–16)

> [Two voices were speaking to me. One, insidious and steadfast,
> Said: 'The Earth is a gâteau full of sweetness;
> I can (and your pleasure would therefore be without end!)
> Give you an appetite of the same size.'
> And the other: 'Come! oh! come and travel into the dreams,
> Beyond the possible, beyond what is known!'
> And that one sang like the offshore wind,
> Wandering ghost, who knows from whence it came,
> Who caresses the ear and nonetheless frightens it.
> I replied to you: 'Yes! sweet voice!' And it's from that day
> That dates what can be called, alas, my scourge
> And my fate.]

The 'fatalité' of replying with a 'yes' is rendered all the more poignant by the initial context that is set by the poem: the poetic 'je' in this poem is still a child ('Mon berceau s'adossait à la bibliothèque' ['My cradle backed onto the library'] v.1), and even though his response may have been naïve, it remains unalterable – and, like Mallarmé's 'orphelin', Baudelaire remembers all too well the response given in this (fictitious) conversation. The child – now grown into the poet who recounts this conversation in verse – must carry the responsibility of saying 'yes' to the voice's temptations, even though he is unable to specify who his interlocutor was (the voices remain abstract with no further indication as to who or what might be speaking to the poet). The injustice of this responsibility is nevertheless accepted, and Baudelaire uses it as a justification for his poetic artifice which subverts traditional expectations:[39]

> Et c'est depuis ce temps que, pareil aux prophètes,
> J'aime si tendrement le désert et la mer;
> Que je ris dans les deuils et pleure dans les fêtes,
> Et trouve un goût suave au vin le plus amer;
> Que je prends très souvent les faits pour des mensonges,
> Et que, les yeux au ciel, je tombe dans des trous. (v.21–26)

> [And it is since this time that, like prophets,
> I love the desert and the sea so tenderly;
> That I laugh at funerals and cry at festivals,
> And find a sweet taste in the most bitter of wines;
> That I often mistake facts for lies,
> And that, eyes to the heavens, I fall into holes.]

In maintaining responsibility for the response he gave to the 'voix', Baudelaire also absorbs into his own voice the voices of the 'voix' who spoke to him, since they, too, are responsible for his 'fatalité'. The implication for the reader is that if he or she also replies with a 'yes' to the challenge of Baudelaire's poetic perversity, then they will also be able to absorb his voice into their own.

By contrast, in the prose poem 'Les Tentations' (B.*OC*.I, pp.307–310), Baudelaire regrets turning down the temptations proffered by 'Deux superbes Satans et une Diablesse' ['Two magnificent Satans and a female Devil']. He takes responsibility for the fact that after rejecting the seemingly persuasive temptations of the three spiritual figures, he is unable to change his reply (even though he tries to). In particular, the voice of the female 'diablesse' – the last to speak – is especially enticing with 'sa voix charmante et paradoxale' ['her charming and paradoxical voice'], and the Baudelairean 'je' is tempted into subjugation by the way she cries out his name. Yet he rejects her, if only then in the following instant to regret his decision:

> Certes, d'une si courageuse abnégation j'avais le droit d'être fier. Mais malheureusement je me réveillai, et toute ma force m'abandonna. 'En vérité, me dis-je, il fallait que je fusse bien lourdement assoupi pour montrer de tels scrupules. Ah! s'ils pouvaient revenir pendant que je suis éveillé, je ne ferais pas tant le délicat!'

---

[39] This passage resonates with the penultimate stanza of 'L'Héautontimorouménos' which I analyse at the beginning of Chapter 5.

Et je les invoquai à haute voix, les suppliant de me pardonner, leur offrant de
me déshonorer aussi souvent qu'il le faudrait pour mériter leurs faveurs. (B.*OC*.
I, p.310)

[Of course, I had the right to be proud of such a courageous self-sacrifice. But
unfortunately I woke up, and all my willpower left me. 'In truth, I told myself,
I had to be particularly drowsy to show such scruples. Ah! if they could come
back when I am awake, I would not be so fussy!'
  And I invoked them out loud, begging them to forgive me, offering to
dishonour myself as often as was necessary in order to merit their favours.]

The attempt to change his reply comes too late: in the waking hours after his
rêverie, the devils have disappeared and cannot be invoked or persuaded to appear
again, even though Baudelaire calls out loud to them (itself an inappropriate way
of addressing them, since they had conversed with him in the mind of his rêverie).
This emphasises the ephemerality of the conversational moment, and explains
why the initial response cannot be altered: the transient moment of conversation
has past (even though it is remembered and reiterated through poetry).

The model of conversational exchange and its inherent transience – even
though it is recorded through poetry – leads both poets to explore the issue of
response. Baudelaire does this especially through his extensive use of rhetorical
questions which thwart conversational exchanges (but which still allow for a
resonant response on the part of the reader), and through his refusal to be swayed
by persuasive rhetoric in other instances; Mallarmé does this through his refusal
to debase poetic language by the use of a colloquial register, and through his
increasing dislocation of subjectivity and voice which destabilises the status of his
conversational protagonists. These various strategies for disrupting conversational
response suggest that both poets actively exploit the threat of incommunicability,
where a particular party to a conversational exchange may fail to take on board
what other voices suggest. By refusing to be swayed by expectation – in the form of
poetic conventions, the rules of conversation, techniques of rhetorical persuasion,
or a moral code – both poets take responsibility for their own voices, and begin
to revel in the prospect that even when other voices (in the form of other poetic
protagonists, or even of the reader) infiltrate their own voices, a certain level of
control is nevertheless carefully maintained.

Chapter 5
'Voix étranges'

È un destino che i pareri de' poeti non siano ascoltati.
[It is fate that poets' opinions are never listened to.]

Alessandro Manzoni, *I promessi sposi*[1]

We speak them all with no apparent anguish,
We speak them all, whatever the language.[2]

The threat posed by strange or foreign voices is one which both Baudelaire and Mallarmé tackle head-on. In certain instances, they are overcome by the fear that their own voices might be subjugated, silenced or lost, at other times they actively seek to take on strange voices. Strategies of personification are rife in Baudelaire's poetry with this end in view; in Mallarmé there is a more self-conscious awareness of how strange voices affect his poetic output. The quality of 'strangeness' – so frequently coupled with an acknowledgement of mortality and human transience in the work of both poets – is not simply a symptom of both poets' indebtedness to the world of the fantastic and extraordinary that Poe inhabited, but is also the mark of a gamble that each poet takes. The more strange or foreign a voice, the greater the potential, surely, for removing that voice from the realm of inevitable mortality. The hope is that by rendering a voice more abstract, there is a greater possibility of achieving a resonant longevity through poetry. The gamble is an uncertain and unbalanced one, and each poet recognises, it seems, that giving over his own voice to more foreign, strange and abstract voices is not a sure guarantee of poetic success, not least of all because the more foreign a voice, the greater also the possibility for failure to elicit any response.

Infiltration, Threats and 'Memoria'

In Baudelaire's 'L'Héautontimorouménos' (B.*OC*.I, pp.78–79), the poetic 'je' is angered by the infiltration of the monster's ironic voice, and senses that his own voice is weakened:

---

[1]   Alessandro Manzoni, *I Promessi sposi* (La Spezia: Fratelli Melita Editori, 1994), p.414.

[2]   From a childhood memory. 'In the throes of his language-anguish, the poet of "Le Démon de l'analogie" gives voice to ... silent words, brings them to life by "revisiting" their potential.' Roger Pearson, *Unfolding Mallarmé* (Oxford: Clarendon, 1996), p.80.

Ne suis-je pas un faux accord
Dans la divine symphonie,
Grâce à la vorace Ironie
Qui me secoue et qui me mord?

Elle est dans ma voix, la criarde!
C'est tout mon sang, ce poison noir! (v.13–18)

[Am I not a note of dissonance
In the divine symphony,
Thanks to voracious Irony
Who shakes me and who bites me?

She is in my voice, the shrieker!
All of my blood is this black poison!]

The negativity of the 'faux accord' is transformed into a powerful positive in the penultimate stanza which, with its series of antitheses which recall the passage from 'La Voix' analysed above, suggests that the discordant tones of the voice of irony, 'la criarde', have reinforced Baudelaire's own voice so that he can cry out:[3]

Je suis la plaie et le couteau!
Je suis le soufflet et la joue!
Je suis les membres et la roue,
Et la victime et le bourreau! (v.21–24)

[I am the wound and the knife!
I am the slap and the cheek!
I am the limbs and the wheel,
Both victim and executioner!]

The reinforcement of his own voice by the voice of irony does not compare with the rich resonance that Baudelaire senses by absorbing the voice of a cat in 'Le Chat (LI)' (B.*OC*.I, pp.50–51) which fills him 'comme un vers nombreux' ['like a well-formed verse'] (v.11). The first section of the poem – which consists of six octosyllabic quatrains, notwithstanding Baudelaire's simile which invokes the 'vers nombreux' of the alexandrine line – is a eulogy to the cat's voice and the power that this grants to the poetic voice (the second section which I do not intend to analyse here focuses on the cat's eyes):

---

³   See Chapter 4, pp.156–157, for an analysis of 'La Voix'.

Dans ma cervelle se promène
Ainsi qu'en son appartement,
Un beau chat, fort, doux et charmant.
Quand il miaule, on l'entend à peine,

Tant son timbre est tendre et discret;
Mais que sa voix s'apaise ou gronde,
Elle est toujours riche et profonde.
C'est là son charme et son secret.

Cette voix, qui perle et qui filtre
Dans mon fonds le plus ténébreux,
Me remplit comme un vers nombreux
Et me réjouit comme un philtre.

Elle endort les plus cruels maux
Et contient toutes les extases;
Pour dire les plus longues phrases,
Elle n'a pas besoin de mots.

Non, il n'est pas d'archet qui morde
Sur mon cœur, parfait instrument,
Et fasse plus royalement
Chanter sa plus vibrante corde,

Que ta voix, chat mystérieux,
Chat séraphique, chat étrange,
En qui tout est, comme en un ange,
Aussi subtil qu'harmonieux! (v.1–24)

[In my head there walks
As though in his apartment
A handsome, strong, sweet and charming cat.
When he meows, you can hardly hear it,

So tender and discreet is the timbre;
But whether his voice is calm or growling,
It is always rich and deep.
That is its charm and its secret.

This voice, which forms into droplets and trickles
Down into the most shadowy depths of my being,
Completes me like a well-formed verse
And delights me like a philtre.

It puts to rest the most cruel evils
And contains all possible ecstasies;
In order to say the longest sentences,
It does not need words.

No, there is no other bow which draws
Across my heart, perfect instrument,
And is able to make most royally
Sing its most resonant string,

Than your voice, mysterious cat,
Seraphic cat, strange cat,
In whom everything is, like in an angel,
As subtle as it is harmonious.]

In all of Baudelaire's work, this is the most extended and detailed description of a voice. Although the precise circumstances of composition are unknown, it was included in the 1857 *Fleurs du Mal*, and seems to have been inspired by the cat belonging to Baudelaire's mistress of the time, Marie Daubrun. Irrespective of whether this poem tells of a real cat or not, the fact that the cat's voice encompasses 24 lines of poetry suggests that Baudelaire is not only aware of the effect that the cat's voice had on him in order to inspire his poem, but he is also aware of the effect that the poetic cat's voice can have on his reader. Three important features of the cat's voice derive from this description: it is an internal, imaginary voice ('Dans ma cervelle' v.1), it presents itself differently at different moments in time ('que sa voix s'apaise ou gronde' v.6), and it is non-verbal ('Pour dire les plus longues phrases, / Elle n'a pas besoin de mots' v.15–16). The implications of these particular vocal attributes for Baudelaire's own poetics reveal themselves over the course of his poetic career, and especially as he considers the influence of music and the effects that this has on his own aesthetics of voice. As Margaret Miner has suggested, the cat's voice in the first section of the poem 'inspires the poet, playing on his heart like a bow on a string, so that the music pent up inside the poet's mind may eventually be released and heard by others'.[4]

That the cat infiltrates Baudelaire's own voice is made explicit in the opening two lines of the poem: the figure of the cat navigates its way through Baudelaire's mind 'ainsi qu'en son appartement' (v.2) prompting the poet to recall and to express the effects of its voice. This image of the cat walking through the compartments of Baudelaire's mind is strongly resonant of the rhetorical tradition of 'memoria': in classical rhetoric, an orator was trained to mentally navigate through the rooms of a house, recalling the ideas, words or images he had placed in each part in order

---

[4]   Margaret Miner, 'Fur in My Brain: "Le Chat"', in *Understanding* Les Fleurs du Mal*: Critical Readings*, ed. by William J. Thompson (Nashville and London: Vanderbilt University Press, 1997), p.98.

to re-extract them and use them in his own discourse. Baudelaire uses the literary conceit of portraying the cat as his navigator: the duality of the cat's position is that he is both an imaginary construction created by Baudelaire (thereby granting responsibility for the poem to Baudelaire) and he is also Baudelaire's muse (thereby granting responsibility for the poem to the cat). The cat's voice is both inherent and extraneous to Baudelaire. The quiet dynamic of the cat's meowing as its voice is introduced to the poem for the first time in the last line of the first stanza makes it difficult to hear ('on l'entend à peine' v.4). The implication is that an astute listener (notably Baudelaire himself) will be able to grasp the cat's conversation. By listening carefully the cat's voice transmits its manifold qualities, expressed by a dual aspect in each of the four lines of the second stanza ('tendre' / 'discret' v.5, 's'apaise' / 'gronde' v.6, 'riche' / 'profonde' v.7, 'charme' / 'secret' v.8). The infiltration of the cat's voice is slow-paced ('qui perle et qui filtre' v.9) and fulfilling ('me remplit' v.11, 'me réjouit' v.12): the parallel structures of this poem take their time to appear, but seem to fulfil expectations. In fact, the implications of this poem go beyond the words on the page themselves, to offer instead an aesthetic interpretation.

What strikes the Baudelairean 'je' about the cat's voice is its non-verbal, musical properties and effects. In stark contrast to the image that Mallarmé posited in his 1867 letter to Léfebure of the chanterelle-squeak of the violin 'dont le son ne réconforte pas dans la boîte' ['the sound of which does not consolidate the body'] (M.*OC*.I, p.720), the voice of the cat resonates fully with the instrument of Baudelaire's heart in the fifth stanza of the poem. This resonance is possible because the cat is unhindered by words (Baudelaire hints at this hindrance by rhyming 'mots' v.16 with 'maux' v.13), and so is able to communicate in a language that goes beyond that of the poem itself. That the cat is 'mystérieux', 'séraphique' and, fundamentally, 'étrange' (v.21–22) implies that it is precisely because of its foreign tongue that it is able to create such a profound effect on the Baudelairean 'je'. The close relationship between being able to comprehend a foreign tongue and exploiting the resonances of the memory forms an important part of Baudelaire's aesthetics of voice. Although any actual moment of the cat 'speaking' to Baudelaire has passed, he is able to exploit his memory – through the imagination – to recollect the effect of the cat's voice. He does not, as he does elsewhere, personify the cat and grant it a speaking voice, but demonstrates that even without words (or precisely because it is without words), the cat is able to communicate with him in an entirely foreign tongue.

The conceit that Baudelaire – in his capacity as a poet – is able to comprehend all languages is reinforced in 'L'Horloge' (B.*OC*.I, p.81) which closes the 'Spleen et idéal' section of *Les Fleurs du Mal*. The temporality of a voice's effect (and therefore the role of the memory in using voice) becomes the central focus of the poem. 'Je suis Autrefois' ['I am Times past'] whispers the voice of the second-hand, speaking 'avec sa voix / D'insecte' ['in its insect-like voice'] (v.10–11). Time's voice, as the time passes by all too rapidly, also takes on many different tongues. Like the apostles at Pentecost (and the religious analogy is no doubt intended by Baudelaire), the 'Horloge' cries out:

> Remember! Souviens-toi, prodigue! Esto memor!
> (Mon gosier de métal parle toutes les langues.) (v.13–14)

> [Remember! Souviens-toi, spendthrift! Esto memor!
> (My metal throat speaks all languages.)]

Whatever the language, the message of time passing is an enduring and self-reflexive one: 'remember', time says, 'that time passes'. The passing of time is a preoccupation for Baudelaire as the self-acclaimed poet of modernity who endeavours to apprehend the eternally transcendent (expressed in the opening line of the poem by the appellation of a 'dieu sinistre' ['sinister god']) within the ephemeral (expressed by the numerous motifs of passing time).[5] And in order to do this, Baudelaire's own voice takes on (or is infiltrated by) the voice of time, thereby exploring what role memory must play in the poetic act.[6] The refrain 'Souviens-toi' is reiterated five times throughout the six-stanza poem, italicised each time as a salient reminder that the call to remember is one that is persistently brought to voice by the poem. Furthermore, this refrain is translated and iterated into the surplus reminders of the English 'Remember' and the Latin 'Esto memor' (v.13). These mutations of the refrain – which come at the central line of the poem – remind the reader that a repetitive refrain can become meaningless if recited without understanding. The introduction of foreign tongues – and the ensuing declaration that the Baudelairean voice of the clock is fluent in every language – not only disrupts the repetition but paradoxically reinforces the meaning of the refrain 'souviens-toi' by drawing attention to their strangeness. This is not a strategy that

---

[5]   Referring, once again to Baudelaire's section on 'La Modernité' in 'Le Peintre de la vie moderne': 'Il s'agit … de tirer l'éternel du transitoire' ['It is a question of … extracting the eternal from the transitory'] (B.*OC*.II, p.694).

[6]   Hiddleston perceives the role of memory as being able to transcend the idea of time passing: 'By spreading out over the three dimensions of past, present, and future, memory brings about a transfiguration of time, which loses its threat, its uncertainties, and its irreversibility. Through the enchantment of memory, the poet finds himself in a time which is, so to speak, circular.' J.A. Hiddleston, *Baudelaire and the Art of Memory* (Oxford: Clarendon, 1999), p.95. Considering Baudelaire's attitude towards time, such as in 'Le Goût du Néant' (B.*OC*.I, p.76): 'Et le Temps m'engloutit minute par minute' ['And Times swallows me up minute by minute'] (v.11); or in 'Enivrez-vous' (B.*OC*.I, p.337): 'Pour ne pas sentir l'horrible fardeau du Temps qui brise vos épaules et vous penche vers la terre, il faut vous enivrer sans trêve' ['In order not to feel the terrible burden of Time which weighs on your shoulders and makes you bend towards the ground, you need to get drunk without ceasing'], demonstrates that the issue of memory is less about circularity, and more about the imperative urgency of recording a poetic idea before its moment has past, in order that it might then be recalled and reiterated through each reading of a poem.

Baudelaire typically employs in his poetry, and both the central positioning and the italicisation of the foreign versions which enclose the 'Souviens-toi' suggest that being able to take on the strange voices is imperative to being able to create a lasting effect. That Baudelaire incorporates foreign words into the verse line by granting them a syllabic value reinforces the status of strange voices in Baudelaire's poetic aesthetic.

Baudelaire incorporates a range of speech acts within this poem by personifying not only the clock (who is apostrophised in the first word of the poem), but also time (v.17) and the second hand (v.9). Each abstract protagonist is granted a voice. The voice of the second hand is able to say the words 'Je suis Autrefois' because it is a voice that is acutely aware of its own transience. The brevity of the voice's presence is able to be recorded in poetry, subverting its transience and establishing a means of being able to endure. The moment of disappearance becomes a moment of memory. However, memory itself equally risks becoming transient, and it is only through the work of an agent of memory, here called a 'mortel folâtre' ['playful mortal'] (v.15), that anything of worth can be extracted ('extraire l'or' ['to extract gold'] v.16).[7] The mortal being in question is the figure of the poet, the gold is his poetry. The poetic act, for Baudelaire, is profoundly engaged in creating a lasting and valuable memory of a fleeting moment. Poetry must take hold of voices at the very moment that they are vanishing – even when that vanishing point is the ultimate vanishing point of death (the poet is, after all, 'mortel', and the voice of time reminds him in the closing line 'tout te dira: Meurs, vieux lâche! il est trop tard!' ['everything will say to you: Die, old weakling! it is too late!'] v.24). The words 'Je suis Autrefois' demonstrate that Baudelaire's strategy for capturing language at its most ephemeral – the spoken word, spoken by the voice of rapidly passing time – is necessarily a poetic strategy, because poetry is the imperishable, enduring substance that is able to speak all languages in order to be understood by all, because poetry is gold, and because golden poetry endures.[8]

---

[7]   'The transmutation of the mud of reality into the gold of poetry … is … for many the essential characteristic of Baudelaire's lyricism.' Hiddleston, *Baudelaire and the Art of Memory*, p.255.

[8]   See also Baudelaire's draft 'Épilogue' for the 1861 edition of *Les Fleurs du Mal* which concludes: 'Tu m'as donné ta boue et j'en ai fait de l'or' ['You gave me muck and I turned it into gold'] (B.*OC*.I, p.192). The importance of 'or' to Mallarmé's poetics has been analysed by numerous critics, but as Pearson reminds us, the importance of a value system within the context of the poet's mortality lead Mallarmé to extract as much as is possible from words: 'Revaluation, not devaluation, is the aim – and achievement – of the Mallarméan verbal economy. … Like Poe, he wanted above all to "Donner un sens plus pur aux mots de la tribu" ("Le Tombeau d'Edgar Poe") – and this in the name of Beauty certainly, but also in the name of Truth. It may be a cliché to say that poetry restores the worn-out currency of everyday language; but it is not yet commonplace to say that, for Mallarmé, literature – "Poetry" – safeguards our ability to talk truthfully – as well as beautifully – about the things that matter in our everyday lives during the countdown to

Death and Disappearing Acts ('en "voix" de disparition')

The strangeness of the clock which speaks in Baudelaire's poem and its ominous reminder of the poet's mortality also signals an important aesthetic tenet. Once the poet himself has disappeared (whether through death, or whether because he is no longer present in the written page), the strange voices of his poetry are still able to converse with the reader. The Renaissance conceit of safeguarding immortality by creating a poetic memorial to a mistress is one that Baudelaire exploits to this end in 'Je te donne ces vers' (B.*OC*.I, pp.40–41).[9] Although, in the quatrains, Baudelaire claims that his poetry will serve her memory, in the tercets, he reclaims his own immortality by suggesting that he is the only one capable of understanding her: 'rien, hors moi, ne répond' ['nothing, apart from me, responds'] (v.10). Baudelaire's ability to resonate with the memory of his mistress (in this instance, probably Jeanne Duval) is the unique domain of the poet. The mistress is always dependent on Baudelaire and must 'Reste comme pendue à mes rimes hautaines' ['Rest as if hanging on my haughty rhymes'] (v.8). Even though the poet may be long dead, he survives through his text in the form of his poetic voices. Yet the status of these poetic voices is still unclear because the poet assumes so many voices, which can both threaten and enrich his own. It is perhaps because of this dichotomy that Mallarmé began to theorise how the poet can disappear from the text even before he is dead, by making language speak for itself. If language is able to take on the role of the most abstract, strange and therefore anonymous voice, then the poet no longer needs to be concerned about losing his voice. Mallarmé displaces the responsibility for poetic resonance onto language itself rather than following the Baudelairean strategy of shifting responsibility onto different vocal protagonists within his poetry.

Mallarmé repeats the mantra of language speaking for itself at various points throughout his career. We have already seen Mallarmé talking to Cazalis in the late 1860s about words speaking for themselves in the 'Sonnet en *yx*', and again in the 1890s in 'Le Mystère dans les lettres'. Two further instances – one from a letter to Verlaine in 1884, and the other from the 1890s 'Crise de vers' – formulate this notion with particular reference to the disappearance of the poet himself. In the letter to Verlaine, which contains a sort of autobiography, Mallarmé claims as an aside about his collection of poetry:

> (à côté de mon travail personnel qui je crois, sera anonyme, le Texte y parlant de lui-même et sans voix d'auteur). (M.*OC*.I, p.789)

> [(alongside my personal work which I think, will be anonymous, the Text speaking for itself and without the voice of an author).]

mortality.' Roger Pearson, '"Les Chiffres et les Lettres": Mallarmé's "Or" and the Gold Standard of Poetry', *Dix-neuf*, 2 (2004), 44–60 (pp.54–55).

[9]   Of course, Mallarmé's 'tombeau' poems are also a part of this aesthetic heritage.

And in 'Crise de vers' he writes:

> L'œuvre pure implique la disparition élocutoire du poëte, qui cède l'initiative aux mots, par le heurt de leur inégalité mobilisés; ils s'allument de reflets réciproques comme une virtuelle traînée de feux sur des pierreries, remplaçant la respiration perceptible en l'ancien souffle lyrique ou la direction personnelle enthousiaste de la phrase. (M.*OC*.II, p.211)

> [The pure work implies the elocutionary disappearance of the poet, who relinquishes initiative to the words, mobilised by the clash of their inequality; they light up with reciprocal reflections like a virtual trail of light across gemstones, replacing the perceptible breathing with the old lyric breath or the enthusiastic personal direction of the phrase.]

Whilst Derrida has famously commented on the letter to Verlaine, suggesting that textual anonymity leads to a vocal or sonorous power (which Derrida calls 'phonique') rather than the power of words themselves, by reading these passages together, it becomes clear that for Mallarmé words do retain a power which is not simply due to their sonorous properties but also to their ability to silently resonate and reply across the irregular interstices of meaning.[10] The passage from 'Crise de vers' reinforces the notion that the power of words for Mallarmé goes beyond the personal intervention of the reading or writing process (together with the breathing spaces that this implies). Mallarmé's increasing dissolution of the relationship between 'voice' and 'subject' grants a paradoxically anonymous subjective potency to words themselves as the poet disappears from the text. The poet's disappearance is of a particular kind. The distinction between claiming that a poem is simply 'sans voix d'auteur' and that a poem is subject to 'la disparition élocutoire du poëte' is revealing. The poet makes his speaking voice disappear, since the poet's own personal 'élocution' or way of speaking is not important to the poetic text, and instead allows the words to speak for themselves.[11]

---

[10] See Chapter 3, recalling also the influence of Poe in his tale 'The Power of Words' which I discussed in Chapter 2. Derrida writes: 'La disparition de la "voix d'auteur" ("le Texte y parlant de lui-même et sans voix d'auteur", comme il fut confié à Verlaine) déclenche une puissance d'inscription non plus verbale mais phonique. Polyphonique. Les valeurs d'espacement vocal sont alors réglées par l'ordre de cette voix sans tain, non par l'autorité du mot ou du signifié conceptuel dont le text ne manque pas – au reste – d'user aussi à sa guise' ['The disappearance of the "voice of the author" ("the Text speaking for itself and without the voice of an author", as it was confided to Verlaine) sets off a power of inscription which is no longer verbal but phonic. Polyphonic. The values of vocal spacing are therefore regulated according to this two-way voice, not by the authority of the voice or the conceptual signified which the text does not fail – in any case – to make use of in its own way']. Jacques Derrida, *La Dissémination* (Paris: Seuil, 1972), p.368.

[11] Dayan comments on Mallarmé's use of the word 'élocutoire' in this context, suggesting that this particular term makes a distinction between 'realistic' language and

Colours, Timbres and the Time Limit of Disembodiment (1859–1864)

Mallarmé wasn't always so sure of language being able to speak for itself, however. In 'L'Azur', for example, composed in the early 1860s before he began these reflections on making language speak for itself, he, like Baudelaire, still demonstrates a concern at the threat of losing his voice in the face of infiltration by other voices. In fact, in the five-year period 1859–1864, the closeness of Baudelaire's and Mallarmé's respective attitudes towards the power which poetic voices possess to overcome the poet himself merits detailed attention. Both poets exploit the strategy of personification, which allows disembodied voices to resonate fully within their texts. The clear timbre and productive vibrancy of these disembodied voices begins to hint at the Mallarméan ideal of what it might mean for language to speak for itself.[12] In Baudelaire's article on Théophile Gautier published in *L'Artiste* in 1859, he famously expresses how poetic language allows colours to speak (for themselves):

> Manier savamment une langue, c'est pratiquer une espèce de sorcellerie évocatoire. C'est alors que la couleur parle, comme une voix profonde et vibrante. (B.*OC*.II, p.118)

> [To skilfully use a language is to practice a form of evocative sorcery. Then colour speaks, like a deep and resonant voice.]

---

poetic language: 'The word "élocutoire", which Mallarmé uses several times, seems, as far as I can tell, to be a neologism from the Latin. Doubtless, as Scherer suggests (*Grammaire de Mallarmé*, p.94), Mallarmé's affection for it is partly explicable by his general predilection for the suffix "oire"; but the word also provides a name for a most useful concept: that quality of discursiveness which is common to all "realistic" language.' Peter Dayan, *Mallarmé's 'Divine Transposition': Real and Apparent Sources of Literary Value* (Oxford: Clarendon, 1986), p.37 (footnote). I would suggest that 'élocutoire' is a specific reflection on the uncertain distinction between speaking out loud and speaking internally through poetic language, and that Mallarmé uses this term in order to distance his own personal way of speaking from that of his readers, in the hope that they will experience the same effect from language that he attains from his poetic composition. That is to say, the issue of 'élocution' or speaking is entirely bound up with Mallarmé's desire to abstract language away from the personal and subjective. This is made clear later on in 'Crise de vers' with the famous reflection on the way that, by speaking personally (through poetry), Mallarmé is able to set in motion the resonances of language itself: 'Je dis: une fleur! et, hors l'oubli où ma voix relègue aucun contour ... musicalement se lève ... l'absente de tous bouquets' ['I say: a flower! and, beyond the oblivion to which my voice relegates any contour ... musically rises up ... the absent one of all bouquets'] (M.*OC*.II, p.213).

[12]   For an analysis of the relationship between disembodied voices and pure sounds, see Ingrid Sykes, 'Sonorous Mechanics: The Culture of Sonority in Nineteenth-century France', *Nineteenth-century Music Review*, 1:1 (2004), 43–66.

The disembodied voice of colour speaks because the poetic voice allows for evocation, a word which by its very etymology (as we have seen in Chapter 3, *ex* + *vocare*) hints at a dislocation between voice and subject that is a feature of disembodiment, and also reinforces the notion that using language is part of an act of remembering (in the sense of evocation as conjuring up times past). The status of the voice of colour remains precarious because it is an allegorical representation of the voice of the poet, which is of course forever beholden to the relentless passing of time.

This relationship between the evocative potential of disembodied voices and their potential to be overcome as time passes is made clear in the prose poem 'La Chambre double' (B.*OC*.I, pp.280–282), published in *La Presse* in 1862. In the opening narrative description, Baudelaire writes:

> Les étoffes parlent une langue muette, comme les fleurs, comme les ciels, comme les soleils couchants.

> [The materials speak a silent language, like flowers, like skies, like sunsets.]

His diction here is oxymoronic. Not only does he personify 'les étoffes' and enable them to speak ('parlent'), but he also specifies that the language they speak is silent ('muette'). This oxymoronic turn seems to suggest that Baudelaire cannot quite fathom what kind of story the materials may have to tell, and this seems to represent a stumbling block in the process which grants an abstract, disembodied voice the ability to speak. The silence that it speaks is a resonant silence because it expresses the dream-like other-worldliness of the practice of 'sorcellerie évocatoire', which is able to persist because it remains out of time:

> Non! il n'est plus de minutes, il n'est plus de secondes! Le temps a disparu; c'est l'Éternité qui règne, une éternité de délices!

> [No! minutes do not exist any more, nor do seconds! Time has disappeared; it is Eternity that reigns, an eternity of delights!]

This idealisation of a language which can speak for itself and resonate silently and out of time is an illusory ideal because language always sparks a memory:

> Horreur! je me souviens! je me souviens! ... Oh! oui! le Temps a reparu; le Temps règne en souverain maintenant.

> [What horrors! I remember! I remember! ... Oh! yes! Time has reappeared; Time now reigns supreme.]

In fact, although the Baudelairean poetic 'je' in this poem had seemingly forgotten all about the oppression of time in his description of the speaking voices of 'les étoffes', his list of similes likening the speaking voices to flowers, skies and sunsets – which are all subject to natural decay – implicitly reminds the reader of the time limits involved in using (spoken) language.

Mallarmé's poem 'L'Azur' (M.*OC*.I, pp.14–15), meanwhile, which was composed initially in 1864 before being revised two years later for publication in *Le Parnasse contemporain*, exploits the same analogy of allowing disembodied voices to speak through poetry whilst yet remaining threatened by the relentless passing of time. Where Baudelaire, in his article on Gautier, perceived the voice of colour to be a productively resonant abstract voice, the ideal voice of poetry, Mallarmé grants voice to the colour 'azur' only to find his own voice threatened by the tolling of the angelus bell in the timbre of the 'L'Azur'. In the opening quatrain, the voice of irony (whose menacing infiltration of the poet's voice has already been encountered in Baudelaire's .'L'Héautontimorouménos' above) takes on the colour blue in order to 'Accable [...] / Le poëte impuissant qui maudit son génie' [Overwhelm [...] / The impotent poet who curses his genius'] (v.2–3). As the poet is overcome with impotence, the word 'l'azur' itself takes on its own voice ('il se fait voix' v.30), to the end of threatening the poet's voice with its own potency:

> En vain! l'Azur triomphe, et je l'entends qui chante
> Dans les cloches. Mon âme, il se fait voix pour plus
> Nous faire peur avec sa victoire méchante,
> Et du métal vivant sort en bleus angélus!
>
> Il roule par la brume, ancien et traverse
> Ta native agonie ainsi qu'un glaive sûr;
> Où fuir dans la révolte inutile et perverse?
> *Je suis hanté*. L'Azur! l'Azur! l'Azur! l'Azur! (v.29–36)
>
> [In vain! the Azure triumphs, and I hear him singing
> In the bells. My soul, he makes himself voice in order
> To make us more afraid with his mean victory,
> And from the living metal the angelus comes out in blue!
>
> He rolls through the fog, old and cuts through
> Your native agony like a steady double-edged sword;
> Where to escape to in the useless and perverse revolt?
> *I am haunted*. The Azure! the Azure! the Azure! the Azure!]

Like the voice of the second hand in Baudelaire's 'L'Horloge' with its 'gosier de métal' (v.14), the metallic timbre of the voice of 'l'Azur' reinforces its menacing regularity of recurrent repetition which chisels away at the poet's own weakened voice. The tolling angelus bell of 'l'Azur', like the ticking of Baudelaire's clock, is bound by time limits. The only voices that can remain in poetry are neither those of the poet, nor those of the disembodied voices he has created in his text, but the voices of language itself. The voices of language proffer the strange, foreign, abstract and disembodied timbres that allow poetry to resonate through the process of 'memoria' which is set in motion by the act of using one's voice in order to re-evoke language's latent resonances.

As Pearson comments, 'Language, for Mallarmé, "recalls" the real world and is itself a memory bank from which particular words shall be invoked'.[13] If language is indeed a memory bank of the real world, then Mallarmé finds himself, in a prose poem from the same period as 'L'Azur', 'Frisson d'hiver' (M.*OC.* I, pp.415–416), calling upon 'la grâce des choses fanées' ['the grace of faded things'] rather than 'les objets neufs' ['new objects'] with their 'hardiesse criarde' ['bawling brazenness']. The timbres of faded language – which could be likened, perhaps, to the fading hues of the image of the setting sun which is so central to the aesthetic world of both Baudelaire and Mallarmé – must remain, for Mallarmé, in conversation with current language. While calling upon the old-fashioned object of an antique Saxon clock (unsurprisingly, given the nature of Mallarmé's exploration of the relationship between the time of language, voice and meaning), Mallarmé patterns this prose poem with refrains set aside in brackets, thus establishing a close rapport between evocation of the past and the current moment of poetic language. A process of appearance and disappearance between past and present language is set in motion at the behest of Mallarmé's female protagonist:

N'as-tu pas désiré, ma sœur au regard de jadis, qu'en un de mes poèmes apparussent ces mots 'la grâce des choses fanées'?

[Did you not wish, dear sister with regard to bygones, that in one of my poems the words 'the grace of faded things' might appear?]

That this poem was originally entitled 'Causerie d'hiver' in its 1867 publication in *La Revue des lettres et des arts* reinforces the notion that poetry is founded on a model of conversation which seeks to isolate and focus on the transience of language, the in-between of its appearances and disappearances. So although the female protagonist has attained that which she desired – 'la grâce des choses fanées' – their appearance is immediately undermined by Mallarmé's insistence on the ephemerality of language. The poetic 'je' replies to the demand of his female interlocutor by promising, in the future, to speak at length of the real objects that surround them:

Viens, ferme ton vieil almanach allemand, que tu lis avec attention, bien qu'il ait paru il y a plus de cent ans et que les rois qu'il annonce soient tous morts, et, sur l'antique tapis couché, la tête appuyée parmi tes genoux charitables dans ta robe

---

[13] Roger Pearson, 'Mallarmé's Homage to Villiers de L'Isle-Adam', in *The Process of Art: Essays on Nineteenth-Century French Literature, Music and Painting in Honour of Alan Raitt*, ed. by Mike Freeman et al. (Oxford: Clarendon, 1998), p.138.

pâlie, ô calme enfant, je te parlerai pendant des heures; il n'y a plus de champs
et les rues sont vides, je te parlerai de nos meubles ...

[Come, shut your old German almanac, which you read attentively, even though
it came out over a hundred years ago and that the kings it speaks of are all dead,
and, lying down on the old-fashioned carpet, your head resting between your
charitable knees in your pale dress, oh calm child, I will speak to you for hours;
there are no more fields and the streets are empty, I will speak to you of our
furniture ...]

The allegory that Mallarmé establishes between the material objects of the room's
furnishings and the language of the real world offers an insight into his aesthetics
of voice in his poetic language: just as the real objects of the room's furnishings
(like those of Baudelaire's 'chambre double') have their own rich background
story, so too do the words that Mallarmé uses in his poem. The irregular patterning
of the bracketed refrains:

'(De singulières ombres pendent aux vitres usées.)'
'(Je vois des toiles d'araignées au haut des grandes croisées.)'
'(Ne songe pas aux toiles d'araignées qui tremblent au haut des grandes croisées.)'
'(Ces toiles d'araignées grelottent au haut des grandes croisées.)'

['(Peculiar shadows hang down over worn-out windows.)'
'(I see spiders' webs at the top of the large casement windows.)'
'(Do not dream of the spiders' webs which tremble at the top of the large casement
    windows.)'
'(These spiders' webs shiver at the top of the large casement windows.)']

trace the possible tale of the trembling ('frisson', 'grelottent') of language itself
which, at each juncture of the spider's web, must face the choices set before it at
the 'grande croisée'. The 'meubles' too, like words, can be re-evoked by exploring
their past in the present moment of the poetic conversation, provided that time
slows down enough, like the 'pendule de Saxe, qui retarde et sonne treize heures'
['Saxon clock, which runs slow and chimes thirteen o'clock'] to capture the effect
of its fleeting transience.[14]

---

[14]   Baudelaire also employs the image of the 'frisson' to designate the capturing of
transient moments, such as in 'Le Crépuscule du matin' (B.*OC*.I, pp.103–104) where he
writes: 'L'air est plein du frisson des choses qui s'enfuient' ['The air is full of the shiver of
things which are running away'] (v.10).

'**Étrangeté**'

The strangeness of disembodied, dead and silent voices – all of which are exploited by both poets in various ways – and the ensuing belief in the resonant force of such strange voices (even if, paradoxically, this means that the poet's voice must disappear) imply that for Baudelaire and Mallarmé, the more foreign the voice, the more productive or creative the poetic effect. This potentially perverse value system, which would grant greater value to a strange voice even though it might be so foreign as to be unable to communicate its meaning, is balanced by each poet's inherent belief in the power of words to communicate more effectively if their surface meaning is distanced. Remembering that Mallarmé, in his 1891 interview with Huret, suggested that 'Il doit y avoir toujours énigme en poésie' ['There must always be an enigma in poetry'] (M.*OC*.II, p.700), the secret that lies behind the surface of poetic language is the ability to communicate notwithstanding (or perhaps precisely because of) its strangeness. We have already seen how the voice of a cat – a 'chat mystérieux / Chat séraphique, chat étrange' (v.21–22) – possessed a 'secret' (v.8), and how Baudelaire's clock was able to speak 'toutes les langues' (v.14). In the verse version of 'L'Invitation au voyage' (B.*OC*.I, pp.53–54), Baudelaire reminds us that the exotic furnishings, like those of 'La Chambre double' and Mallarmé's 'Frisson d'hiver' are able to speak secretively to the poet:

> Tout y parlerait
> À l'âme en secret
> Sa douce langue natale. (v.24–26)

> [Everything would speak
> To the soul in secret
> In its sweet native language.]

These words from the end of the second stanza of the poem suggest that even though the old-fashioned furnishings that inhabit the stanza speak their own mother tongue, they nevertheless communicate profoundly with the Baudelairean poetic voice. As Barbara Johnson comments, 'cette "langue natale", origine de la signification, ... marque le point de disparition du language en tant que tel' ['this "native language", origin of signification, ... signals the moment at which language as such disappears'], suggesting that language's strange disappearing act is precisely what allows communication to take place.[15] Baudelaire emphasises the ability to communicate by describing the evocative perfumes of flowers ('Les plus rares fleurs / Mêlant leur odeurs / Aux vagues senteurs de l'ambre' ['The rarest flowers / Mingling their fragrance / With the faint scent of amber'] v.18–20), and

---

[15]   Barbara Johnson, *Défigurations du langage poétique: la seconde révolution baudelairienne* (Paris: Flammarion, 1979), p.113.

the reflective properties of the polished furniture ('Des meubles luisants / Polis par les ans' ['The gleaming furniture / Polished by the years'] v.15–16) and mirrors ('Les miroirs profonds' ['The deep mirrors'] v.22).[16] The aromas and reflections mysteriously intermingle to create a speaking voice which is foreign to the poetic voice but, as in the reference to the Pentecostal mystery in 'L'Horloge', the fact that everything speaks its own tongue does not preclude the poet and reader from responding to such language(s).

The question, however, remains: what kind of response can be elicited from hearing strange or foreign voices? Three of Mallarmé's sonnets in particular address this question in different yet commensurate ways. Each poem broaches the theme of the death of a poet. 'Le Tombeau d'Edgar Poe' (M.*OC*.I, p.38) dates from 1877 and 'Le Tombeau de Charles Baudelaire' (M.*OC*.I, pp.38–39) and 'Petit Air II' (M.*OC*.I, p.35) date from the early 1890s. The latter poem is the only one which specifically thematises Mallarmé's own (poetic) death, but the homage that he pays to Poe and Baudelaire in the 'Tombeau' poems are not without their self-reflective musings about Mallarmé's own mortality.[17] The poet-figure in each of the sonnets is posited as a strange voice whose poetry serves as his own swan-song prior to death. However, uncertainties arise in Mallarmé's aesthetic: does the swan-song safeguard the poet's voice after death? Is his voice too strange to be heard or understood?

Mallarmé specifically describes Poe's voice as a 'voix étrange' in the final line of the opening quatrain of his sonnet. Poe's death is presented as a triumph because it is after his death that the people of his time (impersonally designated by the words 'son siècle', v.3) come to realise the value of Poe's voice. It is, of course, the usual lot of a poet to be misunderstood in his time. Glory or triumph only comes as his memory lives on through his poetic œuvre: 'enfin l'éternité le change' ['at last eternity changes him'] (v.1). This poetic commonplace is manipulated by Mallarmé in order to emphasise the perverse relationship between the perception of Poe's 'strangeness' and the raw simplicity of the tools of his trade: 'oyant jadis l'ange / Donner un sens plus pur aux mots de la tribu' ['hearing long ago the angel / Give a purer sense to the words of the tribe'] (v.5–6). So the 'étrangeté' of Poe's

---

[16]   The obvious implication of these evocative flowers is that they refer to Baudelaire's own poetry which are, after all, 'fleurs du mal'. On the evocative properties of fragrances, see my analysis of the 'Chevelure' poems in Chapter 3, and also Baudelaire's sonnet entitled 'Le Parfum' which forms the second sonnet of the series under the title 'Un Fantôme' (B.*OC*.I, p.39) – in particular for the relationship between poetic present and past in relation to Baudelaire's own 'fleurs': 'Charme profond, magique, dont nous grise / Dans le présent le passé restauré! / Ainsi l'amant sur un corps adoré / Du souvenir cueille la fleur exquise' ['Profound, magical charm, of the restored past / Which intoxicates us in the present! / So too does the lover from an adored body / Gather the exquisite flower of memory'] (v.5–6).

[17]   Leo Bersani comments that 'Mallarméan death is a state of radically unsettled being, a state in which the poet is always different from whatever may be said about him'. Leo Bersani, *The Death of Stéphane Mallarmé* (Cambridge: CUP, 1982), p.19.

voice was not that he used strange or foreign words, but that he used everyday, unartificial language in such a way as to render it strange (or poetically artificial). The way Mallarmé implicitly links the notion of a 'voix étrange' (v.4) with 'un sens plus pur' (v.6) is indicative of his aesthetics of voice. He seeks the pure ideal of language in its own abstract (or 'étrange') voices. It is because Poe's voice is strange that he can – even after death – expect to continue in his poetic flight ('noirs vols du Blasphème épars dans le futur' ['black flights of the Blasphemy scattered in the future'] v.14). The value of Poe's strange voice, then, lies in his ability to exact a renown even beyond any original instance of ever having used his voice. Both his own poetic output, and Mallarmé's 'tombeau' poem, serve to preserve his memory by exploiting the quality of 'étrangeté' which is specifically qualified as a vocal quality.

The 'étrangeté' of Baudelaire's voice in Mallarmé's sonnet is less explicitly portrayed. The opening quatrain of 'Le Tombeau de Charles Baudelaire' draws attention to the mouth of Baudelaire's poetry: 'Le temple ensevli divulge par la bouche' ['The buried temple divulges from the mouth'] (v.1), and what emerges from this 'bouche' is 'comme un aboi farouche' ['like a wild barking'] (v.4). As in the 'Tombeau de Poe', the wild, untamed quality of the voice of poetry is privileged. Where in the 'Tombeau de Poe', Mallarmé had talked of 'Donner un sens plus pur aux mots de la tribu' (v.6), in the 'Tombeau de Baudelaire', he uses words such as 'farouche' (v.4) and 'hagard' ['wild'] (v.7) to emphasise the relationship between voice and the quality of 'étrangeté'. The struggle between using untamed language and the creation of poetic artifice is nuanced by the distasteful terminology granted to what emerges from the mouth of Baudelaire's poetry ('égout bavant boue et rubis' ['sewer leaking muck and rubies'] v.2, 'Abominablement' ['Abominably'] v.3, 'un aboi' ['a bark'] v.4). If the first quatrain sets up the animality of the poet's voice through the 'aboi', the second quatrain allies this with the vulgarity of prostitution: the poet's voice thus prostitutes itself in its most base state in order to attain the reward of poetic longevity.[18]

The exchange between the two quatrains – from the beast of death Anubis to the prostitute's 'pubis' (v.7) – takes place freely not only because there is no punctuation

---

[18] The notion of prostitution is important to Baudelaire, since it serves as an emblem of a system of exchange whereby Baudelaire offers for sale the most intimate element of his being: his own poetic voice. He writes an ironic syllogism in 'Mon cœur mis à nu': 'Qu'est-ce que l'amour? / Le besoin de sortir de soi. / L'homme est un animal adorateur. / Adorer, c'est se sacrifier et se prostituer. / Aussi tout amour est-il prostitution' ['What is love? / The need to come out of oneself. / Man is an adoring animal. / To adore is to sacrifice oneself and to prostitute oneself. / Therefore all love is prostitution'] (B.*OC*.I, p.692). He also writes in 'Fusées': 'L'amour, c'est le goût de la prositution. Il n'est même pas de plaisir noble qui ne puisse être ramené à la Prostitution. / Dans un spectacle, dans un bal, chacun jouit de tous. / Qu'est-ce que l'art? Prostitution' ['Love is a liking for prostitution. There is not even a noble pleasure which could be brought back to Prostitution. / In a show, at a ball, each person gets pleasure from everyone. / What is art? Prostitution'] (B.*OC*.I, p.649).

to put a stop to syntactical ambiguity, but also because the intensity of the rhymes drives a sense of interchangeability. The ABBA structure of the quatrains is further reinforced by their richness, rhyming 'bouche', 'farouche', 'louche' and 'découche' in the outer lines of the quatrains, and 'rubis', 'Anubis', 'subis' and 'pubis' in the inner lines. The brazenness of the rhyme-words' presence on the page – so unashamedly and so strongly rhyming with one another – almost diverts the attention from the interpretative complexity of the sonnet. The apparent openness of Baudelaire's prostituting of his poetic voice, however, remains bound by a poetic irony: the rhymes mask a significant complexity, just as the violent, untamed 'aboi' of the opening quatrain masks an important subtlety. Baudelaire might give up his poetic voice freely, but he remains omnipresent in the poetic exchange through the 'Ombre' ['Shadow'] of 'un poison' ['a poison'] of which he is 'tutélaire' ['protector'] (v.13). And in fact it is not Baudelaire's voice that disappears in this poetic exchange, but the reader's: the intoxicating poison of Baudelaire's poetic voice, which is 'Toujours à respirer' ['Always to be breathed in'] (even though the reader does not know where to breathe in this poem, since there is no punctuation other than that intimated by the verse-line structure) may cause the reader to disappear or die in the process of inhaling it ('nous en périssons' v.14).

Of course, there is an even greater irony in interpreting the poem as a process of artistic prostitution in which Baudelaire retains the upper hand. Baudelaire himself did not actually compose the poem, and the protection provided for his voice ('un poison tutélaire' v.13) is not created by Baudelaire himself. The question raised by these 'tombeau' poems is: what happens to Mallarmé's voice? In recounting the strange and (to him) foreign voices of Poe and Baudelaire, Mallarmé is able to develop his own 'voix étrange' which allows him to distinguish his poetic voice from himself in a process of 'étrangeté' – which elsewhere, as we have seen, he has defined as a process of 'abstraction'.[19] Mallarmé estranges himself from his own voice by conversing both with himself and with language through poetry. This is why, in 'Petit Air II', there is so much uncertainty as to whose voice is being recounted – or indeed, if any vocal sound was created in the first place. The poetic swan-song that this heptasyllabic Shakespearean sonnet seems to posit is not simply concerned with death and mortality, but also with resonance, music and control:

> Indomptablement a dû
> Comme mon espoir s'y lance
> Éclater là-haut perdu
> Avec furie et silence,
>
> Voix étrangère au bosquet
> Ou par nul écho suivie,
> L'oiseau qu'on n'ouït jamais
> Une autre fois en la vie.

---

[19]   See Chapter 4, pp.115–118.

Le hagard musicien,
Cela dans le doute expire
Si de mon sein pas du sien
A jailli le sanglot pire

Déchiré va-t-il entier
Rester sur quelque sentier!

[In an untamed way must have
Like my hope which throws itself there
Rung out on high lost
With fury and silence,

Voice foreign to the grove
Or followed by no echo,
The bird that we shall never hear
Again in our lives

The wild musician,
That in doubt expires
If from my breast not from his
Has burst forth the worst sob

Torn will he completely
Remain on some path!]

As in the earlier sonnet 'Le vierge, le vivace et le bel aujourd'hui' (M.*OC*.I, p.36), the notion of an 'éclat' is allied with a 'déchirure' ('Éclater' v.3, 'Déchiré' v.13) – both words imply an uncertainty over the status of poetic language by their own semantic uncertainties.[20] The use of the 'éclat' and the 'déchirure' in 'Petit Air II' deliberately raises potential paradoxes of meaning: if the verb 'éclater' in the third line of the sonnet is referring to an uncontrolled sound, then how can this be 'avec … silence' (v.4)? If the adjectival past participle 'déchiré' in the penultimate line of the sonnet is referring to the state of being torn, then how can the subject of the verse line remain 'entier' (v.13)? These provocative semantic uncertainties illustrate and reinforce a more profound uncertainty that resides at the heart of this sonnet, however, and this uncertainty is about the status of Mallarmé's own poetic voice.

Mallarmé's poetic language has often been described by critics as favouring an impersonal ideal, which is why he distances any prevalence of a poetic 'je'.[21] But

---

[20]   See Chapter 4, pp.139–145, for an analysis of 'Le vierge, le vivace et le bel'.

[21]   Peter Dayan, for example, writes: 'It is doubtless because of this sense that the ideal is impersonal, being the same for all men, that Mallarmé normally uses "soi", or "nous", or

why, then, does the first person possessive pronoun 'mon' appear in both the first and the third stanza of this poem which is otherwise so impersonal and distant? The poem is so riddled with doubt that there are uncertainties not only concerning whether the poet-figure, in the form of an undefined 'oiseau' (v.7), has emitted a sound or not, but also concerning whether that sound – if it was indeed emitted – was created by the bird, 'le hagard musicien' (v.9) or the Mallarméan 'moi'. The likelihood that all three possibilities are in fact one and the same person is troubled by the strongly resonant presence of Baudelaire in the second stanza of this poem – Baudelaire's renowned 'Correspondances' sonnet thematises a wooded grove whose words rebound and echo – the voice in Mallarmé's 'bosquet' (v.5) cannot be so sure about its ability to resonate ('par nul écho suivie' v.6) because it is foreign, a 'voix étrangère au bosquet'. This suggests that Mallarmé, for all his aspired-for resonance with the Baudelairean voices of 'Correspondances', seeks to distance himself from such an aesthetic in order to reside in a more uncertain realm which persistently calls into question what it means to use one's voice in poetry. Baudelairean resonances are also present in the first stanza, with the directionless aim of the poetic subject, the violence of the 'furie' (v.4) and the ringing-out of a noise 'là-haut' (v.3) which recall the penultimate quatrain of Baudelaire's 'Spleen' poem 'Quand le ciel bas et lourd' (B.*OC*.I, pp.74–75):

> Des cloches tout à coup sautent avec furie
> Et lancent vers le ciel un affreux hurlement,
> Ainsi que des esprits errants et sans patrie
> Qui se mettent à geindre opiniâtrement. (v.13–16)

> [Bells all of a sudden leap with fury
> And throw out to the heavens a terrible wailing,
> Like errant souls without a country
> Who start to moan relentlessly.]

Just as Baudelaire's poem closes with the defeat of 'l'Espoir / vaincu' ['Hope / beaten'] (v.18–19), so the 'espoir' (v.2) of Mallarmé's poem is, similarly, 'perdu' (v.3). The splenetic nature of 'Petit Air II' is due, in part, to its inability to shake off the well-trodden paths of poetic language (and especially that of Baudelaire): 'Déchiré va-t-il entier / Rester sur quelque sentier!' (v.13–14). The 'sentier' of poetic language, the path that it must follow and has already followed, is of such uncertain value for Mallarmé that he couches it in an open-ended rhetorical question. The overriding sense of doubt that this sonnet puts forward is further reinforced by unconvincing rhymes: rhyming 's'y lance' (v.2) with 'silence' (v.4) seems to be a rather feeble attempt, the 'bosquet' (v.5) / 'jamais' (v.8) rhyme of the

---

"vous", or "l'homme", or "l'âme humaine", or even "toi", to indicate the self considered as source of poetry – but not, as did the Romantics, "moi".' Dayan, *Mallarmé's 'Divine Transposition'*, p.21.

second stanza is particularly weak, and the conflict that arises between 'musicien' (v.9) and 'sien' (v.11) is due to the diaeresis of the [jɛ̃] sound in 'musicien' where metrical constraints would require a synaeresis of the same sound in 'sien'. The selection of the heptasyllabic 'vers impair' metre also lends this sonnet a disjointed aura.

So the foreign, silent and unresonant voice of the 'Voix étrangère au bosquet' (v.5) is one which is hampered by a profound uncertainty concerning its own status. It cannot be allied to a personal 'moi' (although Mallarmé questions whether it might have been his own voice in the third stanza), it does not know whether it actually made itself heard, but it will nonetheless never be heard again ('qu'on n'ouït jamais / Une autre fois en la vie'). The voice dies out *because* of its inherent uncertainty: 'cela dans le doute expire' (v.10). Yet the death of this voice does not mean that it disappears altogether – like the 'voix étrange' of Poe, death poses as a means of potential triumph. The poet's voice may have been overcome, his poetic hopes may have been dashed, but through death he is able to endure: what seemed to be an uncertain rhetorical question in the final couplet is transformed into a proclamation of the certainty of poetic longevity. It is precisely because there is so much uncertainty and strangeness surrounding the voice of this poem that concerns about the inherently transient nature of using one's voice are able to be transcended.

What dies out at the moment of writing can always be re-evoked by a conversational exchange and dialogue which seeks to remember each word's potential past. The more strange, foreign, or abstract the poetic voices, the greater the potential for more profound explorations of possible past meanings. If poetry is posited as an exchange system, it is a system that rapidly develops in sophistication over the course of the careers of Baudelaire and Mallarmé. The potential threats posed to each poet by the infiltration of other voices are countered by their willingness to debase and prostitute their own voices, and to accept that – to a certain extent – their own voices will inevitably die out. It is Mallarmé who hits upon the notion that the quality of vocal strangeness will ultimately overcome any fears of death or loss of voice, and in doing so, he encompasses Baudelaire's more naïve belief in the inherent communicability of poetic language even when the poet speaks in a 'foreign' tongue. For Mallarmé, being able to render his voice 'étrange' is much less about allowing personified voices to infiltrate his poetry, and much more about exploiting the dislocation of certainty in poetic structures, meanings and devices. If poetic language is to communicate with the reader, then it must be able to converse in a resonant exchange which is unhindered by personal agendas or preconceptions (which would lead to misconceptions or misinterpretations, such as Poe's reading public who, as Mallarmé points out in his 'tombeau' poem, accused Poe of drunkenness rather than verbal dexterity). In Mallarmé's poetic equation, the stranger poetry's voices are, the more likely the reader is to engage, question and converse with that poetry.

PART IV
Music

Chapter 6
Songs without Music

Le chant, de plus en plus lié au mot, a fini par devenir une partie de remplissage, affirmant ainsi sa décadence. Dès lors qu'il se donne pour mission d'exprimer le sens du discours il sort du domaine musical et n'a plus rien de commun avec lui.

[Song, more and more bound to words, has finally become a sort of filler, thereby evidencing its decadence. From the moment song assumes as its calling the expression of the meaning of discourse, it leaves the realm of music and has nothing more in common with it.]

Igor Stravinsky, *The Poetics of Music / Poétique musicale*[1]

The quality of 'strangeness' that both poets exploit could lead to the conclusion that the most strange or abstract voices are not those of poetic language, but those of music. Both poets consider the idea that a profound poetic impression resembles the disappearing vibrations or resonances of a musical note or chord; and that the opposite of that profound poetic impression would be found in an un-resonant kind of poetry, described by Mallarmé as the unsatisfying squeak of the highest string of the violin which I discussed above.[2] The contrast between the kind of poetry that resonates and the kind which fails to resonate is elaborated through a musical metaphor in Mallarmé's interview with Jules Huret in 1891. Huret famously quotes Mallarmé as saying:

il faut … qu'il n'y ait qu'allusion. La contemplation des objets, l'image s'envolant des rêveries suscitées par eux, sont le chant: les Parnassiens, eux, prennent la chose entièrement et la montrent: par là ils manquent de mystère. … *Nommer* un objet c'est supprimer les trois quarts de la jouissance du poème qui est faite du bonheur de deviner peu à peu; le *suggérer*, voilà le rêve. (M.*OC*. II, pp.699–700)

[there must … only be allusion. The contemplation of objects, the image flying away from the rêveries inspired by them, are song: the Parnassians, for their part, take the thing in its entirety and show it: by doing this they lack mystery. … To *name* an object is to suppress three quarters of the pleasure of a poem which comprises the delight of guessing little by little; to *suggest*, that is the ideal.]

---

[1]   Igor Stravinsky, *The Poetics of Music / Poétique musicale* (Cambridge, MA: Harvard University Press, 1970), pp.58–59.

[2]   See Chapter 3, pp.108–109.

The terminologies here are binary: on either side of the pivot of poetic enjoyment are 'nommer' and 'suggérer'. Mallarmé heavily weights the balance towards what he deems as resonant or enjoyable poetry, which is one that is governed by allusion, suggestion, mystery, rêverie and song. The non-resonant or unenticing poetry of the Parnassians is left dangling hopelessly in the air in Mallarmé's poetic balancing act because it is a kind of poetry that is governed by unsophisticated strategies of direct naming or revealing. The neatness of the last sentence of the citation above has meant that it has often been cited as encapsulating Mallarmé's aesthetic ideal, and it offers itself as such because of its seemingly self-explanatory binary structure. But it is clear from the context preceding this particular Mallarméan soundbite that music features in this aesthetic ideal, and that it is not just any old music which will do, but rather the kind that Mallarmé refers to specifically as vocal music: *le chant*.

The musical metaphor in both Baudelaire's and Mallarmé's work is, however, a precarious and multi-faceted one which requires detailed attention. Quite apart from the prevalence of musical vocabulary in the poetry and critical writings of both poets, there is a certain degree of slippage between the terms 'musique', 'chant', 'lyre', 'harmonie' and other musically-inspired terminologies. The relationship between vocal music, *le chant*, and the yearned-for mysterious poetic language is particularly uncertain. The 'chant' seems to take precedence over any abstract notion of symbolic language (which is, after all, what Mallarmé is talking about here), that is to say, that it takes precedence over the image or symbol ('l'image s'envolant des rêveries') by providing a different name for the image or symbol. This is the uncertain equation that Mallarmé sets up in the phrase 'La contemplation des objets, l'image s'envolant des rêveries suscitées par eux, sont le chant'. The status of the third-person plural of the verb 'être' is ambiguous because it neither specifically equates nor valorises the relationship between the notion of 'chant' and the 'image' arising from 'la contemplation des objets'. Notwithstanding this uncertainty, this phrase makes it clear that the 'chant' of poetic language is precisely that silent resonance, that persistent yet tremulous ringing-out, which fundamentally constitutes the Mallarméan poetic aesthetic. The 'musicienne du silence' ['musician of silence'] (v.16) of 'Sainte' (M.*OC*. I, p.27) has often been cited to confirm this.[3] As my exploration of the various dynamic ranges exploited by both poets demonstrates, 'silence' is no more a clear-cut notion than 'music' within the aesthetic of either poet. That Mallarmé, then,

---

[3]   Éric Benoit, for example, comments 'le poème "Sainte" ... laisse pressentir alors une nouvelle esthétique, esthétique du "silence", un silence essentiel' ['the poem "Sainte" ... gives a premonition of a new aesthetic, the aesthetic of "silence", an essential silence']. Éric Benoit, *Néant sonore: Mallarmé ou la traversée des paradoxes* (Geneva: Droz, 2007), p.94. Joseph Acquisto, meanwhile, suggests that 'music is present in this poem in an almost haunting way, inspiring the poem's composition yet mentioned explicitly in terms of silence'. Joseph Acquisto, *French Symbolist Poetry and the Idea of Music* (Aldershot: Ashgate, 2006), p.48.

has equated 'chant' with the supposed 'silence' of resonant symbolic language in the Huret interview requires closer attention, not least of all because throughout both poets' writings musical terminologies are not always employed with clear-cut rigour. The first section of this chapter will explore the ramifications of the musical metaphor in its widest sense by focusing first of all on the notion of vocal music and its relation to Baudelaire's and Mallarmé's poetry (such as the poet as singer, or reader as singer), before turning to other kinds of musical metaphors which are not specifically vocal but more predominantly instrumental. Of course the distinction between metaphors pertaining to instrumental music and those pertaining to vocal music is difficult to maintain – Mallarmé does, after all, mention 'l'instrument de la voix' ['the instrument of the voice'] in 'Crise de vers' (M.*OC*.II, p.208) – and I shall take this into account in my exploration of how each poet exploits such metaphors.

Do Baudelaire and Mallarmé believe that certain kinds of musical metaphors, or certain types of music, are more poetic than others? Is vocal music more akin to poetry than instrumental music? Is a band of roving gypsy musicians considered to be more poetic than a military band? Can music, ultimately, be considered an abstract voice par excellence? Can poetry be considered a kind of proto-music? In order to answer these questions, it will be necessary to go via the most prevalent musical theorist of the nineteenth century, Richard Wagner, although I do not explore Wagner's ideas in detail (since this has already been done elsewhere).[4] I draw also from other theories of the relationship between music and poetry, in particular Baudelaire's writings on Banville, and the *Traité du verbe* by René Ghil. The influences of different theories and approaches on Baudelaire and Mallarmé is not consistent – both poets change their minds, for example, about how relevant Wagner is to their poetry; Baudelaire reveres Banville's lyricism but does not follow in his mould; Mallarmé writes a preface to Ghil's treatise but is not an unquestioning adherent of his theories. The underlying reasons behind these shifts in opinion are largely due to the fact that the relationships between poetry and music during the nineteenth century in France were undergoing significant changes. In order to trace these changes, I turn my focus in the second section of this chapter to song settings of poems by Baudelaire and Mallarmé, some of which were composed during the poets' lifetimes, and others a few years later. I consider specific functions that seem to recur both in poetry and song settings, such as

---

[4]   See for example Elwood Hartman, *French Literary Wagnerism* (New York and London: Garland Publishing, 1988); Philippe Lacoue-Labarthe, *Musica ficta (Figures de Wagner)* (Paris: Christian Bourgois, 1991); Heath Lees, *Mallarmé and Wagner: Music and Poetic Language* (Aldershot: Ashgate, 2007); Margaret Miner, *Resonant Gaps between Baudelaire and Wagner* (Athens, GA: University of Georgia Press, 1995); Simon Shaw-Miller, *Visible Deeds of Music: Art and Music from Wagner to Cage* (New Haven and London: Yale University Press, 2002); or Eric Touya de Marenne, *Musique et poétique à l'âge du symbolisme: Variations sur Wagner: Baudelaire, Mallarmé, Claudel, Valéry* (Paris: L'Harmattan, 2005).

dialogue, refrains and breathing spaces, in order to assess whether these functions are what place 'voice' at the heart of each poet's aesthetic.

Although I shall not specifically consider the influence of the prose poem on the relationships between poetry and music during the nineteenth century, it is evident that the notion of music, and particularly of a vocal music, cannot be dissociated from the prose poem form. Baudelaire himself wrote the following in the opening 'Dédicace' to his *Spleen de Paris* prose poems (this is a phrase which is later pilfered by Debussy to describe his own music):

> Quel est celui de nous qui n'a pas, dans ses jours d'ambition, rêvé le miracle d'une prose poétique, musicale sans rythme et sans rime, assez souple et assez heurtée pour s'adapter aux mouvements lyriques de l'âme, aux ondulations de la rêverie, aux soubresauts de la conscience? (B.*OC*.I, pp.275–276)[5]

> [Who amongst us has not dreamed, during his ambitious days, of the miracle of a poetic prose, which is musical without rhythm and without rhyme, supple enough and clashing enough to adapt itself to the lyrical movements of the soul, to the contours of rêverie, to the somersaults of conscience?]

The vocabulary that Baudelaire employs here mirrors that of Mallarmé in the citation from the Huret interview addressed above. The key notion of the 'chant' is expressed here by Baudelaire in vocabulary which reinforces the fact that singing voices are derived from a movement or action, notably the 'mouvements lyriques de l'âme' (the relationship between 'chant', 'lyre' and 'poésie' is, as will be seen, a close-knit one). The process of eliciting a mysterious symbolic language is described in terms of a 'rêverie' (Mallarmé also described this as a 'rêve' in the citation above). It is precisely Baudelaire's seemingly impossible desire for a poetic musicality that is without rhythm or rhyme which suggests that any vocal aesthetic put forward by Baudelaire or Mallarmé is one that needs to move beyond the technicalities of poetry, and towards a notion of 'voice' which is inherently musical because it should be able to sing out silently, and to resonate with the soul.[6]

---

[5]   Debussy writes in a letter to his patron, Henri Vasnier, dated 19 October 1885: 'le genre de musique que je veux faire, j'en veux une qui soit *assez souple, assez heurtée pour s'adapter aux mouvements lyriques de l'âme*, aux caprices de la rêverie' ['the type of music that I want to create is one which will be *supple enough, clashing enough to adapt itself to the lyrical movements of the soul*, to the caprices of rêverie'] (emphasis mine). Claude Debussy, *Correspondance 1884–1918*, ed. by François Lesure (Paris: Hermann, 1993), pp.38–39.

[6]   By acknowledging what Danielle Cohen-Levinas has outlined, namely that 'du dire au chanter, la voix traverse différents stades d'oralité a-grammaticale' ['from speaking to singing, the voice crosses different stages of a-grammatical orality'], it becomes clear that the movement Baudelaire and Mallarmé require of the voice in poetry confounds traditional

By considering the extent to which the process of exchange between poetry and music is always complicated by disruptions, irregular patternings and disappearances, even in the context of forms which supposedly unite the two arts (the song setting, or devices such as the refrain), I seek to complete the picture of Baudelaire's and Mallarmé's aesthetics of voice. Having suggested that for each poet, 'voice' implies a dynamic process of exchange between differing voices which are increasingly difficult to pin down, this final chapter on the role of music in the context of poetry reinforces the fact that neither poet wishes to be prescriptive about the ways in which his poetry is to be read or performed; in fact the aesthetic implications of musical metaphors, techniques and performance scenarios are such that Baudelaire and Mallarmé are careful to accept the constantly shifting nature of what it means to use 'voice' in poetry.

The Musical Metaphor

'Chant et enchantement': a Poetic Heritage

Friend of both Baudelaire and Mallarmé, and poet, dramatist and critic in his own right, Théodore de Banville published his *Petit Traité de Poésie française* in 1872. In the opening pages of the treatise, Banville decisively claims that:

> Le Vers est la parole humain rhythmée de façon à pouvoir être chantée, et, à proprement parler, il n'y a pas de poésie et de vers en dehors du chant.[7]

> [Poetry is human language made rhythmic so as to be sung, and, strictly speaking, there is no poetry without song.]

Banville's justification for this rather grandiose statement is that it is only in modern times (which he calls the era of decadence) that poetry has attempted to distinguish itself from song, as he goes on to say that:

> Ce n'est que par une fiction et par une convention des âges de décadence qu'on admet comme poëmes des ouvrages destinés à être lus et non à être chantés.[8]

> [It is only because of fiction and because of a convention of the years of decadence that we allow to be called poems those works which are destined to be read and not to be sung.]

---

logic systems. Danielle Cohen-Levinas, *La Voix au-delà du chant: une fenêtre aux ombres* (Paris: Vrin, 2006), p.27.

[7] Banville, *Petit Traité de poésie française* (Paris: Librairie de l'Écho de la Sorbonne, [1872?]), p.3.

[8] Banville, *Petit Traité*, p.3.

In this way, Banville claims (albeit in potentially tongue-in-cheek way) a heritage for poetry which is profoundly bound up with vocal music. What, however, does Banville mean by 'chant'? It is only in the paragraph that follows that his meaning becomes clearer, as he grants greater importance to 'chant' by capitalising the word and talking of 'le Chant'. He claims that the purpose of modern poetry is to re-discover a lost art:

> A quoi donc servent les vers? A chanter. A chanter désormais une musique dont l'expression est perdue, mais que nous entendons en nous, et qui seule est le Chant.[9]

> [What, then, is poetry for? For singing. For singing henceforth a music whose expression has been lost, but which we hear within us, and which alone is Song.]

The notions expressed in this citation recall the Mallarméan idea, described above in the citation from the Huret interview, that the relationship between poetry and music is both complicated and mysterious. Yet for Banville it is also fundamental and necessary. Indeed, he goes on to say of 'le Chant', in truly hyperbolic fashion, that:

> l'homme en a besoin pour exprimer ce qu'il y a en lui de divin et surnaturel, et, s'il ne pouvait chanter, il mourrait.[10]

> [man needs it in order to express the divine and supernatural within him, and, if he were unable to sing, he would die.]

That Banville immediately establishes a relationship between the divine and supernatural and the idea of song at once harks back to the ancient classical model of poetry being a divinely-inspired lyric tradition. For Baudelaire and Mallarmé, however, the 'divin et surnaturel' element of the poetic song has less to do with a classical tradition (although they recognise this poetic heritage), and more to do with a more modern idea of symbolic language: 'le mystère'.

The fact that both Baudelaire and Mallarmé recognise poetry's heritage as a musical art form, and specifically as a vocal musical art form in the form of song is evident from some of the titles they select for their poetry. In *Les Fleurs du Mal*, Baudelaire presents us with 'Chanson d'après-midi', 'Chant d'automne', 'Hymne', 'Hymne à la beauté', 'Madrigal triste', and Mallarmé in his *Poésies* presents us with 'Chansons bas', 'Petit air', and in his earlier theatrical version of 'Hérodiade', he included the poem 'Cantique de saint Jean'. Whilst such titles do not constitute a particularly significant portion of either poet's work, their use

---

[9]   Banville, *Petit Traité*, p.4.
[10]   Banville, *Petit Traité*, p.4.

is sufficient to indicate that both poets were aware of poetry's heritage as song.[11] Nevertheless, as Mallarmé elaborates in the Huret interview, accepting poetry as song in the nineteenth-century France was dependent on an understanding that poetry was no longer unduly beholden to an ancient, classical ideal, although Banville was attracted by this idea. It is Baudelaire himself who elaborates how the idea of poetry as song, or lyric poetry, for Banville, is not simply a return to an ancient means of poetic expression. In his 1861 article on Banville, which he brings together with other articles under the title *Réflexions sur quelques-uns de mes contemporains*, Baudelaire writes that Banville is a lyric poet (emphasis Baudelaire's own):

> si je trouve dans ses œuvres un mot qui, par sa fréquente répétition, semble dénoncer un penchant naturel et un dessein déterminé, j'aurai le droit de conclure que ce mot peut servir à caractériser, mieux que tout autre, la nature de son talent, en même temps que les sensations contenues *dans les heures de la vie où l'on sent le mieux vivre.*
>
> Ce mot, c'est le mot *lyre*, qui comporte évidemment pour l'auteur un sens prodigieusement compréhensif. La *lyre* exprime en effet cet état presque surnaturel, cette intensité de vie où l'âme *chante*, où elle est *contrainte de chanter*, comme l'arbre, l'oiseau et la mer. (B.*OC*.II, p.164)

> [if I find within his works one word which, because of its frequent repetition, seems to reveal a natural penchant and a pre-meditated plan, I would have to say that this word would serve to characterise, better than any other, the nature of his talent, at the same time as those sensations which are to be found *in the times of our lives when we feel the most alive.*
>
> This word is the word *lyre*, which clearly bears for the author a exceptionally comprehensive meaning. The *lyre* expresses, in fact, that almost supernatural state, that intensity of life whereby the soul *sings*, whereby it is *compelled to sing*, like the tree, the bird and the sea.]

Baudelaire's vocabulary demonstrates that he considers the lyre to be fundamental not just to Banville, but also to humanity in general. The universal applicability of the lyric state – which is defined by Baudelaire as an all-encompassing sensation – is here expressed by generalising terms such as 'l'on sent', or 'l'âme chante'. Baudelaire reinforces the idea that the lyric state can be experienced by everybody and gives an example:

---

[11] Pierre Brunel goes so far as to suggest that 'l'hymne [est] la célébration lyrique par excellence' ['the hymn is the lyric celebration par excellence']. Pierre Brunel, *Baudelaire et le 'puits des magies': six essais sur Baudelaire et la poésie moderne* (Paris: José Corti, 2003), p.182.

Il y a, en effet, une manière lyrique de sentir. Les hommes les plus disgraciés de la nature, ceux à qui la fortune donne le moins de loisir, ont connu quelquefois ces sortes d'impressions, si riches que l'âme est comme illuminée, si vives qu'elle en est comme soulevée. (B.*OC*.II, p.164)

[There is, in fact, a lyric way of feeling. Even the most ugly men, those to whom fortune gives the least leisure, have sometimes felt these sorts of impressions, which are so rich that the soul is as if illuminated, so alive that it is as if raised up.]

Baudelaire's plethora of similes within these passages are indicative of his own sense of what it means for poetry to sing. Lyric poetry, or poetry which sings, is able to express a profoundly spiritual moment.

Furthermore, the potential for these kinds of lyric experiences is entirely innate, and man's ability to experience a poetic singing is unavoidably correlated to the way that nature sings ('comme l'arbre, l'oiseau et la mer'). The natural inclination to experience a lyric sensation in Banville's eyes can only be elicited from a return 'aux moyens anciens d'expression poétique' ['to the oldest means of poetic expression']. As Baudelaire recognises in Banville's work, the modern poetic lyricist finds these ancient means of poetic expression to be 'parfaitement adaptés à son but' ['perfectly adapted to his goal']. What is the aim of the modern poetic lyricist if not to 'enchanter l'esprit' ['enchant the mind']? (B.*OC*.II, p.168). The etymological link between 'chanter' and 'enchanter' is not lost on Baudelaire, and although Baudelaire's own tendencies in his creation of a poetic magic, or 'une magie suggestive' ['a suggestive magic'] (B.*OC*.II, p.598) veer towards the more melancholic and demoniacal style of 'enchantement' rather than the noble and classical style of 'enchantement' that Banville employs, the close rapport that he discerns between creating a poetic song and a poetic enchantment suggests that the musical metaphor of 'chant' is more complicated than the classical Banvillian lyric poet would allow for.[12]

Although from his article on Banville it is possible to discern some of Baudelaire's own attitudes to 'chant' in relation to poetry, it is only through looking in more detail at how he employs the verb 'chanter' or the noun 'chant'

---

[12]   Mallarmé also employs the terms 'chant' and 'enchantement' in close proximity in his own writings on Banville in 'Quelques médallions et portraits en pied', where he also associates Banville with the 'lyre': 'aux heures où l'âme rythmique aspire à l'antique délire du chant, mon objet est Théodore de Banville, qui n'est pas quelqu'un, mais le son même de la lyre. ... il marche à travers l'enchantement édéen' ['during the times when the rhythmic soul aspires to the old delirium of song, my object is Théodore de Banville, who is not someone, but the sound of the lyre itself. ... he walks amongst the Edenic enchantment'] (M.*OC*.II, pp.142–143). That Mallarmé de-subjectifies the notion of the 'lyre' by using the name of Banville not to designate a person but a sound is, itself, a significant feature of Mallarmé's own aesthetic.

within his *Fleurs du Mal* that his perception of what it means for poetry to sing can be discerned. Baudelaire uses the idea of 'chant' in a number of different ways, which I have schematised in Table 6.1.[13]

Table 6.1   Baudelaire's use of 'chant' / 'chanter'

within the context of other senses	'Comme l'ambre, le musc, le benjoin et l'encens, Qui chantent les transports de l'esprit et des sens' ('Correspondances' v.13–14) 'Pendant que le parfum des verts tamariniers, (/) Se mêle dans mon âme au chant des mariniers' ('Parfum exotique' v.12 and 14)
to express a non-human singing voice	'l'âme du vin chantait dans les bouteilles' ('L'Âme du vin', v.1) 'des oiseaux chantant soir et matin' ('Paysage' v.19)
to grant a singing voice to musical instruments	'chant des instruments' ('L'Amour du Mensonge' v.2) 'chant des violons' ('Danse macabre' v.25) 'chants du cuivre' ('Le Goût du Néant' v.8)
to indicate religious ceremony / transcendence	'chanter des Te Deum' ('La Muse vénale' v.11) 'chanter ses louanges' ('Que diras-tu' v.5) '[…] vous chantez le Réveil Vous marchez en chantant le réveil de mon âme' ('Le Flambeau vivant' v.12–13)

Baudelaire's use of the word 'chant' / 'chanter', therefore, is not confined to the notion of a human singing voice, even though in his article on Banville, he used the verb 'chanter' solely in relation to the idea of singing as a human universal. In fact Baudelaire discerns song in a range of scenarios, and all of these serve to create what he defined in his Banville article as the 'manière lyrique de sentir'. That singing is primarily an emotive quality in Baudelaire's vocabulary ('Il y a, en effet, une manière lyrique de sentir') is indicative of how he perceives the relationship between 'chant' and 'enchantement'. The ability to make poetry sing, therefore, does not rely specifically on a verbal song; rather it can be a song without words which is able to create the impression of singing without being overly bound by semantics. Since vocal music or song would traditionally remain

---

[13]   Together 'chant' (n.) and 'chanter' (v.) occur 30 times in *Les Fleurs du Mal*. The examples are not exhaustive, but are intended to be representative. The categories are also not exclusive: certain examples could also fit into more than one category.

beholden to words – and therefore to meaning – Baudelaire and Mallarmé begin to explore a poetic song that is devoid of over-laden semantics.[14]

This attitude towards song as an enchantment of the senses stems from the prevailing aesthetic idea that music which was free from words was able to touch in a more absolute, pure way than music with words, which is bound up by the old aesthetic regime of mimesis. This aesthetic ideal of 'absolute music' played a significant role in the battle between poetry and music, and in the question about which art was to be afforded the greater predominance. The fact that Verlaine, for example, entitled his 1874 collection of poetry *Romances sans paroles*, is indicative of a prevailing sense in nineteenth-century France that words were somehow a hindrance to effective poetry.[15] Of course, in the context of Mallarmé's work – which draws much from Baudelaire's own poetic language – it is not words that are a hindrance, but only the kind of words which name too directly (or are over-burdened semantically with a representational aim).[16] So the relationship between words and music, between a poetry that sings and a poetry that is pure (instrumental) music is complicated by the fact that poetry can never release itself from words, and that, fundamentally, poetry cannot release itself from a vocal enactment, because there is no instrument that can 'play' the poetry other than the human voice itself.[17] Mallarmé gets round this problem in his 1894 Oxford and Cambridge lecture entitled 'La Musique et les lettres' by exploiting the idea that music and poetry are 'la face alternative' ['the alternate side'] of each other.[18] Peter

---

[14]   I refer back to my analysis of meaning in relation to Mallarmé's use of the word 'sensation' in Chapter 3.

[15]   The 'song without words' was, of course, initially developed by the German composer Mendelssohn in the early stages of the nineteenth century, and his innovations prompted important aesthetic discussions about the status of song and music. This builds on the late eighteenth-century Rousseauian perspective in chapter twelve of the *Essai sur l'origine des langues* that 'les vers, les chants, la parole, ont une origine commune' ['poems, songs, the spoken word, have a common origin']. Jean-Jacques Rousseau, *Essai sur l'origine des langues* (Paris: Aubier Montaigne, 1974), p.144.

[16]   Mallarmé did, after all, according to Valéry in his 1939 Oxford lecture 'Poésie et pensée abstraite', say to the painter Edgar Degas that poetry is not made up of ideas but of words. 'Il [Degas] dit un jour à Mallarmé, "Votre métier est infernal. Je n'arrive pas à faire ce que je veux et pourtant, je suis plein d'idées …" Et Mallarmé lui répondit "Ce n'est point avec des idées, mon cher Degas, que l'on fait des vers. C'est avec des mots"' ['He [Degas] said one day to Mallarmé, "Your art is infernal. I cannot manage to do what I want and nonetheless, I am full of ideas …" And Mallarmé replied to him "You do not make poems with ideas, my dear Degas, but with words"']. Paul Valéry, *Œuvres*, ed. by Jean Hytier, Bibliothèque de la Pléiade, 2 vols (Paris: Gallimard, 1957–1960), II, p.1324.

[17]   See Chapter 2, pp.54–57.

[18]   'La Musique et les Lettres sont la face alternative ici élargie vers l'obscur … L'un des modes incline à l'autre et y disparaissant, ressort avec emprunts' ['Music and Literature are the alternate side here expanded towards the mysterious darkness … One of the modes

Dayan picks up on this particular phrase in his article on 'La Musique et les Lettres chez Barthes' and suggests:

> Ainsi la musique est cette *absence* du sens où nous voyons la face alternative de la littérature; la musique instrumentale est cette *absence* de la voix humaine où nous voyons la face alternative du chant.[19]

> [Just as music is that *absence* of meaning in which we see the alternate side of literature; instrumental music is that *absence* of the human voice in which we see the alternate side of song.]

Because of this 'face alternative' which operates in the domain of poetry and music in order to distance any excess of meaning (in the old representational model), the musical metaphor of 'chant' in the poetry of both Baudelaire and Mallarmé is inextricably linked to the musical metaphor of instrumental music. Banville's old-fashioned lyric poetry was unable to attain the aesthetic ideal of a mysterious and magical symbolic language because it was too closely bound to the idea of a song with words. Whilst Baudelaire and Mallarmé both discerned that the 'chant' cannot be eradicated from poetry (since poetry is an unavoidably vocal art, and since the heritage of 'chant' in relation to poetry weighs heavily on the poetic art), both poets began to turn increasingly towards the idea of instrumental music as a musical metaphor for poetry because of its (apparent) ability to cast semantics aside.

'L'instrumentation et l'orchestration': the Modern Ideal?

Where Baudelaire, in his article on Banville cited above, talked of 'sensations' and 'impressions' in relation to the poetic song, Mallarmé uses similar terminologies in relation to the idea of poetry as instrumental music. During the period when he was still teaching in Tournon, at a time when his poetic 'crise' was looming, Mallarmé wrote to his friend Henri Cazalis in 1865 about a new dramatic poem that he was creating, entitled 'Hérodiade':

> Et mon vers, il fait mal par instants et blesse comme du fer! J'ai, du reste, là, trouvé une façon intime et singulière de peindre et de noter des impressions très fugitives. Ajoute, pour plus de terreur, que ces *impressions* se suivent comme dans une symphonie, et que je suis souvent des journées entières à me demander si celle-ci peut accompagner celle-là, quelle est leur parenté et leur effet ... (M.*OC*.I, p.666)

---

inclines towards the other and disappearing within it, emerges again with borrowings'] (M.*OC*.II, p.69).

[19]   Peter Dayan, 'La Musique et les Lettres chez Barthes', *French Studies*, 57:3 (2003), 335–348 (p.341).

[And my poetry hurts sometimes and hurts like an iron rod! Besides, I have found an intimate and particular way of painting and noting very fleeting impressions. Add to this, by way of even greater terror, that these *impressions* follow on from each other like in a symphony, and that I often spend entire days asking myself if this one can accompany that one, what is their relationship and their effect ...]

Mallarmé recognises that the way he is using language in his 'Hérodiade' is innovative because it is peculiar to his own self. Yet he perceives that his attempts to note down what he calls his fugitive impressions are especially unnerving because they resemble symphonic music. The instrumental metaphor here does not calm Mallarmé's terror in the face of his own poetry, but does precisely the opposite. It is quite different from the kind of reassuring, uplifting, enchanting impressions and sensations that Baudelaire described as resulting from Banville's lyre. And it indicates that the instrumental metaphor, for all its positive attributes – such as being free of semantics – does not necessarily serve to assuage poetic composition, and can instead trouble it. Mallarmé here has chosen to talk of a symphony, that is to say, of a musical work which has many different instrumental voices which work together across time, or in his own words, follow on from one another ('se suivent').[20] He extends the instrumental analogy further by talking of the days he spends in trying to decide what element can satisfactorily accompany another element. The verb 'accompagner' hints at a number of ideas, but in particular the idea that one voice or musical line takes precedence over another which is subordinate or an accompaniment to the first. Perhaps Mallarmé is referring to the specifics of rhyme here – whether one word can appropriately 'accompany' another – but in fact the context is more generic (and the referent 'celle-ci' suggests otherwise). In fact, he is concerned about what impression can successfully accompany another impression. That is to say, if the symphonic analogy is followed through, he equates impression with an instrumental voice or line, and is concerned therefore about which instruments he can use to accompany the prevailing instrumental voice.

Although Mallarmé in this passage does not specifically elaborate different elements of instrumentation, it is an idea that is entirely familiar to him. He recognises that different instruments have different qualities, as will be evidenced in my analysis of the prose poem 'Plainte d'automne' below. Moreover, he has seen an elaboration of the relationship between different instrumental qualities and different poetic impressions in the treatise by his friend René Ghil, the *Traité du*

---

[20] 'La symphonie est la plus pure manifestation du génie musical; elle est l'idéal de l'art, le poème par excellence' ['The symphony is the purest manifestation of musical genius; it is the ideal of art, the poem par excellence']. *Grand dictionnaire universel du XIXe Siècle*, 14:1317, cited in David Evans, *Rhythm, Illusion and the Poetic Idea: Baudelaire, Rimbaud, Mallarmé* (Amsterdam and New York: Rodopi, 2004), p.220.

Verbe published initially in 1885 and again in subsequent years.[21] As outlined in Chapter 1, Mallarmé himself prefaced the 1886 edition (the preface now forms the final paragraphs of 'Crise de vers'). In the treatise, Ghil suggests that the poet needs to understand the idea of 'l'Instrumentation poétique' ['poetic Instrumentation'] in order to compose musical poetry. In the final chapter of his treatise, he elaborates how different vowels have different colours (in a Rimbaldian fashion) and how these relate to particular instruments, which in turn relate to particular impressions or emotions.[22] This notion is presented as the culmination of his argument, and the system can be outlined in Table 6.2 as follows.[23]

Table 6.2   Ghil's 'instrumentation-Verbale'

A	Orgues [Organs]	Noir [Black]	Gloire, Tumulte [Glory, Turmoil]
E	Harpe [Harp]	Blanc [White]	Sérénité [Calm]
I	Violon [Violin]	Bleu [Blue]	Passion, Prière à l'aigu [Passion, High-pitched prayer]
O	Cuivres [Brass]	Rouge [Red]	Souveraineté, Gloire, Triomphe [Sovereignty, Glory, Triumph]
U	Flûte [Flute]	Jaune [Yellow]	Ingénuité, Sourire [Innocence, Smile]

Whilst Mallarmé's opinions on this system are not entirely self-evident, it is known nonetheless that he was familiar with Ghil's work as an important work in progress. As Jean-Pierre Bobillot outlines, whilst Ghil's attempts at the systematisation of the effects of language may be problematic, or at the very least questionable, nonetheless 'la tentative demeure en elle-même cohérente – et, au moins, potentiellement, féconde –, se situant toute au plan de l'organisation phonique du matériau verbal' ['the attempt remains coherent of itself – and, at least, potentially, productive –, situating itself along the lines of the phonic organisation of

---

[21]   René Ghil, *Traité du Verbe: états successifs (1885 – 1886 – 1887 – 1888 – 1891 – 1904),* ed. by Tiziana Goruppi (Paris: Nizet, 1978).

[22]   The relationship between sound and colour is traditionally explored under the auspices of 'synaesthesia'. I do not aim to surmise which poets or theorists in nineteenth-century France may or may not have been synaesthetic, but Baudelaire is recognised to have understood the notion, and Rimbaud parodied it in his 1870s sonnet 'Voyelles' and then later in 'Délires II. Alchimie du verbe'. Certain composers, such as the influential Russian composer Scriabin (1872–1915), devised an entire system of keys and colours. See Shaw-Miller, *Visible Deeds of Music,* p.67. As Suzanne Bernard points out, Ghil's system was mocked in *La Revue indépendante* of 13 June 1889 by Delaroche, Mockel and A. Saint-Paul. See *Mallarmé et la musique* (Paris: Nizet, 1959), p.17.

[23]   I build on Suzanne Bernard's schematisation in *Mallarmé et la musique,* p.16.

the verbal material'].[24] The difficulties that arise from Ghil's theories relate to how, precisely, this system of instrumentation can be put into practice, or 'orchestrated'. Joseph Acquisto points out that 'poetry is never really meant to be orchestrated' and reminds us that this notion of an 'instrumentation-Verbale' represents 'the pinnacle of Ghil's theory that allows one to "orchestrate" a poem even though he tells us that actually doing so would be ludicrous'.[25] According to Louis Marvick's analysis of Ghil's work, however, this notion of using instruments together reveals an important underlying feature of Ghil's theories which are in fact founded on the human voice:

> the 'mariage caractéristique d'Instruments' can then be located in the human voice, which alone is capable of reproducing the timbre of every instrument.[26]

Whilst this places a very great onus on the capabilities of the human voice, it nevertheless offers a perspective on how nineteenth-century poets and theorists considered the relationships between voice(s) and instruments, and therefore between vocal music and instrumental music. Both the human voice and instrumental voices are able to express particular emotive states such as those outlined by Ghil in his *Traité du Verbe*.

Mallarmé himself explores the relationship between certain instruments and certain impressions or emotions in the prose poem 'Plainte d'automne' (M.*OC*.I, pp.414–415). In the second paragraph of the prose poem, Mallarmé talks primarily of a single instrument (as opposed to a symphonic group) which he terms 'l'orgue de Barbarie'. This is presumably intended to designate a barrel organ being played outside in the street below, and the music played by the organ creates an aura of

---

[24]   René Ghil, *Le Vœu de Vivre et autres poèmes*, ed. by Jean-Pierre Bobillot (Rennes: Presses Universitaires de Rennes, 2004), p.36.

[25]   Acquisto, *French Symbolist Poetry and the Idea of Music*, p.106.

[26]   Louis Marvick, *Waking the Face That No One Is* (Amsterdam and New York: Rodopi, 2004), p.95. That instruments, conversely, are supposedly capable of reproducing the sound of the human voice is a long-standing aesthetic commonplace. One of the standard stops on French classical organs is a 'voix humaine' stop, a reed stop that supposedly mimics the human voice by its undulating quality. Interest in this organ stop during the nineteenth century in France is evidenced by a short two-act opera premièred on 30 December 1861, by the composer Alary and set to a libretto by Mélesville, entitled *La Voix humaine* which tells the story of an organist's search for the perfect organ stop. He comes up with a 'voix humaine' stop which is modelled on the voice of the woman he loves, and the stage directions announce: 'Tout à coup, Didier fait entendre le motif du chant, et touche le jeu nouveau; aussitôt la voix humaine retentit; c'est une voix de femme qui ne profère que des sons soutenus, et ne prononce pas de paroles' ['All of a sudden, Didier makes heard the motif of the song, and starts playing the new stop; straight away the voix humaine rings out; it is the voice of a woman which only makes high sounds, and does not pronounce any words']. Mélesville (pseudonym for Anne Honoré Joseph Duveyrier), *La Voix humaine: opéra en deux actes* (Paris: Beck, 1861), p.8.

melancholy for the Mallarméan poetic 'je'. That Mallarmé uses the verb 'chanter' for the organ is in itself pertinent, because it comes in the double context of two poems; the familiar poem that he was reading, and the prose poem that he is in the process of writing. In this poetic environment, the singing of the organ intervenes above any potential singing of the poetry itself:

Je lisais donc un de ces chers poèmes ... quand un orgue de Barbarie chanta languissamment et mélancoliquement sous ma fenêtre.

[So I was reading one of those dear poems ... when a barrel organ started singing listlessly and with melancholy beneath my window.]

The emotion of sadness that the sound of the instrument creates for Mallarmé is reinforced by a climax of related terms, offset by a series of contrasts. For him, 'l'orgue de Barbarie' sings 'languissament', 'mélancoliquement', and is later described as 'l'instrument des tristes' ['the instrument of sad people'] which has made him 'désespérément rêver' ['dream despairingly']. The climactic force of the despairing sadness is offset by the contrast created by other instruments:

L'instrument des tristes, oui, vraiment: le piano scintille, le violon donne aux fibres déchirées la lumière, mais l'orgue de Barbarie, dans le crépuscule du souvenir, m'a fait désespérément rêver.

[The instrument of sad people, yes, in truth: the piano sparkles, the violin gives light to torn fibres, but the barrel organ, in the shadows of memory, made me dream despairingly.]

If Mallarmé's attitude towards the correlation between instruments and emotions were to be set out in a table, however, it would have very little correlation with Ghil's analysis elaborated above. The organ here for Mallarmé creates sadness – a far cry from the 'gloire' or 'tumulte' that Ghil writes of.[27] And the violin creates light, which is neither a 'passion' nor a 'prière à l'aigu' as Ghil would suggest. The piano, of course, is not represented in Ghil's system, but then nor does Mallarmé's 'system' in 'Plainte d'automne' incorporate vowels or colours as Ghil's does. This demonstrates that any perceived (or rationalised) correlation between instruments and emotions is in fact entirely arbitrary.

Yet the arbitrariness of relationships between instruments and poetic language is precisely what Mallarmé exploits. When he talks of 'violon' or 'harpe' or even the more antiquated 'viole' or 'clavecin' within his poetry, he recognises that there

---

[27]   The difference between Ghil's (presumably traditional) organ and Mallarmé's barrel organ is also a question of register – Mallarmé's is a much less refined instrument, and so produces a very different kind of emotive response. This notion of register is significant in Mallarmé's use of the musical metaphors which draw on instruments.

are distinctions that can be made between these instruments, but that there is no clear-cut designation as to what effect each instrument creates, notwithstanding the suggestions he makes in 'Plainte d'automne'. Instead he recognises that, as a metaphor, the instruments serve to designate a more general poetic idea. This is why, in 'Don du poème', the voice of the female dedicatee of the poem is described as 'rappelant viole et clavecin' ['recalling viol and harpsichord'] (v.11). Mallarmé does not suggest that the voice he hears resembles one specific instrument (and thereby one specific impression); instead he couples two instruments together, intimating that the 'voix' that he hears presents him with more than one vocal line through the 'viole' accompanied by the 'clavecin', if this is indeed how the two instruments are intended to be working together in this metaphor. Whilst it is true to say that the 'viole' and the 'clavecin' are considered more outmoded instruments than, for example, 'violon' or 'piano', Mallarmé's use of the terms 'viole et clavecin' here is not presented in a context which grants any particular relevance to the fact that they are instruments of the past. David Evans reads this differently, however, suggesting that:

> In the mid-1860s poems, as Mallarmé's musical metaphor evolves from simple melodies of phonetic patterns towards the silent structural notion, the 'flûte' and 'viole' symbolize an outdated poetics. In 'Don du poème' as the poet takes his frail new poem to his wife, 'la berceuse' (1.9), for resuscitation, her voice recalls the 'viole et clavecin' (1.11) of yore.[28]

Evans' suggestion that the antiquated instruments symbolise an outdated poetics is rendered problematic by his inclusion of the 'flûte' under such a designation, since this is an instrument still very much in use both in the nineteenth century and today. The 'viole et clavecin' in 'Don du poème', on the other hand, whilst they are tinged with a certain old-fashionedness, are in fact presented here not as referring specifically to poetry or poetics, but rather to the voice of the female addressee 'Et ta voix rappelant viole et clavecin' ['And your voice recalling viol and harpsichord'].[29] This is Mallarmé's way of symbolising how the addressee 'speaks' upon receiving the 'don du poème'; her speech is instrumental, in the

---

[28]   Evans, *Rhythm, Illusion and the Poetic Idea*, p.259.

[29]   As David Rowland makes clear in his book, *Early Keyboard Instruments: a Practical Guide* (Cambridge: CUP, 2001), the harpsichord was used in concerts in Paris in the 1860s, though usually under the guise of 'historical' concerts. It is likely that the viol was similarly used in 'historical' concerts. As with the choice of the 'orgue de Barbarie' in 'Plainte d'automne', Mallarmé's diction here is designating a particular register. By the time he was writing, the piano, for example, had become a bourgeois status-symbol: Flaubert's Emma Bovary did, after all, have piano lessons, and Mme Josserand in Zola's *Pot-bouille* was adamant that her daughters become suitably accomplished pianists. By talking of the 'viole et clavecin' in 'Don du poème', Mallarmé employs a more refined register of language that averts any bourgeois connotations.

sense that it is poetically symbolised by non-verbal ways of creating music. The relationship between the 'voix' and 'viole et clavecin', therefore, is almost as arbitrary as Ghil's system of interrelations above, because the 'voix' does not use verbal language, but musical language.[30] Furthermore, as is clear from the lack of correlation between Mallarmé's 'Plainte d'automne' and Ghil's system, musical language does not follow the same logic as verbal language.

This, therefore, is the key to understanding the instrumental musical metaphor, and why it is at times privileged by Baudelaire and Mallarmé over the vocal music metaphor within their poetry. The fact that the instrumental metaphor frees the musical one from words also suggests that it frees poetry from words. That is to say, Mallarmé's strategy of presenting the voice of the female addressee as sounding like a 'viole et clavecin' is an indirect, non-verbal and musical way of symbolising whatever she might actually have said upon receiving the poem brought to her after the 'nuit d'Idumée' ['Idumean night'] (v.1). In exploiting the metaphor of instrumental music, Mallarmé presents the reader with an interpretative dilemma. If, in choosing the metaphor of 'viole et clavecin', Mallarmé was averting direct language, then any verbal reasoning about the significance of the 'viole et clavecin' is problematised. The relationship between musical instruments and particular emotions or colours, or even specific interpretative meanings, remains both naïve and arbitrary. The undecidability of the instrumental music metaphor points towards a broader scope of possible non-verbal responses to poetic language such as a lingering impression or sensation, whether emotional or otherwise.

Baudelaire's use of the metaphor of instrumental music reveals a similar tendency to associate a particular instrument with a particular mood. In the prose poem 'Les Vocations' (B.*OC*.I, pp.332–335), Baudelaire presents the fourth boy of a group of 'quatre garçons, las de jouer sans doute' ['four boys, no doubt tired of playing'] who 'causaient entre eux' ['were chatting amongst themselves'], as being intoxicated and enchanted by the music of a band of roving gypsy musicians. The relationship between the music he hears and the fact that the three men who are playing the music are wandering musicians constitutes a large part of the appeal for the boy. Baudelaire creates the conceit also that none of the other three boys with whom he is conversing has paid any attention to the gypsies' music: 'Vous

---

[30]   In fact, the voice does not, and cannot, speak at all. The temporal scenario of this poem further problematises the possibility of the voice ever speaking. The present-tense opening verb 'Je t'apporte' is an impossibility because at no point in the present moment can the action actually happen – he is either writing the poem or bringing the poem, and he cannot do both at once. For this reason, the 'voix' in v.11 is placed in an uncertain temporal scenario. Either this poem has been written after the poem was actually brought to the woman's feet (in which case he is recounting a past event in the present), or else the poetic voice is merely creating a hypothesis for how the woman might react to his poem (in which case he is recounting a future moment that has not yet happened). In either scenario, the 'voix' which recalls 'viole et clavecin' is forbidden to speak – which further heightens the musical metaphor which denies her voice a verbal basis.

n'y avez pas fait attention, vous autres' ['You weren't paying attention, you lot'].
This conceit hints at the idea that only certain kinds of people – amongst them the
fourth boy – are capable of comprehending the appeal of the instrumental music
at stake here, which is:

> une musique si surprenante qu'elle donne envie tantôt de danser, tantôt de pleurer,
> ou de faire les deux à la fois, et qu'on deviendrait comme fou si on les écoutait
> trop longtemps. L'un, en traînant son archet sur le violon, semblait raconter un
> chagrin, et l'autre, en faisant sautiller son petit marteau sur les cordes d'un petit
> piano suspendu à son cou par une courroie, avait l'air de se moquer de la plainte
> de son voisin, tandis que le troisième choquait, de temps à autre, ses cymbales
> avec une violence extraordinaire.

> [a music so surprising that it makes you either want to dance or to cry, or to do
> both at once, and you would go mad if you listened to it for too long. One of
> them, drawing his bow across the violin, seemed to be recounting a tale of woe,
> and the other, making his little hammer hop over the strings of a little piano
> hanging from his neck by a strap, gave off the impression of mocking the woes
> of his neighbour, whereas the third one was smashing together, from time to
> time, his cymbals with an extraordinary violence.]

Where in the prose poem 'Portraits de Maîtresses' analysed above, the lower
register of the 'causerie' was emphasised by a musical metaphor, here the fourth
boy's intervention describing the rather extraordinary music is in direct contrast
to the banality of the 'causerie' of the other boys.[31] Baudelaire adds an element of
extraordinariness ('surprenante', 'extraordinaire') to this conversational exchange
by exploiting musical metaphors in the fourth boy's description of the impressions
left on him by the music he heard.

That Baudelaire in the opening lines of the description of the music offers two
alternative reactions – either to dance or to cry – indicates once again the arbitrary
nature of the relationship between music and emotions, even though he then goes
on to talk about the tale of 'chagrin' which the violin recounts. Baudelaire uses
diction which is anti-prescriptive: the impressions that he recounts remain no
more than that ('semblait raconter', 'avait l'air de'). What is significant here in
Baudelaire's description of this band of instrumental musicians is that he describes
the relationships between the musicians, which is presented as a relationship
between the different instruments. The 'causerie' between the four boys is sidelined
in favour of a more mysterious and extraordinary conversation. The violin's tale
of 'chagrin' is mocked by the 'petit piano', and the 'violence' of the cymbals
counteracts both this 'chagrin' and 'moquerie'. The musical conversation that is
taking place is intractable – the musicians are so absorbed in their own playing that

---

[31]   See Chapter 4, pp.122–126.

they are barely aware of each other, let alone of the effect that they may be creating. What keeps them playing is their intense satisfaction at the music-making:

> Ils étaient si contents d'eux-mêmes, qu'ils ont continué à jouer leur musique de sauvages, même après que la foule s'est dispersée.

> [They were so happy with themselves that they carried on playing their barbaric music, even after the crowd had dispersed.]

The crowd disperses because they, unlike the fourth boy protagonist of 'Les Vocations', are not taken in by this surprising music. For the boy, the music has a Pied Piper effect, and he follows the players to find out where they come from:

> Moi, voulant savoir où ils demeuraient, je les ai suivis de loin, jusqu'au bord de la forêt, où j'ai compris seulement alors, qu'ils ne demeuraient nulle part.

> [As for me, because I wanted to know where they lived, I followed them at a distance, to the edge of the forest, at which point I only then realised that they did not live anywhere.]

The fact that the musicians have no fixed abode, that they are wandering musicians, is central to Baudelaire's use of the instrumental metaphor. He sets up a clear distinction between the boy and anyone else who hears the music. Neither the 'foule' nor the other boy protagonists of the prose poem were drawn to this music because they had no interest in the mysteriousness and complexities surrounding its origins or its transient nature.

The contrast between the provincial crowd's lack of interest in the music of the roving gypsy musicians and the Parisian crowd's intense interest in the music of a military band in another prose poem, 'Les Veuves' (B.*OC*.I, pp.292–294), is indicative of the complexity of the instrumental music metaphor for Baudelaire. In 'Les Veuves', Baudelaire's description of the kind of music being performed – and its appeal to the crowd – is disparaging:[32]

> un de ces concerts dont la musique des régiments gratifie le peuple parisien.

> [one of those concerts in which military music satisfies the Parisian crowd.]

---

[32] The scene depicted in this prose poem is similar to that which Rimbaud paints in his poem 'À la Musique', although in this latter poem, the setting is a provincial town rather than Paris. Nevertheless, Rimbaud similarly makes the distinction between the unappreciative ignorant crowd and the poetic 'moi' who is set apart from the rest of the crowd. See Arthur Rimbaud, *Poésies. Une saison en enfer. Illuminations* (Paris: Gallimard, 1965–1999), p.59.

As in 'Les Vocations', Baudelaire sets up a distinction between the 'foule' and the individual protagonist listening to the music. In 'Les Veuves', the single figure that listens to the music is a widow, who 's'assit à l'écart' ['sits apart'] and attains some consolation from the concert because she is 'sans ami, sans causerie, sans joie, sans confident' ['without a friend, without someone to chat to, without joy, without a confidant'] and the music fills the gaps left by this plethora of absences. For her, the music of the military band has a purpose and import far greater than any it may have for the crowd who throng around the barriers trying to catch the strains of the music. The crowd purports to appreciate the music, but really grasps very little of its potential meaning:

> les oisifs, fatigués de n'avoir rien fait, se dandinent, feignant de déguster indolemment la musique.

> [lazy people, tired because they have done nothing, shift from one foot to the other, pretending to enjoy the music with indifference.]

The music for the widow has a restorative, consoling meaning grasped from the way that:

> L'orchestre jette à travers la nuit des chants de fête, de triomphe ou de volupté.

> [The orchestra throws into the night its festive, triumphant or voluptuous songs.]

Not only is 'la nuit' describing the vespertine setting of the concert, but it also hints at the death of her husband; for the widow, the music of the 'orchestre' offers a means of communication with him. That Baudelaire also employs the noun 'chants' to describe the music suggests that the way instruments work together through their different voices is related to the vocal art – and, tentatively, therefore, related to the possibility of conveying a meaning (even if that meaning is unstable and different for each poetic protagonist). The fact that the verbal meaning conveyed by music can take on so many different forms – 'fête', 'triomphe' or 'volupté' – points towards the Mallarméan interpretation of the relationship between instrumental music and verbal meaning. The metaphor of instrumental music can, and must, convey a series of impressions or sensations which are not just emotive ideas, but also contain possibilities for meanings which necessarily remain irregular, unusual and unstable. It is in this way that music affects poetic language, because the 'meaning' of instrumental music gleans its semantic possibilities from the notion of music as a 'chant' with or without words. So when Mallarmé writes in the preface to Ghil's treatise (reiterated in 'Crise de vers'):

Je dis: une fleur! et, hors de l'oubli où ma voix relègue aucun contour, en tant
que quelque chose d'autre que les calices sus, musicalement se lève, idée même
et suave, l'absente de tous bouquets. (M.*OC*.II, p.213)

[I say: a flower! and, beyond the oblivion to which my voice relegates any
contour, in the sense of something other than known calices, musically rises up,
same and sweet idea, the absent one of all bouquets.]

he expresses a relationship between two musical metaphors: vocal music and
instrumental music. The adverb 'musicalement' takes over from the 'voix'
not simply as a 'chant' or as an 'instrument', but as both at once. The 'chant-
instrument' of the voice of poetic language, which here pronounces the word
'fleur', is precisely that intangible linguistic-musical moment that is neither verbal
language nor verbal music, or even non-verbal music, but rather a suspended,
vibrating, transient and disappearing moment in between language and music, the
'entre' of the 'rythme entre des rapports' ['rhythm between relationships'] (M.*OC*.
I, p.807) perhaps.[33]

Precarious Proto-music

The way music distances meaning through the interaction between the 'chant'
and the 'instrument' illustrates how the balance of poetry's vocal equation
is persistently being tipped first one way and then the other. The interrelations
between 'sens', 'son' and 'sensation' ['sense', 'sound' and 'sensation'], in a
musical context privileges 'sensation' and 'son' in particular over the notion of
'sens'. This does not imply that meaning is done away with altogether, but that it
takes on a different status. This offers an attractive vocal aesthetic if poetry is still
allowed to sing, but in a manner free from any over-laden semantic burden (hence
the 'chant' is persistently tinged by the 'instrument' and becomes a combined
'chant-instrument' for Baudelaire and Mallarmé). The attraction of this vocal
aesthetic is what both Baudelaire and Mallarmé recognised in the aesthetic theory
propounded by Richard Wagner.[34] In his monumental *Oper und Drama* of 1852

---

[33] See Chapter 3.

[34] Although I cite from Wagner below, Wagner's more extended German texts were in
fact virtually unread in France. French readers had access to his 1861 French text, the *Lettre
sur la musique* which introduces his key ideas. However, as Edouard Dujardin points out, it
was a text that was 'peu et mal lue'. See Dujardin, 'Richard Wagner et la Poésie française
contemporaine', *La Revue de Genève*, 1ère année, 2me semestre, Tome 11 (1886), p.262.
Heath Lees suggests that 'It seems unthinkable that Mallarmé was not amongst those who
read this 100-page introduction around the time of its publication, considering his contact
with Baudelaire's circle, his early acquaintance with the wagnerist musician Léon Marc,
his two *echt*-wagnerian friends Mendès and Villiers – and indeed the evidence of his 1860s
poems and correspondence, where reference is often made to music-poetic ideas whose

Wagner recognised that instrumental music was an echo of the human voice, and that within instrumental music – free from the hindrance of consonants – the 'pure' human voice could be discerned:

> Das musikalische Instrument ist gewissermaßen ein Echo der menschlichen Stimme von der Beschaffenheit, daß wir in ihm nur noch den in den musikalischen Ton aufgelösten Vokal, nicht aber mehr den wortbestimmenden Konsonanten vernehmen. In dieser Losgelöstheit vom Worte gleicht der Ton des Instrumentes jenem Urtone der menschlichen Sprache.[35]

> [By its very nature, the musical instrument is, to an extent, an echo of the human voice, in that we still hear in it only the vowel dissolved into a musical tone, but no longer the word-defining consonants. By being released from words, the tone of the instrument is like the Ur-tone of human speech.]

That Wagner considers the human voice as the basis of instrumental voices is an aesthetic standpoint which also influences Baudelaire and Mallarmé. For Wagner, understanding how the sounds of the human voice are able to 'become' wordless instrumental music is an important feature of how words and music relate to one another. Commenting on this same passage from Wagner, Simon Shaw-Miller suggests that:

> Wagner makes it clear that for him the setting of word to music is ultimately the product of the musicality of language itself, the means of expressing feelings. In other words, poetry is a kind of proto-music – verse's measure as rhythm and rhyme as melody. Words are understood as sensual presentation or expression.

---

content and formulation inescapably suggest the Wagner of the *Lettre sur la Musique*'. See 'Mallarmé and the All-Embracing Word Work', in *Situating Mallarmé*, ed. by David Kinloch and Gordon Millan (Bern: Peter Lang, 2000), p.15. Louis Marvick points out that Mallarmé's familiarity with Wagner probably came through Baudelaire's own 1861 essay on Wagner: 'In the decade preceding 1871 ... the greatly complicating presence of Wagner had made itself felt, and by 1885, the year of Mallarmé's two contributions to the *Revue Wagnérienne*, Wagner's theories, with their pedigree from Schopenhauer, had become part of the intellectual baggage of Symbolism. Mallarmé certainly knew these theories at second hand (through Baudelaire's article of 1861 and the advocacy of Catulle Mendès and Edouard Dujardin, among others), but his direct knowledge was probably limited to what he could gather from Wagner's *Zukunftsmusik*, published in French as the preface to a translation of his opera-poems. This work, known in French as the *Lettre à M. Villot sur la musique*, contains a number of striking parallels with Mallarmé's thought, and also some striking points of difference.' See Marvick, *Waking the Face That No One Is*, p.1.

[35] Richard Wagner, 'Dichtkunst und Tonkunst im Drama der Zukunft', in *Oper und Drama* (Leipzig: Weber, 1852), Project Gutenberg. Online, available at: http://gutenberg. spiegel.de/wagner/operdram/operd341.htm [accessed 14 October 2005].

Music is thus the prime vehicle of emotive communication, containing within it the '*Ur*-tone of all human speech'.[36]

Music, for Wagner, takes over where the human voice becomes 'hindered' by 'word-defining consonants', and it is in this sense that music which is free from words is able to create profound, lasting sensations of an emotive state. Wagner's concern to relate the emotive responses derived from instrumental music back to the human voice, is the point at which Baudelaire (and later Mallarmé) would re-claim poetry's privilege over music, turning poetry into a complex 'chant-instrument'. Both poets are eager to reinforce poetry's position by granting it the status of a musical genre which is capable of orchestrating the mystery of language.[37]

However, Baudelaire recognises that instrumental music's privilege – its freedom from words – stems from its ability to provoke emotive responses that are not reliant on a subjective involvement which seeks to explain or understand the meaning of feelings. As Philippe Lacoue-Labarthe elaborates:

> Seule la musique est à même d'exprimer, c'est-à-dire de signifier, mais au-delà de la signification, cet au-delà subjectif du sujet: ce qui, du sujet, mais en lui aussi bien et comme lui, passe le sujet.
>
> Ce n'est pas simplement parce que la musique se définit comme le mode d'expression privilégié du sentiment ou même de ce que Baudelaire appelle, plus rigoureusement, 'la partie indéfinie du sentiment'.[38]

> [Only music is capable of expressing, that is to say, signifying, but beyond signification, this subjective beyond of the subject: the aspect of the subject that, in the subject and as the subject as well, moves beyond the subject.
>
> This is not only because music defines itself as the privileged mode of the expression of feeling or even of what Baudelaire more rigorously calls 'the undefined part of feeling'.]

The ideal of the abstract voice of instrumental music aims to move beyond the grip of subjective interpretation (and it is because they avert subjective preconceptions that both poets are attracted by strange voices[39]). Metaphors of instrumental music are almost invariably presented within the context of feelings and sensations in the work of Baudelaire and Mallarmé because such music is able to release the

---

[36]   Shaw-Miller, *Visible Deeds in Music*, p.41.

[37]   Cf. Catani who writes in relation to Mallarmé's 'Solitude' that the writer who will achieve the most success is the one who is 'best able to orchestrate "le mystère" – an explanation of the human condition'. Damian Catani, *The Poet in Society: Art, Consumerism and Politics in Mallarmé* (Bern: Peter Lang, 2003), p.209.

[38]   Lacoue-Labarthe, *Musica ficta (Figures de Wagner)*, p.74; trans. Felicia McCarren (Stanford: Stanford University Press, 1994), p.29.

[39]   See Chapter 5.

dual bonds of semantics and subjectivity in order to convey a poetic idea in a way that can be sensed by all. The effects of instrumental music must always return to vocal music because, as Baudelaire discerned in his article on Banville, there is a 'manière lyrique de sentir' (B.*OC*.II, p.164). So if poetry is a proto-music then it is a precarious proto-music. The poet who hankers after a musical state, rich with profound sensations and impressions of analogous and suggestive language, always runs the risk of failing to attain this aesthetic ideal. The precarious balance between music and poetry, hinged around the idea of poetry as a proto-music or indeed of music as a proto-poetry, is persistently tipped first one way and then the other by the fact that both arts necessarily continue to borrow from one another in a process of exchange that seeks to abstract the ideal response by creating a lingering sensation.

Both Baudelaire and Mallarmé explore this complex balancing act in sonnets centred on the image of a bell. Baudelaire's 'La Cloche fêlée' (B.*OC*.I, pp.71–72) and Mallarmé's 'Le Sonneur' (M.*OC*.I, p.13) both present moments of a poetic experience where the resonant voices they expect to be able to produce in fact falter. Written about 10 years apart from each other (the earliest version of Baudelaire's sonnet dates from 1851, Mallarmé's from 1862), the quatrains of both sonnets explore the symbolic tolling of a bell, and the religious connotations that this entails (Mallarmé talks of 'un angélus' ['an angelus'] v.4, Baudelaire of a 'cri religieux' ['religious cry'] v.7). At the 'volta' of both sonnets, however, the sudden introduction of the voice of the poetic 'je' sets up a contrast to the ringing out of the bell. The shift from the third person description of the bell to the voice of the first-person singular also signals a distinctive change in mood – the poetic 'je' of each poem recognises that the ability to ring out as clearly as the symbolic incantation of the bell is not a given. The two sonnets, for all their differences, employ a similar narrative in this respect, because the resonant voice of the bell has a greater force than the weakened voice of the poetic 'je'. This narrative can be summarised as follows:

	Baudelaire, 'La Cloche fêlée'	Mallarmé, 'Le Sonneur'
ringing out of bell (quatrains)	la cloche au gosier vigoureux (v.5) [the bell with a vigorous throat]	la cloche éveille sa voix claire (v.1) [the bell awakens its clear voice]
insertion of first-person / 'je' (opening tercet)	Moi, mon âme est fêlée (v.9) [Me, my soul is cracked]	Je suis cet homme (v.9) [I am that man]
desire to ring out like bell	Elle veut de ses chants peupler l'air froid des nuits (v.10) [It wants with its songs to populate the cold air of the nights]	J'ai beau tirer la câble à sonner l'Idéal (v.10) [I pull the rope in vain to sound the Ideal]
weakened voice	Il arrive souvent que sa voix affaiblie (v.11) [It often happens that its weakened voice]	Et la voix ne me vient que par bribes et creuse! (v.12) [And the voice only reaches me in snatches and erodes!]

The weakened poetic voice can find no felicitous resolution to his fate; it ends in death. This is, however, a symbolic death of an overly-subjective poetic voice which fails to resonate or ring out. Of course, the poems themselves are still able to resonate: implicitly, therefore, these sonnets indicate that both Baudelaire and Mallarmé sought to make their poems ring out as a proto-music by borrowing the instrumental music metaphor of the bell whose voice is more abstract. Both poets recognise that any poetic voice that fails to resonate must be annihilated in order to allow the mysterious resonances of poetic language to take place. Neither sonnet objurgates the bell for its resonant vigour: both sonnets express the desire to become like the bell, and for the poetic 'je' to absent itself in order to let the persistent tolling express its plentiful and rich sensations. This persistent tolling of the bell is like a Wagnerian 'leitmotiv' that makes music's presence felt more intensely than the voice of the poet himself.[40]

Unexpected Returns: Dialogues, Refrains and the Song Setting

If both poets are increasingly drawn, over the course of their poetic careers, to exploit stranger and more abstract voices by rendering the subjective involvement of poetic protagonists more oblique, then it is no surprise that music becomes such an important part of their aesthetics of voice. Having considered the extensive recurrence of musical metaphors in the work of both poets, and their awareness of the aesthetic standpoints of Poe, Wagner, Banville and Ghil, it is important also to analyse whether such metaphorical interpretations also relate to particular musical techniques or forms. Where musical metaphors may falter in their effect, musical techniques which privilege repetitive motifs might be able to create more long-lasting effects. What music seems to offer to Baudelaire and Mallarmé – beyond the ideal of abstracting voices so that they become strange, rarified and free from subjective preconceptions – is an indispensable strategy for remembering and recognising poetry.

In the 'Salon de 1846' Baudelaire expresses the importance of memory in art:

> J'ai déjà remarqué que le souvenir était le grand criterium de l'art; l'art est une mnémotechnie du beau. (B.*OC*.II, p.455)

> [I have already mentioned that memory was the great criterium of art; art is a mnemonic of the beautiful.]

What strategies for remembering poetry are available to Baudelaire and Mallarmé? Both poets are aware of the incantatory properties of poetry: this stems from their acknowledgment of the influence of spiritual and religious ritual on their poetic

---

[40]   This is also why, perhaps, Wagner's own voice is silenced by Mallarmé in his sonnet 'Hommage (à Wagner)' (M.*OC*.I, p.39–40).

art. Mallarmé, for example, writes in the 'Ouverture' to the 1866 draft theatrical version of 'Hérodiade' (v.38–40):

> Ombre magicienne aux symboliques charmes!
> Une voix, du passé longue évocation,
> Est-ce la sienne prête à l'incantation? (M.*OC*.I, p.136)

> [Magician's shadow with symbolic charms!
> A voice, long evocation of the past,
> Is it yours ready for incantation?]

These words come from an incantation by Hérodiade's 'Nourrice': the ritual of recitation has the seemingly magical effect of evoking the past. As we have seen, being able to remember past voices is central to Mallarmé's aesthetics of voice, since these voices influence each new reading of his poetry. The incantatory effects produced by reading poetry are not the only ways of evoking past voices.[41] Exploiting repetitive devices such as small-scale sound repetitions (alliteration, assonance, rhyme) or larger-scale repetitions such as refrains are inherent to the poetic art, but the way Baudelaire and Mallarmé exploit these in relation to their aesthetics of voice reveals an important indebtedness to music. Such indebtedness is not simply retrospective; both poets look towards forms which unite poetry and music such as the song setting. As I shall demonstrate, however, the supposed conjoining of poetry and music in the form of a song setting can open up even deeper divisions and particular interpretative dilemmas that affect the possibility of creating a memorable response.

The opening line of Baudelaire's 'Le Balcon' (B.*OC*.I, pp.36–37) is replete with repetitive strategies, incorporating the strong alliteration of both 'm' and 's' sounds, as well as semantically sparking off a set of memories:

> Mère des souvenirs, maîtresse des maîtresses (v.1)

> [Mother of memories, mistress of all mistresses]

Furthermore, 'Le Balcon' is in 'strophe encadrée' form, with this line repeated at the end of the stanza. This hints at the idea that the repetitive devices in Baudelaire are not just intended to serve as an evocative 'leitmotiv', but also to create a particular sense that what is being performed, spoken or sung has already been heard before. Being able to spark off a sense of recognition is an important feature of repetitive devices, as they serve the memory by recalling past experiences. Lacoue-Labarthe calls this process 'anamnesis', the ability to recall and identify with past occurrences. Lacoue-Labarthe suggests that Baudelaire's strong sense of

---

[41]   The etymology of 'incantation', like 'enchantement', is of course derived from 'chant', which reinforces the close rapport between 'chant' and poetry.

appreciation of Wagner's music is due to the fact that he recognises himself within it. He cites Baudelaire's own sense of recognition:

> [dans la lettre de Baudelaire à Wagner] le [motif le] plus décisif est évidemment le motif de l'*anamnèse*. Si la subjugation de Baudelaire est si forte, c'est en réalité parce que cette musique, *il l'avait déjà entendue*: 'Je connaissais cette musique'; 'Cette musique était la mienne, et je la reconnaissais comme tout homme reconnaît les choses qu'il est destiné à aimer'. L'anamnèse est la *reconnaissance* elle-même, et il y va de la *destination du sujet*.[42]

> [[in Baudelaire's letter to Wagner], the most definitive motif is that of *anamnesis*. If Baudelaire's subjugation is so strong, it is in reality because *he had already heard this music*: 'I knew this music'; 'This music was my own, and I recognized it as any man recognizes those things he is destined to love.' Anamnesis is *recognition* itself; it is a matter of the *destination of the subject*.]

In his poetry, Baudelaire exploits repetitive devices in order to activate this 'I have already heard this' sensation, or the process of 'anamnesis'.[43] Baudelaire is quick to recognise that – as is the case with religious incantation – an over-use of repetition will dissolve into a meaningless and ineffective babble.

In his 'Notes Nouvelles sur Edgar Poe' Baudelaire places particular emphasis on the use of rhyme patterns and refrains in Poe's blank verse whilst also highlighting the importance of surprise, or the quality of 'étrangeté':

> Poe attachait une importance extrême à la rime, et … dans l'analyse qu'il a faite du plaisir mathématique et musical que l'esprit tire de la rime, il a apporté autant de soin, autant de subtilité que dans tous les sujets se rapportant au métier poétique. De même il avait démontré que le refrain est susceptible d'applications infiniment variées, il a aussi cherché à rajeunir, à redoubler le plaisir de la rime en y ajoutant cet élément inattendu, *l'étrangeté*, qui est comme le condiment indispensable de toute beauté. Il fait surtout un usage heureux des répétitions du même vers ou de plusieurs vers, retours obstinés de phrases qui simulent les obsessions de la mélancolie ou de l'idée fixe – du refrain pur et simple, mais amené en situation de plusieurs manières différentes – du refrain-variante qui joue l'indolence et la distraction – des rimes redoublées et triplées, et aussi d'un genre de rime qui introduit dans la poésie moderne, mais avec plus de précision et d'intention, les surprises du vers léonin. (B.*OC*.II, pp.335–336)

---

[42] Lacoue-Labarthe, *Musica ficta. (Figures de Wagner)*, pp.61–62; trans. Felicia McCarren, p.21.

[43] See Graham Chesters's work *Some Functions of Sound Repetition in 'Les Fleurs du Mal'* (Hull: University of Hull, 1975) for a detailed exploration of Baudelaire's repetitive devices.

[Poe attached a great importance to rhyme, and … in the analysis that he carried out of the mathematical and musical pleasure that the mind derives from rhyme, he used as much care and as much subtlety as in all subjects relating to the poetic art. Just as he showed that the refrain can be applied in infinitely varied ways, so too did he seek to update, and to intensify the pleasure of rhyme by adding this unexpected element to it, *strangeness*, which is like the essential condiment of all beauty. In particular he makes effective use of repetitions of the same verse or of several verses, obstinate returns of phrases which simulate the obsessions of melancholy or of a fixation – of the pure and simple refrain, but also brought into use in several different ways – of the variant-refrain which plays with indolence and distraction – doubled or tripled rhymes, and also of a type of rhyme which introduces into modern poetry, but with more precision and intention, the surprises of the leonine verse.]

The attraction of carefully-employed repetitive devices is that they are 'susceptible d'applications infiniment variées', and they are able to exploit anamnestic possibilities.[44] Poe's craft is successful because he varies his repetitive devices by using internal rhymes and by ensuring that a line repetition exploits the effects created by different contexts. Baudelaire's admiration of this technique is indicative of how he uses repetitive devices in his own poetry to serve a process of 'memoria'. The 'actio' of using voice in poetry, then, becomes inextricably linked to 'memoria' because in bringing a poem to voice the reader begins to recognise past encounters with words, sounds and the evocative feelings that these can create. What takes place in poetry is an exchange between past and present uses of voice. The exchange must, however, create unexpected returns – to be found in the quality of 'étrangeté' – if poetry is to be deemed to be truly resonant. By exploiting the blurred line between poetry which is spoken and poetry which is sung (in the form of incantatory devices), both poets acknowledge that the abstract and strange voice of music serves their poetic art. For poetry to sing out silently in such a way as to create a lasting impression, it must both meet and confound the expectations of the memory.

It is not the act or repetition per se that creates such an effect, but the exchange of unexpected returns derived from a new encounter with a sound, word or phrase already encountered. Graham Robb has noted that 'la forme dialogique … est un des traits de la chanson' ['dialogic form … is one of the features of song'].[45] The

---

[44]   'L'esthétique du refrain, outre son rôle cyclique, consiste dans la manière dont il s'inscrit à chaque fois dans un nouveau contexte, ce qui nuance son jeu de significations' ['The aesthetic of the refrain, beyond its cyclical function, consists of the manner in which it inscribes itself each time within a new context, which nuances its game of possible meanings']. *Dictionnaire de Rhétorique et Poétique*, ed. by Michèle Aquien and Georges Molinié (Paris: Librairie Générale de France, 1996), p.640.

[45]   Graham Robb, *La poésie de Baudelaire et la poésie française 1838–1852* (Paris: Aubier, 1993), p.257.

conversational exchange, or 'forme dialogique', for Baudelaire and Mallarmé, as I have explored above, is a complex system which seeks to exploit the more extraordinary or strange qualities of the exchange process, seeking out unexpected responses.[46] Just as Baudelaire is much more explicit in his strategies for designating voice in his poetry than Mallarmé, so too is he more explicit about his repetitive devices in his verse poems. Baudelaire exploits line repetitions and refrains in a number of poems, where Mallarmé's 'refrains' are confined to the tripartite repetition of 'L'Azur, l'azur, l'azur ...' (v.36) in 'L'Azur' (M.*OC*.I, pp.14–15) or to the recurrent phrase 'Nommez-nous ...' (v.9, 12 and 15) in 'Placet futile' (M.*OC*. I, p.8).[47] That Mallarmé is more oblique or subtle in his use of conversational and repetitive devices signals an important development in the attitude towards how the quality of 'étrangeté' is able to function in poetry: Baudelaire had already begun to explore how conversational and repetitive devices might be rendered more oblique, Mallarmé then took this to further extremes.

Whilst I do not suggest that the devices of dialogue and line repetition are what define poetry as 'musical', the heritage of poetry as a musical art seems to have retained, in Baudelaire at least, these traits as indicators of poetry's ability to sing. For example, in 'Hymne' (B.*OC*.I, p.162), Baudelaire uses a rhetorical question as a trait of a thwarted conversation and a refrain which is modified. The rhetorical question is a direct address to his mistress and its content draws attention to the stylistic traits of Baudelaire's poem:

> Comment, amour incorruptible,
> T'exprimer avec vérité? (v.13–14)

> [How can I, oh incorruptible love,
> Express you truthfully?]

Baudelaire's self-conscious questioning about the techniques he might use to express his love for his mistress directly relates to the refrain that he uses in this poem, since the refrain stanzas are the only other stanzas in which Baudelaire directly addresses her. The opening and last stanzas are the 'refrain' stanzas, and these, in turn borrow from the third line of the sonnet 'Que diras-tu'.[48] Baudelaire subtly modifies both the first and the second line of the refrain upon repetition in the final stanza:

---

[46]   See Chapter 4.

[47]   Claude Debussy's setting of this poem fills in the ellipsis that follows the first two instances of the imperative 'Nommez-nous ...' by citing, in the piano accompaniment, the opening phrase of the piano introduction to the song. See Songs of Claude Debussy, ed. by James R. Briscoe, 2 vols (Milwaukee: Hal Leonard, 1993), II, pp.164–167.

[48]   Both poems were composed in the same year, 1854, and dedicated to the same woman, Madame Sabatier. See Chapter 4, pp.128–130, for an analysis of 'Que diras-tu'.

First stanza	Final stanza
À la très chère, à la très belle	À la très bonne, à la très belle
Qui remplit mon cœur de clarté,	Qui fait ma joie et ma santé,
À l'ange, à l'idole immortelle,	À l'ange, à l'idole immortelle,
Salut en l'immortalité!	Salut en l'immortalité!
[To the very dear one, to the very beautiful one	[To the very good one, to the very beautiful one
Who fills my heart with light,	Who is my joy and my health
To the angel, to the immortal idol,	To the angel, to the immortal idol
All hail in immortality!]	All hail in immortality!]

These careful modifications prevent the repetition from being too exact, prompting the reader instead to reflect on the effect created by the thwarted repetition, which is, in turn, reinforced by the thwarted exchange of the rhetorical question which requires the reader to supply a response.

There are, however, conflicts which arise from other 'readings' of this poem. Where Baudelaire has been careful to manipulate his repetitive strategies according to an apparently 'musical' technique, when this poem was later set to music by Gabriel Fauré, the composer ignores the subtle modifications of the repeated stanza, and, furthermore, opts to repeat the line 'Salut en l'immortalité' twice at the end of the first stanza, and three times at the end of the song.[49] In addition, he decides to preserve the same melodic line and accompaniment for the repetition, thereby refusing to acknowledge the important nuances of the modifications that Baudelaire's altered refrain had presented. The conflicts that arise from the composer's musical setting of the poem suggest that there is a conflict between a musician's perspective on 'musical' techniques such as the refrain, and the poet's perspective on such techniques. Fauré's decision may be in line with his expectation of what a refrain in a song should do. Traditionally, a refrain in a song was the moment at which the chorus or audience could join in: if there were changes to the refrain, this would make it harder for an audience (who would not have the words in front of them) to take part. This theory does not, however, necessarily stand up to the test of other Baudelaire poems which have been set to music.

Although during Baudelaire's lifetime relatively few of his poems were ever set to music, those that were set to music either before his death or afterwards have tended to be the ones which contain large-scale repetitive devices. Within Baudelaire's verse poetry line-repetition is employed in a range of different ways.

First, the 'strophe encadrée' form is used in four poems from *Les Fleurs du Mal*: 'Le Balcon', 'Réversibilité', 'L'Irréparable' and 'Mœsta et errabunda' (all from the 'Spleen et Idéal' section) use this strategy, which repeats the opening line of a stanza as the final line of the same stanza. The same device is used in a fifth poem which was banned from the collection following the 1857 trial, 'Lesbos' (which like 'Le Balcon' opens with the word 'Mère').

---

49 Gabriel Fauré, *Mélodies*, 3 vols (Paris: Hamelle, [n.d.]), I, pp.71–77.

Another poem which uses line repetition on a more complex and extensive scale is 'Harmonie du soir'. This poem employs the Malay pantoum form (introduced to France by Victor Hugo with *Les Orientales*), which repeats the second and fourth lines of each stanza as the first and third of the subsequent stanza. Baudelaire's pantoum is in fact irregular, because it does not also conclude with the opening line of the poem, as the form would typically require. 'Harmonie du soir' is therefore an unusual poem on many levels – not only is it the only example of a very strictly repetitive form, which alternates only two rhymes '-oir' and '–ige', but it is also an irregular example of the form.

Line repetition also takes the form of repetition of entire stanzas. Another poem which takes an unusual form is 'Le Beau navire'. The first three stanzas of the poem are reiterated later in the poem, although each time separated by two new stanzas so that the stanza pattern becomes A-B-C-A-D-E-B-F-G-C. Following on directly from 'Le Beau navire', 'L'Invitation au voyage' repeats the two-line stanza or couplet 'Là, tout n'est qu'ordre et beauté, / Luxe, calme et volupté' as the poem's refrain. Two further examples of a refrain can be found in Baudelaire's work, first of all the one-line refrain in 'Les Litanies de Satan' from the 'Révolte' section, and in the second instance in 'Le Jet d'eau' which was published in *Le Parnasse contemporain* in 1866, where Baudelaire repeats a six-line refrain. 'Hymne' repeats the first stanza as the last stanza, but with modifications.

Smaller-scale repetitions, but still not on the level of individual phonemes, include the anaphoric 'Abel et Caïn', which alternates the opening of each couplet with either 'Race d'Abel' or 'Race de Caïn', and also 'L'Horloge' which incorporates the refrain '*Souviens-toi!* ' four times (v.10, 13, 17, 19).

Of these 13 poems which incorporate large-scale repetitive patternings, one is known to have been set to music in Baudelaire's lifetime ('L'Invitation au voyage' by Jules Cressonnois, which was also later set by Emmanuel Chabrier and, most famously, Henri Duparc), and at least a further five of these poems were set to music by French composers after his death ('Le Balcon', 'Harmonie du soir' and 'Le Jet d'eau' by Claude Debussy, 'Hymne' by Gabriel Fauré, and 'Réversibilité' by Louis Vierne). Whilst this analysis is not intended to address the complete corpus of song settings of Baudelaire's poetry, there is evidence that poems with large-scale repetitive devices lend themselves more readily to a song setting (even if ultimately conflicts arise) because the repetition serves as a structuring device which is reminiscent of poetry's originary heritage as song.[50]

Although we know that Jules Cressonnois and Villiers de l'Isle-Adam set Baudelaire's poetry to music during his lifetime, Baudelaire's reaction to this

---

[50] For recordings of settings of Baudelaire, see, for example, the CD recording by Felicity Lott (soprano) and Graham Johnson (piano), *Mélodies sur des poèmes de Baudelaire* (Arles: Harmonia mundi, 2003).

is unknown.[51] He writes in a letter dated 1865 or 1866 and probably addressed to Madame Charles Hugo, pianist and singer and daughter-in-law of Victor Hugo:

> Madame, Voici des mélodies de mon ami Cressonnois, que je n'ai jamais entendu exécuter. Je compte un peu sur vous pour me faire cette grâce. (B.*Corr.* II, p.559)

> [Madam, Here are the songs by my friend Cressonnois, which I have never heard performed. I hope I can count on you to do me this favour.]

Even if the 'mélodies' to which he refers in this letter included Cressonnois' setting of 'L'Invitation au voyage', there is no further correspondence reflecting Baudelaire's opinion on the setting. That the same poem was then set only three years after Baudelaire's death by Emmanuel Chabrier and Henri Duparc suggests that this is a poem that particularly attracts the attention of composers. Chabrier, on hearing Duparc's masterful setting of the poem, withdrew his own composition out of deference. By contrast with the Cressonnois setting, however, both Chabrier and Duparc only set the first and last stanzas, and repeat only two refrains, missing out the middle stanza and refrain. Where the Cressonnois setting retains one tune for verses and another for the refrains (with only some minor modifications to the piano accompaniment), Chabrier and Duparc are much more inventive in their settings (the Cressonnois setting also distorts the metrical accents of the Baudelairean verse line by rigidly adhering to 3/4 time).

Baudelaire's own prose poem version of 'L'Invitation au voyage' (published in *Le Présent* in August 1857) points towards the so-called 'musicality' of the poem and the desire to hear 'L'Invitation au voyage' set to music; but here the focus moves away from the supposed 'musicality' of repetitive techniques, and turns instead to more aesthetic reflections. He refers first of all to Weber's similar-sounding 'L'Invitation à la valse' which hints at his desire for a musical setting of his own poem:

> Oui, c'est là qu'il faut aller respirer, rêver et allonger les heures par l'infini des sensations. Un musicien a écrit l'*Invitation à la valse*; quel est celui qui composera l'*Invitation au voyage*, qu'on puisse offrir à la femme aimée, à la sœur d'élection? (B.*OC*.I, p.302)

---

[51] Jules Cressonnois, 'L'Invitation au voyage' in *Harmonies*, 4 vols ([Paris?]: [n.pub.], 1862–1865), III, pp.27–33. For the Villiers setting, see *Lettres à Baudelaire*, ed. by Claude Pichois (Neuchâtel: La Baconnière, 1973), p.385 which reproduces Villiers' setting of 'La Mort des amants' dating from *c*.1865 as transcribed by Charles de Sivry and published in *Les Quat'z'arts*, 3 April 1898.

[Yes, that is where one must go to breathe, to dream and to extend time through infinite sensations. A musician has written *Invitation to the waltz*; who will be the one to compose the *Invitation to the voyage*, which could be offered to the adored woman, to the chosen sister?]

The relationship between 'sensations' and 'musique' is made explicit by the way Baudelaire places the desire for a musical version of 'L'Invitation au voyage' immediately after the word 'sensations'. The imagined sensations feed the musical idea, but both are elusive because they have not yet been attained. Rather like the boy's desire in the prose poem 'Les Vocations', where he not only wanted to follow the roving gypsy musicians, but also wanted 'de les prier de m'emmener avec eux et d'apprendre à jouer de leurs instruments' (B.*OC*. I, p.335), the poetic voice in 'L'Invitation au voyage' is aspirational, seeking to escape the quotidian through an admixture of music and travel. The irony conveyed in the paragraph cited, however, is that Baudelaire knows only too well that he has already written two 'Invitations au voyage' – the verse poem, and the prose poem. That he considers these to be 'musical' is made explicit not only by the choice of the verb 'composera' but also by his placing the title side-by-side with Weber's, as if Baudelaire considers a 'voyage' to be a musical form like the 'valse'.

If the 'musicality' of 'L'Invitation au voyage' is more easily discerned in the verse form (B.*OC*.I, pp.53–54) rather than the prose poem, it is because of the inclusion of the two-line refrain:

> Là, tout n'est qu'ordre et beauté,
> Luxe, calme et volupté. (v.13–14, 27–28, 41–42)

> [There, all is order and beauty,
> Luxury, calm and voluptuous pleasure.]

The heptasyllabic lines of the refrain's couplet are distinct from other heptasyllabic lines in the poem (the verse stanzas alternate between lines of five and seven syllables, itself perhaps a 'dialogue' between different verse line lengths) because of the structure of the line. By inserting the comma immediately after 'Là', Baudelaire creates a moment of stasis, followed by a seemingly regular hemistich of six syllables. The second line of the refrain also has a clear moment of stasis created by the comma after 'Luxe', this time after two syllables instead of one (forcing a 'coupe lyrique' with the mute 'e' being pronounced), thus creating a sense of imbalance between the two lines of the refrain. A rapport between the two lines is established, however, by the build-up of five nouns which elaborate what is meant by the opening word of the refrain, 'Là': 'ordre', 'beauté', 'luxe', 'calme', 'volupté'.

Example 6.1 Duparc, 'L'Invitation au voyage', bars 31–40

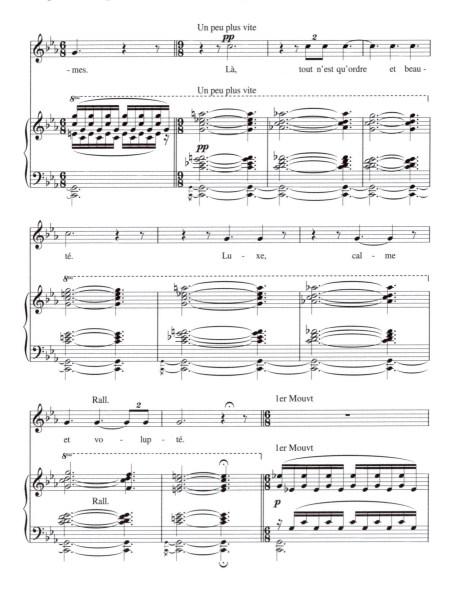

The stasis created by the commas in the Baudelairean line is mirrored in Duparc's musical setting of the poem (see Example 6.1).[52] (Cressonnois, by contrast, does not incorporate any moment of stasis in his setting of the refrain). Duparc creates a moment of stasis at the refrain first of all by a change in metre

---

[52]   Duparc, *Mélodies*, 2 vols (Paris: Salabert, 1988), I, pp.1–8.

from 6/8 to 9/8, and then by suddenly replacing the continuous semiquavers of the underlying accompaniment of the verses with long tied notes. He also signals a change in pulse, suggesting that the refrain should be 'Un peu plus vite' ['A little faster']. Although this may seem to contradict the sense of stasis he creates at the refrain, the indication of a change in pulse in fact serves to disrupt any sense of continuity from the preceding verse passage. In the first bar of the refrain, not only are there now long tied notes and a new metre, but the change in pulse also means that the timing of the entry of the voice following on from the piano chord does not follow from the preceding pulse. Duparc retains the quality of stasis throughout the two lines of the refrain by adhering to the texture of chordal tied notes in the piano part, beneath a vocal line which remains on one note (c") for the first line, and drops down a fifth for the second line. After a pause at the end of the refrain, the metre returns to 6/8, the pulse returns to the '1ᵉʳ Mouvement' and the continuous semiquavers start up again to signal the return of the verse element.

The clear distinction between verse and refrain in the Duparc setting is, however, only maintained in the first instance of the appearance of the refrain. On its second occurrence, the vocal line remains the same, but the piano accompaniment is different, retaining the semiquaver patternings from the verse element of the song setting. Duparc demonstrates a sensitivity to the way in which a refrain can be used in order to recall, to remember and yet also to introduce an element of surprise.

The fact that Duparc's setting, for example, is a much more mature interpretation of Baudelaire's poem than Cressonnois' setting, is not only a mark of Duparc's skill as a composer, but also illustrates that the composer, like any reader of Baudelaire's poetry, is free to make interpretative decisions about pauses, breathing spaces, pacing, tempo, timbre and colour. It is for this reason that it is problematic to suggest that Duparc's setting ought to be privileged over Cressonnois', or even Chabrier's, setting. Each different musical 'reading' of the poem confirms that the relationship between poetry and music is necessarily subject to disruptions and distortions. 'L'Invitation au voyage' was not specifically written to be set to music although it has prompted a number of settings. There is evidence, by contrast, that 'Le Jet d'eau' was originally intended as a song, perhaps in conjunction with Pierre Dupont, himself poet and composer. This hypothesis is significant because Dupont's songs follow a more naïve, popular genre which might, on the surface, seem to be at odds with the Baudelairean aesthetic which prompted the development of the more complex art song. Baudelaire is quick to point out that although Dupont's songs are more naïve than his own, the fact that they were performed by Dupont with such 'sentiment' is an important mark of what it means to set poetry to music. Although Baudelaire himself was no composer, his admiration of Dupont's skill lies in the fact that Dupont was able to combine poetry and music effectively. Baudelaire writes in his 'notice' which appeared in the 1851 edition of Pierre Dupont's *Chants et Chansons*:

> L'édition à laquelle cette notice est annexée contient, avec chaque chanson,
> la musique, qui est presque toujours du poète lui-même, mélodies simples et

d'un caractère libre et franc, mais qui demandent un certain art pour bien être exécutées. Il était véritablement utile, pour donner une idée juste de ce talent, de fournir le texte musical, beaucoup de poésies étant admirablement complétées par le chant. (B.*OC*.II, p.35)

[The edition to which this preface is attached contains the music together with each 'chanson' [poem], almost all of which have been composed by the poet himself, simple melodies, of a free and frank nature, which nevertheless require a certain skill to be executed effectively. Having the musical text is particularly useful, since a lot of poems are admirably completed by song.]

Baudelaire's comment that poetry can be 'admirablement complété[e] par le chant' illustrates his awareness of the role of music in poetic composition, but the sub-text here is that Dupont's poetry is lacking something which is fulfilled or completed by the musical element.[53] It demonstrates Baudelaire's wariness of what it means to set a poem to music: not every poem needs to be 'completed' by music.

Baudelaire's comments about Dupont's *Chants et Chansons*, however, do illustrate an important element of Baudelaire's own aesthetics of voice. Rather like Roland Barthes' comments in 'Le Grain de la voix' about how much he preferred Charles Panzéra's voice to Dietrich Fischer-Dieskau's, already Baudelaire had spotted in Dupont's voice certain qualities which lend themselves more appropriately to the type of song he sings:[54]

Ainsi que beaucoup de personnes, j'ai souvent entendu Pierre Dupont chanter lui-même ses œuvres, et comme elles, je pense que nul ne les a mieux chantées. J'ai entendu de belles voix essayer ces accents rustiques ou patriotiques, et cependant je n'éprouvais qu'un malaise irritant. Comme ce livre de chansons ira chez tous ceux qui aiment la poésie … je leur ferai part d'une réflexion qui m'est venue en cherchant la cause du déplaisir que m'ont causé beaucoup de chanteurs. Il ne suffit pas d'avoir la voix juste ou belle, il est beaucoup plus important d'avoir du sentiment. (B.*OC*.II, p.35)

[Like many people, I often heard Pierre Dupont sing his own works, and like them, I believe that nobody else could have sung them better. I have heard good voices trying to capture these rustic or patriotic accents, and yet all I could feel was an irritating discomfort. Since this book of chansons will go to all those who like poetry … I would like to share a thought which occured to me when trying to work out the reason for the displeasure that lots of singers have caused

---

[53]   Rosemary Lloyd points out that Baudelaire's comment here concurs with the opinions of other contemporary critics of Dupont's work, such as Champfleury and Sainte-Beuve. See Rosemary Lloyd, *Baudelaire's Literary Criticism* (Cambridge: CUP, 1981), p.30.

[54]   See Roland Barthes, *Œuvres complètes*, ed. by Éric Marty, 3 vols (Paris: Seuil, 1994), II, pp.1436–1442.

me. It is not enough to simply have a good or beautiful voice, it is much more
important to have some sentiment.]

If poetry is to be performed as a song, the poetic song is not to be devoid of
sentiment, but replete with the profound sensations that the resonances between
poetry and music can create. Baudelaire's recognition that not all singers are adept
at performing songs to Baudelaire's own taste is mirrored also by the Goncourt
brothers who recall an evening chez Daudet in June 1883 where the poet and
composer Maurice Rollinat performed his own settings of Baudelaire's poetry.
Where previously Rollinat had not been to the Goncourt taste, his performance of
settings of Baudelaire prompt an unexpected response:

> Je n'avais jusqu'ici qu'un goût médiocre pour Rollinat. Je le trouvais tantôt trop
> macabre, tantôt trop *bête à bon Dieu*. Aujourd'hui, il me prend par de la musique
> qu'il a faite sur quelques pièces de Baudelaire. Cette musique est vraiment d'une
> compréhension tout à fait supérieure. Je ne sais pas quelle est sa valeur près des
> musiciens; mais ce que je sais, c'est que c'est de la musique de poète et de la
> musique parlant aux hommes de lettres. Il est impossible de mieux faire valoir,
> de mieux *monter en épingle* la beauté des mots; et quand on entend cela, c'est la
> sensation d'un coup de fouet, donné à ce qu'il y a de littéraire en vous.[55]

> [Up until now I didn't especially like Rollinat. I sometimes found him too
> macabre, sometimes too banal. Today he swept me away through the music
> which he has written for some Baudelaire poems. This music is of a very superior
> understanding. I don't know what musicians will think of it; but what I do know
> is that it is a poet's music, and music that speaks to men of letters. There is no
> better way to emphasise, no better way *to show off* the beauty of the words; and
> when you hear it, it gives you the sensation of being whipped up, reinforcing the
> literary sentiment within you.]

Where Baudelaire had spoken of the necessity for 'sentiment' on the part of singers
performing Dupont's songs, here the Goncourts are surprised by the impact of the
sensation created by hearing Rollinat's music. Song settings of poetry are able,
then, to exploit strategies such as dialogue and refrain since these are techniques
which stem from poetry's heritage as song; more important to the effectiveness
of a song setting is not that it must contain dialogue or refrains, but that it is
able to lend itself to a musical performance that creates a profound and lasting
impression.

Music for both Baudelaire and Mallarmé provides not only a complex metaphor
for their own respective aesthetics of voice, but also a complex engagement and
interaction with different techniques and performance possibilities. Poetry's

---

[55] Edmond and Jules de Goncourt, *Journal: Mémoires de la vie littéraire*, 3 vols
(Paris: Flammarion, 1956–1989), II, p.1011.

relationship with vocal music is problematised because it remains beholden to words; and yet the relationship with instrumental music is problematised because it is entirely non-verbal. Each poet, therefore, endeavours to find ways which allow for an admixture of 'chant' and 'instrument' within their poetry, by exploring the interaction with music not just through musical metaphors within the poetry, but also through strategies of patterning and unexpected disruptions on either a larger or smaller scale. This way of understanding the relevance of music to poetry as a 'chant-instrument', allows Baudelaire to say of the female protagonist in 'Tout entière' (B.*OC*.I, p.42) 'son haleine fait la musique' (v.23), and Mallarmé to say in 'Crise de vers' that 'Toute âme est une mélodie qu'il s'agit de renouer; et pour cela, sont la flûte ou la viole de chacun' (M.*OC*.II, pp.207–208). The relationship between vocal music and instrumental music and the voice of poetry is maintained through the ideal of a vocal aesthetic that is neither music nor poetry in the traditional sense. As Jacques Rancière elaborates in his extended essay on Mallarmé in which he also quotes from a letter written by Mallarmé to Edmund Gosse dated 10 January 1893:

> La poésie est plus musicale que la musique pour deux raisons données comme équivalentes: parce qu'elle est l'art du verbe, de la pensée exprimée, qui s'oppose au 'mutisme' de l'orchestre, et parce qu'elle est l'art du silence, du 'tacite concert' ou du 'tacite envol d'abstraction' qui s'oppose à son fracas – 'la même chose que l'orchestre sauf que littérairement ou silencieusement'.[56]

> [Poetry is more musical than music for two reasons given as equivalent: because it is the art of the word, of expressed thought, which is opposed to the 'silence' of the orchestra, and because it is the art of silence, of the 'silent concert' or the 'silent flight of abstraction' which is opposed to its roar – 'the same thing as the orchestra except in a literary or silent fashion'.]

In order to create a poetry that sings, therefore, the poets must work with both language and with silence, with the words on the page and the empty breathing space surrounding them. In doing so, the poet's voice gives way to the voices of language, of music as both song and instruments, and of the reader, exploiting the patternings and disruptions that the breathing spaces between each of these voices entail:

> L'œuvre pur implique la disparition élocutoire du poète, qui cède l'initiative aux mots, par le heurt de leur inégalité mobilisés; ils s'allument de reflets réciproques comme une virtuelle traînée de feux sur des pierreries, remplaçant la respiration perceptible en l'ancien souffle lyrique ou la direction personnelle enthousisate de la phrase. (M.*OC*.II, p.211)[57]

---

[56]   Jacques Rancière, *Mallarmé: la politique de la sirène* (Paris: Hachette, 1996), p.89.

[57]   Barbara Johnson says of these words: 'Céder l'initiative aux mots, c'est avoir la voix de l'Autre, s'éclipser comme sujet, devenir soi-même autre' ['To relinquish initiative

[The pure work implies the elocutionary disappearance of the poet, who relinquishes initiative to the words, mobilised by the clash of their inequality; they light up with reciprocal reflections like a virtual trail of light across gemstones, replacing the perceptible breathing with the old lyric breath or the enthusiastic personal direction of the phrase.]

In this respect, the problem of subjectivity, or the question 'whose voice is it?' is overcome. The traces of all of poetry's voices are necessarily alternately disembodied and profoundly human, because in order to exploit the 'mystère' which is so indispensable to poetry's effectiveness, poetry must not over-determine the vocal scenarios. Whether Baudelaire's or Mallarmé's poetry was intended to be read out loud, either as a public recitation or to oneself, or to be read internally to oneself, or whether indeed it was intended ever to be set to music is not a question of any great import: the overriding concern for both poets – which they expressed in their different ways – was to create a vocal aesthetic that offers a subtle interaction between the human voice and abstract voices, between poetry's voices and music's voices, between the poet's voice and the reader's voice, in order to allow the mysterious resonances of language to ring out like the persistent – though at times irregular – oscillation of a tolling bell.

---

to the words, is to possess the voice of the Other, to eclipse oneself as subject, to oneself become other']. *Défigurations du langage poétique: la seconde révolution baudelairienne* (Paris: Flammarion, 1979), p.204.

Conclusion

In 1863 the German scientist Hermann Helmholtz published groundbreaking work on physiological acoustics. In his chapter on the relationship of musical tones, he remarked that:

> attentive observations on ordinary conversation show us that regular musical intervals involuntarily recur, although the singing tone of the voice is concealed under the noises which characterise the individual letters, and the pitch is not held firmly, but is frequently allowed to glide up and down.[1]

His analysis of the 'musicality' of conversation is founded on his preliminary hypothesis, expounded in the opening chapter of his work which explores the 'composition of vibrations':

> The first and principal difference between various sounds experienced by our ear, is that between *noises* and *musical tones*. ... Noises and musical tones may certainly intermingle in very various degrees, and pass insensibly into one another, but their extremes are widely separated.[2]

By recognising that we can distinguish between noises, the speaking voices of ordinary conversation and the sung musical notes, even though the distinction between these elements is always based on a sliding scale and is often based on frequent modulation between elements, Helmholtz has encapsulated the complexity of what it means to use one's voice (and how it resonates within the ear and according to human perception).[3]

---

[1] Hermann Helmholtz, *On the Sensations of Tone*, trans. by Alexander J. Ellis (New York: Dover Publications, 1954), p.238. The original German title is: *Die Lehre von den Tonempfindungen als physiologische Grundlage für die Theorie der Musik*. The first French translation appeared in 1868 as *Théorie phsyiologique de la musique fondée sur l'étude des sensations auditives*. For an analysis of the significance of this work in France, see Peter Dayan, *Music Writing Literature, from Sand via Debussy to Derrida* (Aldershot: Ashgate, 2006), p.51.

[2] Helmholtz, *On the Sensations of Tone*, p.7.

[3] The desire to notate words musically became an important preoccupation in the latter stages of the nineteenth century. For example, in the section of 'Crise de vers' which was originally written as an article published in *The National Observer* on 26 March 1892 and entitled 'Vers et musique en France', Mallarmé comments on Gustave Kahn's writings,

Although Baudelaire predates the publication of Helmholtz's work in French, and Mallarmé does not appear to have directly encountered Helmholtz's work, his comments on the extent to which we can identify musical notes in ordinary conversation point towards the kind of aesthetics of voice that both poets sought to promulgate. Since poetry itself is not an 'ordinary' conversation (and, as we have seen, Baudelaire in particular exploited the extraordinary in conversational exchanges, and Mallarmé was troubled by the problems of conversing poetically with those unattuned to his aesthetic ideals), it seems reasonable to suggest that in poetry the 'musical intervals' that Helmholtz discerns in ordinary conversation are intensified and rendered more prevalent. Helmholtz specifically talks of the ways in which the voice naturally rises or falls at the end of a sentence:

> The end of an affirmative sentence followed by a pause, is usually marked by the voice falling a Fourth from the middle pitch. An interrogative ending rises, often as much as a Fifth above the middle pitch. ... Emphasised words are also rendered prominent by their being spoken about a Tone higher than the rest.[4]

Whilst these observations are not universally applicable to all languages and ways of speaking, there is evidence that the speaking voice modulates according to emphasis. In poetry the emphases of metrical accents and rhyme structures are more prevalent than in 'ordinary' conversation (of course prose poetry follows more nebulous criteria, but the broad scope of these observations nevertheless apply). Although I am wary of using Helmholtz as 'proof' that poetic language is more 'musical' than ordinary language (and indeed my purpose has not been to demonstrate the 'musicality' or otherwise of poetry), his important observations remind us that the human voice is able to create the same kind of physical sensations through both speaking and singing because they are founded on the same basis. The ear detects pitch in both speaking and singing voices because the ear responds to the frequency of vibrations which Poe had termed 'an impulse on the air'.[5]

No wonder, then, that Baudelaire and Mallarmé were so preoccupied with poetry's relationship with music. The attention that both poets paid to the way in which voice can be used in poetry, and to how a poem can be brought to voice, offers a different view on acoustical perception to the scientific approach employed by Helmholtz. Various French theorists in the nineteenth century endeavoured to capture the closeness of the relationship between speaking and singing voices, between poetry and music – René Ghil, for example, was undoubtedly influenced by Helmholtz's work, but the lesser-known Louis Becq de Fouquières, writing in 1879, may not yet have encountered Helmholtz's important text. Where Helmholtz

---

in which Kahn proposes 'une très savante notation de la valeur tonale des mots' ['a very skilled notation of the tonal value of words'] (M.*OC*.II, p.207 and p.301).

[4]   Helmholtz, *On the Sensations of Tone*, p.238.

[5]   Edgar Allan Poe, *The Penguin Complete Tales and Poems of Edgar Allan Poe* (London: Penguin, 1982), p.442.

was concerned to identify the pitches of the speaking voice in terms of accepted musical notation, Becq de Fouquières endeavoured to use musical notation to capture the rhythms of spoken verse. In the ninth chapter of his *Traité général de versification française*, entitled 'Notation musicale des rythmes' ['The musical notation of rhythms'], he states that 'composer un vers, c'est construire une phrase musicale' ['to compose a verse is to construct a musical phrase']. According to the theories he propounds, if a musician is to set a poem to music, he remains bound to the given rhythms of the verse line proposed by the poet:

> on doit affirmer qu'un vers quelconque n'est autre chose qu'une phrase musicale, et que son rythme, noté musicalement, est le point de départ obligé du musicien. Celui-ci, sans parler ici du mode et de la hauteur des sons, peut augmenter ou diminuer le temps des vers, et par suite le temps des éléments rythmiques et la durée des syllabes; il peut, au moyen de riches variations, développer le thème qui lui est fourni par le poète; mais, sous la plus compliquée et la plus nombreuse instrumentation, on doit toujours retrouver le rhythme du vers inaltéré. L'inspiration musicale doit jaillir du vers, comme l'âme et la vie du germe qui les contient.[6]

> [it must be said that any verse is nothing other than a musical phrase, and that its rhythm, noted musically, is the required point of departure for the musician. This latter, without mentioning here the key or the pitch of the sounds, can increase or diminish the length of each line, and as a result the length of the rhythmic elements and the duration of the syllables; he can, through rich variations, develop the theme which is provided to him by the poet; but, even with the more complicated and more numerous instrumentation, the rhythm of the verse must always remain unaltered. The musical inspiration should gush forth from the verse line, like the soul and life from the seed which contains them.]

He goes on to give examples of verse rhythm notated in musical rhythms of quavers and crotchets (some of which are more convincing than others) supposedly by way of advising would-be composers how to set verse to music. The fact that both Helmholtz's musical notation of the pitch of speaking voices and Becq de Fouquières' musical notation of the rhythm of speaking voices ultimately fail to capture the complexity of what is actually going on when poetry is brought to voice is, however, an important indicator of the aesthetic conundrums that poets, musicians and theorists endeavoured to unravel.

What Baudelaire and Mallarmé do through their poetry is to exploit the closeness of speaking voices to singing voices, and of voices with words to voices without words. They do this not simply in order to provide a better notation system than that proferred by Helmholtz or Becq de Fouquières, but in order to furnish a

---

[6]   Louis Becq de Fouquières, *Traité général de versification française* (Paris: Charpentier, 1879), pp.181–182.

much more profound aesthetic truth: the most unspeakable and mysterious element of poetry is its most aesthetically rewarding. In order for poetry to retain its value, it must retain its mystery and its complexity, defying graspable explanations that would shatter the illusion of poetry's transporting effects. If, in order to do this, poetry must borrow from music, then neither poet shies away from this (indeed, as we have seen, they often do quite the contrary). By showing how both poets idealise the notion of poetry as deriving both from a 'chant' and from an 'instrument' – and that this 'chant-instrument' emerges from the use of the human voice in their poetic aesthetic – I have shown that both poets distanced themselves from contemporary aesthetic theories which sought to define, in a puportedly scientific way, how poetic language relates to musical language by proposing more sophisticated and complex models within their verse and prose poetry. I have not sought to 'prove' that their poetry is either a 'musical' or an 'oral' poetry, but rather that both poets are profoundly aware of the aesthetic value of using one's voice through poetry by drawing on the heritage of both music and oratory.

The art of oratory, stemming from the rhetorical tradition, influences the work of both poets insofar as they are aware of the ways in which a wider range of different performance scenarios are available for their poetry, in the voice of so many different possible readers. Whilst neither poet specifies precisely what kind of reader he envisages for his poetry, or how his poetry ought to be read, both are aware of potential pitfalls in reading scenarios. Mallarmé's preference for a softer dynamic range suggests a more intimate setting for the reading of his poetry, but this is not to the exclusion of public recitation: he is, however, wary of any reader who approaches his poetry with pre-conceived ideas. Baudelaire's poetry, on the other hand, incorporates (both thematically and stylistically) a broader dynamic range, but he, like Mallarmé, is also wary of overly prejudiced approaches to reading, speaking and performing poetry. Important to both poets is a careful attention to register and context. Mallarmé, for example, seeks more refined registers in his conversational exchanges in order to avoid the inconsequential utterances of 'bavardage' ['chattering']. Although Baudelaire accepts that 'bavardage' has a place within his poetry, he also recognises that in order to use one's voice effectively, it is important to take context into account. In the prose poem 'La Solitude' (B.*OC*. I, pp.313–314), for example, Baudelaire reminds the reader that those who, when speaking in public, are unable to adapt to the situation around them, or unable to adapt to who their listener might be, will use their voice in vain:

> Il est certain qu'un bavard, dont le suprême plaisir consiste à parler du haut d'une chaire ou d'une tribune, risquerait fort de devenir fou furieux dans l'île de Robinson. Je n'exige pas de mon gazetier les courageuses vertus de Crusoé, mais je demande qu'il ne décrète pas d'accusation les amoureux de la solitude et du mystère.
>
> Il y a dans nos races jacassières des individus qui accepteraient avec moins de répugnance le supplice suprême, s'il leur était permis de faire du haut de

l'échafaud une copieuse harangue, sans craindre que les tambours de Santerre ne leur coupassent intempestivement la parole.

Je ne les plains pas, parce que je devine que leurs effusions oratoires leur procurent des voluptés égales à celles que d'autres tirent du silence et du recueillement; mais je les méprise.

[It is true that a chatterbox, whose primary pleasure consists of speaking from the pulpit or from the rostrum, would run a very strong risk of going completely mad on Robinson's island. I do not require my journalist to possess the courageous virtues of Crusoe, but I ask that he does not impose accusations on those who like solitude and mystery.

There are some individuals within our chattering classes who would accept the ultimate torture with less repugnance if they were allowed to deliver a lengthy harangue from the top of the scaffold, without having to worry that the Santerre's drums might cut off their speech at an inopportune moment.

I do not complain about them, because I imagine that their oratory effusions procure the same kind of voluptuous pleasures for them as others manage to derive from silence and recollection; but I despise them.]

Baudelaire does not decree that the 'races jacassières' should not speak, but he recognises that there is of course no point in trying to give a public oration when alone, just as there is no point trying to speak in public when no one will listen. Baudelaire, then, is in line with Mallarmé in his abhorrence of contributing to the babble of mindless chattering, since this is at odds with an aesthetics of voice which not only uses voice carefully, but also listens carefully.

According to the kind of aesthetic regime propounded by Baudelaire and Mallarmé, using one's 'voice' in poetry should enable the creation of (suspended) vibrations, oscillations and echoes. And whilst neither poet had recourse to the recent developments in neuroscience that have now begun to explain why the sensation elicited from using and hearing voices can be as profound as when a voice has not specifically been expressed out loud, it is clear that they were aware of this phenomenon. Mallarmé in particular sought to privilege this 'sensation' in his poetic aesthetic by looking for the 'in-between' moments of language, those moments between speaking out loud and silence, between meanings and non-meanings, between poetry and music. So the significance granted to the sensation created by poetic language does not denigrate a poem's meaning, but supplements it by resonating with the memory of other words and meanings. In order for this resonant exchange to take place, both poets encourage the action of trying out language in different guises, in order to exploit fleeting moments where different sounds, words and meanings both coincide and conflict. In this respect, an aesthetics of voice for Baudelaire and Mallarmé becomes a conversation not between reader and poet, or between protagonists within the poem (although it relies also on these strategies) but a conversation between moments of language themselves. The reader's role, then, is to activate and listen to these moments in order to seek out the strange voices of language that are beyond the reader's (or poet's) own voice and beyond the poetic text itself. It is upon each reading that unexpected responses can be drawn out from the trembling sensation of language's own voices.

As the century progresses, fellow poets acknowledge this approach to an aesthetic formulation of the notion of 'voice', contributing not only to the theoretical formulations by treatise-writers, but also engaging with the importance of 'voice' in the context of the wavering status of poetry. Villiers de l'Isle-Adam, for example, uses 'voice' to propound a poetico-political manifesto by exploiting the technique of the refrain in his prose poem 'Vox populi'.[7] Valéry meanwhile reinforces the concept of 'voice' as a dynamic process which oscillates between the extremes of sound and sense in order to create a particular aesthetic sensation:

> Pensez à un pendule qui oscille entre deux points symétriques. Supposez que l'une de ces propositions extrêmes représente la forme, les caractères sensibles du langage, le son, le rythme, les accents, le timbre, le mouvement – en un mot la Voix en action. Associez, d'autre part, à l'autre point, au point conjugué du premier, toutes les valeurs significatives, les images, les idées; les excitations du sentiment et de la mémoire, les impulsions virtuelles et les formations de compréhension – en un mot, tout ce qui constitue le fond, le sens d'un discours. Observez alors les effets de la poésie en vous-mêmes.[8]

> [Think of a pendulum which oscillates between two symmetrical points. Imagine that one of these extremities represents the form, the appreciable characteristics of language, sound, rhythm, accents, timbre, movement – in a word, the Voice in action. Assign to the other point, to the point conjugated from the first, all values of signification, images, ideas, stimulations of feeling and of memory, virtual impulses and the formations of understanding – in a word, everything which constitutes the basis, the meaning of discourse. Observe, then, the effects of poetry within yourselves.]

It is other poets' acknowledgements of the care that needs to be taken when using 'voice' in poetry that confirms the significance of the aesthetic effects that can be drawn out from poetry's voices.

To return, then, to my initial suggestion that the burgeoning symbolist aesthetic entailed a renewed focus on the notion of 'voice', my analysis has explored the different ways in which Baudelaire and Mallarmé increasingly refine what 'voice'

---

[7]   Villiers de l'Isle-Adam, *Œuvres complètes*, ed. by Alan Raitt, Bibliothèque de la Pléiade, 2 vols (Paris: Gallimard, 1986), I, pp.562–565. See also my article: 'Politics or Poetics? The Battle Cry of the Refrain in Villiers de l'Isle-Adam's "Vox populi"', *Romance Studies*, 26:2 (2008), 126–135.

[8]   Paul Valéry, *Œuvres*, ed. by Jean Hytier, Bibliothèque de la Pléiade, 2 vols (Paris: Gallimard, 1957–1960), I, p.1332.

can mean in the context of nineteenth-century poetry. 'Voice' cannot simply be defined as an individual, human, physical trait; nor can it be defined as an entirely abstract or textual trait. The ways in which Baudelaire and Mallarmé carefully manipulate the interaction between the individual, human and physical attributes of voice and the more abstract, symbolic and textual qualities, especially with recourse to musical properties, confirm their aesthetic preoccupations. For each poet, 'voice' must necessarily be a *process* of interaction and exchange rather than something stable, static and clearly-defined. It is only within the context of a dynamic and resonant exchange, which takes place in the interstices between differing designations of voice (whether human, textual or performative, whether internal or external), that the yearned-for aesthetic effect can be drawn out from poetic language. To converse with Baudelaire or Mallarmé, then, is to engage productively with their poetry. As both poets are careful to point out, however, it is only the fully conversant reader – one who is well-versed in poetry and particularly attentive to the poetic text, and one who is able to set aside individual preconceptions – who will be able to achieve such profound aesthetic resonances by listening carefully to the dynamic range of voices that emerge from poetry.

Bibliography

Primary Works

Baudelaire, Charles, *Correspondance*, ed. by Claude Pichois, Bibliothèque de la Pléiade, 2 vols (Paris: Gallimard, 1966–1973).
——, *Curiosités esthétiques, L'Art romantique et autres Œuvres critiques*, ed. by Henri Lemaitre (Paris: Bordas, 1990).
——, *Les Fleurs du Mal*, ed. by Antoine Adam (Paris: Garnier Frères, 1959).
——, *Les Fleurs du Mal*, ed. by Claude Pichois (Paris: Gallimard, 1972–1996).
——, *Les Fleurs du Mal*, ed. by Jacques Dupont (Paris: Flammarion, 1991).
——, *Œuvres complètes*, ed. by Claude Pichois, Bibliothèque de la Pléiade, 2 vols (Paris: Gallimard, 1975–1976).
——, *Petits Poëmes en prose (Le Spleen de Paris)*, ed. by Robert Kopp (Paris: Gallimard, 1973).
Mallarmé, Stéphane, *Igitur, Divagations, Un Coup de dés* (Paris: Gallimard, 1976).
——, *Œuvres complètes*, ed. by Henri Mondor and G. Jean-Aubry, Bibliothèque de la Pléiade (Paris: Gallimard, 1945).
——, *Œuvres complètes*, ed. by Bertrand Marchal, Bibliothèque de la Pléiade, 2 vols (Paris: Gallimard, 1998–2003).
——, *Poésies*, ed. by Bertrand Marchal (Paris: Gallimard, 1954–1992).

Other Poetic Works

Hugo, Victor, *Œuvres poétiques*, ed. by Pierre Albouy, Bibliothèque de la Pléiade, 2 vols (Paris: Gallimard, 1967).
Gautier, Théophile, *Poésies complètes*, ed. by René Jasinski, 3 vols (Paris: Nizet, 1970).
Ghil, René, *Le Vœu de Vivre et autres poèmes*, ed. by Jean-Pierre Bobillot (Rennes: Presses Universitaires de Rennes, 2004).
Lamartine, Alphonse de, *Œuvres poétiques complètes*, ed. by Marius-François Guyard, Bibliothèque de la Pléiade (Paris: Gallimard, 1963).
Le Parnasse contemporain, 3 vols (Farnborough: Gregg International, 1970).
Louÿs, Pierre, *Les Chansons de Bilitis* (Paris: Fayard, 1930).
Poe, Edgar Allan, *Histoires extraordinaires*, trans. by Charles Baudelaire (Paris: Gallimard, 1973–2004).
——, *Nouvelles Histoires extraordinaires*, trans. by Charles Baudelaire (Paris: Gallimard, 1951–1974).

————, *The Penguin Complete Tales and Poems of Edgar Allan Poe* (London: Penguin, 1994).

Rimbaud, Arthur, *Poésies. Une saison en enfer. Illuminations*, ed. by Louis Forestier (Paris: Gallimard, 1965–1999).

Valéry, Paul, *Œuvres*, ed. by Jean Hytier, Bibliothèque de la Pléiade, 2 vols (Paris: Gallimard, 1957–1960).

Verlaine, Paul, *Fêtes galantes, Romances sans paroles*, ed. by Jacques Borel (Paris: Gallimard, 1973).

Villiers de l'Isle-Adam, *Œuvres complètes*, ed. by Alan Raitt, Bibliothèque de la Pléiade, 2 vols (Paris: Gallimard, 1986).

Rhetorical or Poetical Treatises

Aristotle, *Poetics*, trans. by Michael Heath (London: Penguin, 1996).

Banville, Théodore de, *Petit Traité de poésie française* (Paris: Librairie de l'Écho de la Sorbonne, [1872?]).

Becq de Fouquières, Louis, *Traité général de versification française* (Paris: Charpentier, 1879).

Dubroca, Louis, *Traité de prononciation des consonnes finales des mots français* (Paris: Dubroca, 1808).

Fontanier, Pierre, *Les Figures du discours*, ed. by Gérard Genette (Paris: Flammarion, 1977), combining the original publications *Manuel Classique pour l'étude des tropes, ou Élemens de la science du sens des mots* (Paris: Maire-Nyon, 1830) and *Des Figures du discours autres que les tropes* (Paris: Maire-Nyon, 1827).

Ghil, René, *Traité du Verbe: états successifs (1885 – 1886 – 1887 – 1888 – 1891 – 1904)*, ed. by Tiziana Goruppi (Paris: Nizet, 1978).

Gossart, Alexandre, *Traité complet de la versification française renfermant une nouvelle théorie de la rime, la prosodie, la déclamation, les gestes, des observations sur la mise en musique de la poéise, une description de toutes espèces de poèmes, un précis historique* (Paris: Maire-Nyon, [1859?]).

Gramont, Ferdinand de, *Les Vers français et leur prosodie* (Paris: Hetzel, 1875).

Pierrot-Deseilligny, Jules-Amable, *Choix de compositions françaises et latines ou Narrations, scènes, discours, lieux communs, développements historiques, vers latins des meilleurs élèves de l'université moderne, avec les matières et les arguments* (Paris: Hachette, 1860).

————, *Cours d'éloquence française*, 2 vols (Paris: [n.pub.], 1820–1822).

Quicherat, Louis, *Petit Traité de versification française*, 8th edn (Paris: Librairie Hachette, 1882).

Quintilian, *Institutio oratoria*, 2 vols (Oxford: Clarendon, 1970).

Ténint, Wilhem, *Prosodie de l'école moderne* (Paris: Didier, 1844).

Secondary Works

Abbate, Carolyn, *Unsung Voices: Opera and Musical Narrative in the Nineteenth Century* (Princeton: Princeton University Press, 1991).

Acquisto, Joseph, *French Symbolist Poetry and the Idea of Music* (Aldershot: Ashgate, 2006).

Agamben, Giorgio, *Language and Death: the Place of Negativity* (Minneapolis: University of Minnesota Press, 1991).

Aquien, Michèle, and Georges Molinié, eds, *Dictionnaire de Rhétorique et Poétique* (Paris: Librairie Générale de France, 1996).

Austin, J.L., *How to Do Things with Words* (Oxford: Clarendon, 1962).

Barthes, Roland, *Œuvres complètes*, ed. by Éric Marty, 3 vols (Paris: Seuil, 1994).

Benjamin, Walter, *Charles Baudelaire: un poète lyrique à l'apogée du capitalisme*, trans. by Jean Lacoste (Paris: Payot, 1979 and 2002).

Benoit, Éric, *Néant sonore: Mallarmé ou la traversée des paradoxes* (Geneva: Droz, 2007).

Bernard, Suzanne, *Mallarmé et la musique* (Paris: Nizet, 1959).

——, *Le Poème en prose de Baudelaire jusqu'à nos jours* (Paris: Nizet, 1959).

Bernstein, Susan, *Virtuosity of the Nineteenth Century: Performing Music and Language in Heine, Liszt and Baudelaire* (Stanford: Stanford University Press, 1998).

Bersani, Leo, *The Death of Stéphane Mallarmé* (Cambridge: CUP, 1982).

Beugnot, Bernard, *Poétique de Francis Ponge* (Paris: PUF, 1990).

Bolla, Peter de, *The Discourse of the Sublime: Readings in History, Aesthetics and the Subject* (Oxford: Blackwell, 1989).

Bonnefoy, Yves, *La Poésie à voix haute* (Condeixa-a-Nova: Ligne d'ombre, 2007).

Bourjea, Serge, 'Paul Valéry: "un certain regard"', *Poétique*, 113 (1998), 29–43.

Bowie, Malcolm, *Mallarmé and the Art of Being Difficult* (Cambridge: CUP, 1978).

Bowie, Malcolm, Alison Fairlie and Alison Finch, eds, *Baudelaire, Mallarmé, Valéry: New Essays in Honour of Lloyd Austin* (Cambridge: CUP, 1982).

Breatnach, Mary, *Boulez and Mallarmé. A Study in Poetic Influence* (Aldershot: Scolar, 1996).

Briscoe, James, ed., *Debussy in Performance* (New Haven and London: Yale University Press, 1999).

Brunel, Pierre, *Baudelaire et le 'puits des magies': six essais sur Baudelaire et la poésie moderne* (Paris: José Corti, 2003).

Cassagne, Albert, *Versification et Métrique de Charles Baudelaire* (Geneva and Paris: Slatkine Reprints, 1982).

Catani, Damian, *The Poet in Society: Art, Consumerism and Politics in Mallarmé* (Bern: Peter Lang, 2003).

Cellier, Léon, *Parcours initiatiques* (Neuchâtel: La Baconnière, 1977).

Chesters, Graham, *Some functions of Sound Repetition in 'Les Fleurs du Mal'* (Hull: University of Hull, 1975).

Chion, Michel, *La Voix au cinéma* (Paris: Éditions de l'Étoile, 1982).

Cocteau, Jean, *La Voix humaine* (Paris: Librairie Stock, Delamain & Boutelleau, 1930).

Cohen-Levinas, Danielle, *La Voix au-delà du chant: une fenêtre aux ombres* (Paris: Vrin, 2006).

Cohn, Robert Greer, *Mallarmé's 'Divagations': A Guide and Commentary* (Bern: Peter Lang, 1990).

Cornulier, Benoît de, *Théorie du vers: Rimbaud, Verlaine, Mallarmé* (Paris: Seuil, 1982).

Crow, Christine, *Paul Valéry and the Poetry of Voice* (Cambridge: CUP, 1982).

Dayan, Peter, *Mallarmé's 'Divine Transposition': Real and Apparent Sources of Literary Value* (Oxford: Clarendon, 1986).

——, *Music Writing Literature, from Sand via Debussy to Derrida* (Aldershot: Ashgate, 2006).

——, 'La musique et les lettres chez Barthes', *French Studies*, 57:3 (2003), 335–348.

——, 'Nature, Music, and Meaning in Debussy's Writings', *19th-Century Music*, 28:3 (2005), 214–229.

——, 'De la traduction en musique chez Baudelaire', *Romance Studies*, 18:2 (2000), 145–155.

Debussy, Claude, *Correspondance 1884–1918*, ed. by François Lesure (Paris: Hermann, 1993).

Declercq, Gilles, *L'Art d'argumenter: structures rhétoriques et littéraires* (Paris: Éditions Universitaires, 1992).

Derrida, Jacques, *La Dissémination* (Paris: Seuil, 1972).

——, *De la Grammatologie* (Paris: Minuit, 1967).

——, *Ulysse gramophone* (Paris: Galilée, 1987).

——, *La Voix et le phénomène: introduction au problème du signe dans la phénoménologie de Husserl* (Paris: PUF, 1989).

Descombes, Vincent, *La Denrée mentale* (Paris: Minuit, 1995).

Ducard, Dominique, *La Voix et le miroir: Une étude sémiologique de l'imaginaire et de la formation de la parole* (Paris: L'Harmattan, 2002).

Evans, David, *Rhythm, Illusion and the Poetic Idea: Baudelaire, Rimbaud, Mallarmé* (Amsterdam and New York: Rodopi, 2004).

Fauquet, Joël-Marie, ed., *Musiques Signes Images: liber amicorum François Lesure* (Geneva: Minkoff, 1988).

Florence, Penny, ed. and trans., *Mallarmé on CD-ROM: Un Coup de dés jamais n'abolira le hasard* (Oxford: Legenda, 2000).

Foyard, Jean, *Le Vers et sa musique* (Dijon: Centre de Recherches Le Texte et l'Edition Université de Bourgogne, 2001).

Freeman, Mike, and Elizabeth Fallaize, Jill Forbes, Toby Garfitt, Roger Pearson with Janis Spurlock, eds, *The Process of Art: Essays on Nineteenth-Century*

French Literature, Music, and Painting in Honour of Alan Raitt (Oxford: Clarendon, 1998).

Fumaroli, Marc, ed., *Histoire de la rhétorique dans l'Europe moderne 1450–1950* (Paris: PUF, 1999).

Galand, René, *Baudelaire: poétiques et poésie* (Paris: Nizet, 1969).

Gautier, Théophile, *Baudelaire*, ed. by Jean-Luc Steinmetz (Bordeaux: Le Castor Astral, 1991).

Genette, Gérard, *Figures III* (Paris: Seuil, 1972).

Gill, Austin, *The Early Mallarmé*, 2 vols (Oxford: Clarendon, 1980 and 1986).

Goehr, Lydia, *The Quest for Voice: On Music, Politics, and the Limits of Philosophy* (Oxford: Clarendon, 1998).

Goldman, David Paul, 'Esotericism as a Determinant of Debussy's Harmonic Language', *The Musical Quarterly*, 75:2 (1991), 130–147.

Goncourt, Edmond, and Jules de Goncourt, *Journal: mémoires de la vie littéraire*, 3 vols (Paris: Flammarion, 1956–1989).

Guichard, Léon, *La Musique et les lettres en France au temps du wagnérisme* (Paris: PUF, 1963).

Hartman, Elwood, *French Literary Wagnerism* (New York and London: Garland Publishing, 1988).

Helmholtz, Hermann, *On the Sensations of Tone*, trans. by Alexander J. Ellis (New York: Dover Publications, 1954).

Hertz, David, *The Tuning of the Word: the Musico-literary Poetics of the Symbolist Movement* (Carbondale: Southern Illinois University Press, 1987).

Hiddleston, J.A., *Baudelaire and the Art of Memory* (Oxford: Clarendon, 1999).

Hillery, David, *Music and Poetry in France from Baudelaire to Mallarmé* (Bern: Peter Lang, 1980).

Holloway, Robin, *Debussy and Wagner* (London: Ernst Eulenberg, 1979).

Holmes, Anne, 'Counterpoint in Mallarmé's "L'Après-midi d'un faune"', *French Studies*, 57:1 (2003), 27–37.

Howells, Christina, *Derrida: Deconstruction from Phenomenology to Ethics* (Cambridge: Polity Press, 1998).

Jackson, John E., 'Le Jeu des voix: de l'interpellation et de quelques autres formes énonciatives dans *Les Fleurs du Mal*' in John E. Jackson, Claude Pichois and Jean-Paul Avice (eds), *L'Année Baudelaire*, 6 (Paris: Champion, 2002), 69–87.

Jankelevitch, Vladimir, *Debussy et le mystère* (Neuchâtel: Éditions de la Baconnière, 1949).

Johnson, Barbara, *Défigurations du langage poétique: la seconde révolution baudelairienne* (Paris: Flammarion, 1979).

Kibédi-Varga, Aron, *Les Constantes du poème: à la recherche d'une poétique dialectique* (The Hague: Van Goor Zonen, 1963).

——, *Rhétorique et littérature: étude de structures classiques* (Paris: Didier, 1970).

Kinloch, David, and Gordon Millan, eds, *Situating Mallarmé* (Bern: Peter Lang, 2000).

Kramer, Lawrence, *Music and Poetry: The Nineteenth Century and After* (Berkeley and Los Angeles: University of California Press, 1984).

Kristeva, Julia, *Polylogue* (Paris: Seuil, 1977).

———, *La Révolution du langage poétique* (Paris: Seuil, 1974).

Lacoue-Labarthe, Philippe, *Musica ficta (Figures de Wagner)* (Paris: Christian Bourgois, 1991).

Laver, John, *The Phonetic Description of Voice Quality* (Cambridge: CUP, 1980).

Lees, Heath, *Mallarmé and Wagner: Music and Poetic Language* (Aldershot: Ashgate, 2007).

Lloyd, Rosemary, *Baudelaire's Literary Criticism* (Cambridge: CUP, 1981).

———, 'Hypocrite Brother, Hypocrite Sister: Exchanging Genders in *Les Fleurs du Mal*', *French Studies*, 53:2 (1999), 167–175.

Loncke, Joycelynne, *Baudelaire et la musique* (Paris: Nizet, 1975).

McCombie, Elizabeth, *Mallarmé and Debussy: Unheard Music, Unseen Text* (Oxford: Clarendon, 2003).

McGuinness, Patrick, 'From Page to Stage and Back: Mallarmé and Symbolist Theatre', *Romance Studies*, 26 (1995), 23–40.

———, ed., *Symbolism, Decadence and the Fin de siècle: French and European Perspectives* (Exeter: University of Exeter Press, 2000).

Maclean, Marie, *Narrative as Performance: The Baudelairean Experiment* (London and New York: Routledge, 1988).

Man, Paul de, *Blindness and Insight* (London: Methuen, 1983).

Marchal, Bertrand, *La Religion de Mallarmé: poésie, mythologie et religion* (Paris: José Corti, 1988).

Marchal, Bertrand, and Jean-Luc Steinmetz, eds, *Mallarmé ou l'obscurité lumineuse* (Paris: Hermann, 1999).

Marder, Elissa, *Dead Time: Temporal Disorders in the Wake of Modernity (Baudelaire and Flaubert)* (Stanford: Stanford University Press, 2001).

Marvick, Louis, *Waking the Face That No One Is* (Amsterdam and New York: Rodopi, 2004).

Méchoulan, Eric, *Le Corps imprimé: essai sur le silence en littérature* (Montréal: Les Editions Balzac, 1999).

Meschonnic, Henri, *Critique du rythme: anthropologie historique du langage* (Lagrasse: Verdier, 1982).

———, *Mallarmé au delà du silence* in *Mallarmé: Ecrits sur le livre* (Paris: Éditions de l'éclat, 1985).

———, *Pour la poétique I* (Paris: Gallimard, 1970).

———, *Pour la poétique II* (Paris: Gallimard, 1973).

Milner, Jean-Claude, *Mallarmé au tombeau* (Lagrasse: Verdier, 1999).

Milner, Jean-Claude, and François Regnault, *Dire le vers* (Paris: Seuil, 1987).

Miner, Margaret, *Resonant Gaps between Baudelaire and Wagner* (Athens, GA: University of Georgia Press, 1995).

Murat, Michel, *Le Coup de dés de Mallarmé: un recommencement de la poésie* (Paris: Belin, 2005).

Murphy, Steve, *Logiques du dernier Baudelaire: Lectures du Spleen de Paris* (Paris: Champion, 2003).

——, ed., *Lectures des 'Fleurs du Mal'* (Rennes: Presses Universitaires de Rennes, 2002).

Pearson, Roger, '"Les Chiffres et les Lettres": Mallarmé's "Or" and the Gold Standard of Poetry', *Dix-neuf*, 2 (2004), 44–60.

——, *Mallarmé and Circumstance: The Translation of Silence* (Oxford: OUP, 2004).

——, *Unfolding Mallarmé: The Development of a Poetic Art* (Oxford: Clarendon, 1996).

Pensom, Roger, *Accent and Metre in French* (Bern: Peter Lang, 1998).

Perrin, Laurent, ed., *Le sens et ses voix: dialogisme et polyphonie en langue et en discours*, Recherches Linguistiques, 28 (Metz: Université Paul Verlaine, 2006).

Pichois, Claude, ed., *Lettres à Baudelaire* (Neuchâtel: La Baconnière, 1973).

Pizzorusso, Arnaldo, *Da Montaigne a Baudelaire: prospettive e commenti* (Roma: Bulzoni, 1971).

Poe, Edgar Allan, *Essays and Reviews* (New York: The Library of America, 1984).

Porter, Lawrence, *The Crisis of French Symbolism* (Ithaca and London: Cornell University Press, 1990).

Rancière, Jacques, 'The Aesthetic Revolution and its Outcomes: Emplotments of Autonomy and Heteronomy', *New Left Review*, 14 (2002), 133–151.

——, *Le Destin des images* (Paris: La Fabrique, 2003).

——, *Mallarmé: la politique de la sirène* (Paris: Hachette, 1996).

——, *La Parole muette: essai sur les contradictions de la littérature* (Paris: Hachette, 1998).

Ratcliffe, Stephen, *Listening to Reading* (Albany: State University of New York Press, 2000).

Reynolds, Deirdre, 'Mallarmé and the Decor of Modern Life', *Forum for Modern Language Studies*, 42:3 (2006), 268–285.

——, *Rhythmic Subjects: Uses of Energy in the Dances of Mary Wigman, Martha Graham and Merce Cunningham* (Alton: Dance Books, 2007).

Rice, Donald, and Peter Schofer, *Rhetorical Poetics: Theory and Practice of Figural and Symbolic Reading in Modern French Literature* (Madison: University of Wisconsin Press, 1983).

Ridley, Aaron, *The Philiosophy of Music* (Edinburgh: Edinburgh University Press, 2004).

Riffaterre, Michael, 'Le Poème comme représentation', *Poétique*, 4 (1970), 401–418.

Robb, Graham, *La Poésie de Baudelaire et la poésie française 1838–1852* (Paris: Aubier, 1993).

———, *Unlocking Mallarmé* (New Haven and London: Yale University Press, 1996).

Rousseau, Jean-Jacques, *Essai sur l'origine des langues* (Paris: Aubier Montaigne, 1974).

Rowland, David, *Early Keyboard Instruments: A Practical Guide* (Cambridge: CUP, 2001).

Sartre, Jean-Paul, *Baudelaire* (Paris: Gallimard, 1947 and 1975).

———, *Mallarmé: la lucidité et sa face d'ombre* (Paris: Gallimard, 1986).

Scher, Steven P., ed., *Music and Text: Critical Inquiries* (Cambridge: CUP, 1991).

Scherer, Jacques, *Le Livre de Mallarmé* (Paris: Gallimard, 1978).

Scott, Clive, *Channel Crossings: French and English Poetry in Dialogue 1550–2000* (Oxford: Legenda, 2002).

———, '"État Présent": French Verse Analysis', *French Studies*, 60:3 (2006), 369–376.

———, *The Poetics of French Verse: Studies in Reading* (Oxford: Clarendon, 1998).

Scott, David H.T., *Sonnet Theory and Practice in Nineteenth-century France: Sonnets on the Sonnet*, Occasional Papers in Modern Languages, 12 (Hull: University of Hull Publications, 1977).

Shaw, Mary Lewis, *Performance in the Texts of Mallarmé: The Passage from Art to Ritual* (Pennsylvania: Pennsylvania State University Press, 1993).

Shaw-Miller, Simon, *Visible Deeds of Music: Art and Music from Wagner to Cage* (New Haven and London: Yale University Press, 2002).

Stephens, Sonya, *Baudelaire's Prose Poems: The Practice and Politics of Irony* (Oxford: OUP, 1999).

Stravinsky, Igor, *The Poetics of Music / Poétique musicale* (Cambridge, MA: Harvard University Press, 1970).

Sugano, Marian Zwerling, *The Poetics of the Occasion: Mallarmé and the Poetry of Circumstance* (Stanford: Stanford University Press, 1992).

Sykes, Ingrid, 'Sonorous Mechanics: The Culture of Sonority in Nineteenth-century France', *Nineteenth-century Music Review*, 1:1 (2004), 43–66.

Temple, Michael, *The Name of the Poet: Onomastics and Anonymity in the works of Stéphane Mallarmé* (Exeter: University of Exeter Press, 1995).

———, ed., *Meetings with Mallarmé: In Contemporary French Culture* (Exeter: University of Exeter Press, 1998).

Thompson, William J., ed., *Understanding Les Fleurs du Mal: Critical Readings* (Nashville and London: Vanderbilt University Press, 1997).

Tibi, Laurence, *La Lyre désenchantée: l'instrument de musique et la voix humaine dans la littérature française du XIXe siècle* (Paris: Champion, 2003).

Touya de Marenne, Eric, *Musique et poétique à l'âge du symbolisme: Variations sur Wagner: Baudelaire, Mallarmé, Claudel, Valéry* (Paris: L'Harmattan, 2005).

Trione, Aldo, *The Aesthetics of the Mind after Mallarmé* (Lewiston, NY: Edwin Mellen Press, 1996).

Wagner, Jacques, *La Voix dans la culture et la littérature françaises: 1713–1875* (Clermont-Ferrand: Presses Universitaires Blaise Pascal, 2001).

Wagner, Richard, *Oper und Drama* (Leipzig: Weber, 1852), Project Gutenberg. Online, available at: http://gutenberg.spiegel.de/wagner/operdram/operdram. htm.

Wenk, Arthur B., *Claude Debussy and the Poets* (Berkeley: University of California Press, 1976).

Wieckowski, Danièle, *La poétique de Mallarmé: la fabrique des iridées* (Paris: Sedes, 1998).

Williams, Heather, *Mallarmé's Ideas in Language* (Bern: Peter Lang, 2004).

Yates, Frances, *The Art of Memory* (London: Routledge and Kegan Paul, 1966).

Zumthor, Paul, *Introduction à la poésie orale* (Paris: Seuil, 1983).

——, *Performance, réception, lecture* (Longueuil: Éditions du Préambule, 1990).

Music Scores

Cressonnois, Jules, *Harmonies*, 4 vols ([Paris?]: [n.pub.], 1862–1865).

Duparc, Henri, *Mélodies*, 2 vols (Paris: Salabert, 1988).

Debussy, Claude, *Songs of Claude Debussy*, ed. by James R. Briscoe, 2 vols (Milwaukee: Hal Leonard, 1993).

Fauré, Gabriel, *Mélodies*, 3 vols (Paris: Hamelle, [n.d.]).

Discography

Lott, Felicity (soprano) and Graham Johnson (piano), *Mélodies sur des poèmes de Baudelaire* (Arles: Harmonia mundi, 2003).

Index